Management for Professionals

For further volumes:
http://www.springer.com/series/10101

Peggy Chaudhry · Alan Zimmerman

Protecting Your Intellectual Property Rights

Understanding the Role of Management, Governments, Consumers and Pirates

Springer

Peggy Chaudhry
Villanova School of Business
Villanova University
Villanova, PA, USA

Alan Zimmerman
City University of New York
College of Staten Island
Staten Island, NY, USA

ISSN 2192-8096 ISSN 2192-810X (electronic)
ISBN 978-1-4614-5567-7 ISBN 978-1-4614-5568-4 (eBook)
DOI 10.1007/978-1-4614-5568-4
Springer New York Heidelberg Dordrecht London

Library of Congress Control Number: 2012951629

Printed on acid-free paper

Springer is part of Springer Science+Business Media (www.springer.com)

I would like to devote the book to my family. I want to recognize my husband, Sohail, for his endless encouragement of my research endeavors. I sincerely acknowledge my parents, Dave and Evelyn, who always supported my career aspirations. Finally, I thank my children, Matt and Aeysha, for giving me the motivation to succeed.

Dr. Peggy Chaudhry

This book is dedicated to my family whose interest and help has been invaluable. First, to my wife Lori for her unstinting encouragement. Also to the next generation: Craig, Dan, Howie, Karen, and Matt and their respective partners. And the next: Alex, Abby, Emma, Hannah, Lily, Luke, Natalie, Owen, Phoebe, Sophia, and Samantha. With this collective intelligence we can solve any problem.

Dr. Alan Zimmerman

Preface

The expansion of world trade has brought with it an explosive growth in counterfeit merchandise. Estimates put the world total for counterfeit products at about one half trillion dollars annually, although it is impossible to accurately determine the true size of the counterfeit market. What is known is that this illicit trade has infected nearly every industry from pharmaceuticals to aircraft parts. Software and music piracy are easy targets widely reported in the media. In 2011, the Business Software Alliance (BSA) estimated that 42% of personal computer software installed worldwide was illegal and the losses to the software industry were $63 billion. These figures represent a significant increase from 2007 when about 38% of software was pirated costing the industry about $48 billion. Overall, a wide range of industries agree that there is a severe problem with the protection of intellectual property rights (IPR) throughout the world, yet there have been virtually no attempts to describe all aspects of the problem.

This work aims to give the most complete description of various characteristics of the IPR environment in a global context. We believe a holistic understanding of the problem must include consumer complicity to purchase counterfeit products, tactics of the counterfeiters (pirates) as well as actions (or inaction) by home and host governments, and the role of international organizations and industry alliances. This book establishes the full environmental aspects of piracy, describes successful anticounterfeiting actions, and then prescribes measures IPR owners should take to protect their intellectual property.

While there have been many articles in the popular and business press that focus on counterfeit trade, there have been only a small number of books published on the subject that address the predicament facing nearly every industry in a dispassionate, intellectual manner. We believe this book fulfills a unique need for a thorough review of all aspects of the IPR problem.

This book is not targeted at consumers although we hope they will find it enlightening. This is a research-based book that can serve as the basis for further inquiries by academics, institutional researchers, and professionals in the international business and legal communities. We believe it should be a useful reference for government officials, managers, and law professionals who are combating counterfeiting as part of their everyday responsibilities in countries throughout the world.

This work is a result of our continuing interest in the subject of counterfeit products. Extensive travel to China and other countries or just walking the streets of New York reminds us that this is a pervasive problem. For 20 years we have been working on various aspects of the problem and we have each published journal articles and delivered conference presentations based on the research we have been doing over that period. We would be remiss if we did not thank Victor Cordell and Michael Walsh for stimulating our interest in the subject and contributing to our early publications. In addition we would like to recognize the involvement of Jonathan Peters whose facility with statistics has been invaluable. A special thanks to Dr. Stephan Schläfereit for reviewing our work. We are also most grateful to Tom Snelling, Partner, and his colleagues, Jen Yang and Jillian Caldwell, at Freshfields Bruckhaus Deringer LLP for all their insights and help. Finally, we appreciate the assistance of Stephen Stumpf, Fred J. Springer Chair in Business Leadership, for sponsoring the funding of research and conference presentations through the Villanova School of Business. Overall, it is evident from the preceding remarks and forthcoming acknowledgments that this book is a result of the inspiration and support of many colleagues. Nevertheless we accept complete responsibility for the text including any errors that may have inadvertently occurred.

Villanova, PA, USA Peggy Chaudhry
Staten Island, NY, USA Alan Zimmerman

Author Bios

Dr. Peggy Chaudhry is an associate professor of International Business at the Villanova School of Business, Villanova University, Villanova, Pennsylvania. She received her Ph.D. in International Business with minors in International Economics and Marketing at the University of Wisconsin at Madison. She is considered an expert in intellectual property, illicit trade issues (particularly, counterfeit/gray markets and distribution channels), and international business management. Her research interests include managerial tactics to curb counterfeit trade, consumer complicity with counterfeit goods, and gray markets for consumer goods, including impacts for the pharmaceutical industry. She currently serves on the Editorial Board of *Business Horizons* and has published articles in the areas of intellectual property rights in business trade publications, such as *Advertising Age* and *The Wall Street Journal.* Her academic research has appeared in many journal outlets such as *Advances in International Marketing*, *Business Horizons*, *Columbia Journal of World Business*, *Enterprise Information Systems*, *European Management Journal*, *Journal of Business Strategy*, *Journal of Business & Technology Law*, *Journal of International Marketing*, *Multinational Business Review*, and *Virginia Journal of International Law*. In 2009, she published her first book (with Alan Zimmerman), *The Economics of Counterfeit Trade*: *Governments, Consumers*, *Pirates and Intellectual Property Rights.* She has been invited to speak before various audiences on the topic of the protection of intellectual property rights and consumer complicity with counterfeit goods including the US International Trade Commission and the University of Maryland's Francis King Carey School of Law. She was also interviewed by *The Wall Street Journal* for her views of the growth in counterfeit trade.

Dr. Alan Zimmerman is professor of International Business and Marketing at City University of New York, College of Staten Island, Director of the International Business Program, and Advisor to the International Business Society. Zimmerman is a two-time Fulbright Scholar and three-time president of the New Jersey American Marketing Association Chapter. In January 2011 he taught at the Shanghai Institute of Language and Commerce in the People's Republic of China, his fourth visit to that country.

He is also the founder and president of three businesses including Radley Resources, a business to business market research and consulting practice. The firm's extensive list of clients includes American Express, DuPont, and Owens-Corning. He worked for more than 30 years in international and domestic marketing with the consultancy and with Westinghouse Electric Corporation. He served as vice president of marketing for E.F. Hauserman, a $100-million interior wall manufacturer. He is a frequent speaker and author on international business and marketing. His text book, *Business Marketing Management: A Global Perspective*, written with UK professor Jim Blythe, and now in its second edition, is being used by colleges around the world. His academic research has appeared in many journals including *Business Horizons*, *Multinational Business Review*, *Science and Engineering Ethics*, *Journal of Asia Pacific Business*, *Journal of Business & Industrial Marketing*, and the *Journal of Global Marketing*.

He holds a doctorate in international business and marketing from the Lubin School of Business at Pace University, New York, an MBA from Duquesne University in Pittsburgh, and a BS in Communications from Temple University in Philadelphia. In January 2010, he spent three weeks in India on a second Fulbright award, lecturing in Delhi and rural Rajasthan. In 2005, he held a semester-long Fulbright assignment at the Dublin Institute of Technology, with whom CSI has an established exchange program.

Acknowledgments by the Authors

Dr. Peggy Chaudhry

I would like to express my gratitude to Alan Zimmerman, my coauthor, who is an outstanding scholar and colleague—we successfully merged our vision for this book. I sincerely thank Jeffrey Snyder, Partner at Crowell & Moring, and Francis Sweeney, President, TDK USA, for their willingness to counsel me on the legal and global business realities of protecting intellectual property rights. Next, I give special thanks to my academic coauthors, Steve Stumpf and Michael Walsh, who have been exceptional researchers on IP issues. I appreciate my reference librarian, Linda Hauck, for her zealous aptitude to assist me with the research required for this book. I am grateful to Dean Patrick Maggitti, my previous Dean, Dr. Kevin Clark, and my chair, Dr. Daniel Wright, of the Villanova School of Business for instilling a research-centered culture that gave me the necessary support to focus on the book. I want to thank my assistant, Pat Cunningham, for her exceptional support. Finally, I must bestow gratitude to former graduate and undergraduate students for expressing such enthusiastic interest in my intellectual property research—I have learned from you also.

Dr. Alan Zimmerman

First I would like to acknowledge my dedicated coauthor, Peggy Chaudhry, no doubt one of the leading scholars in this field, who made this process so pleasant. We have been working for several years on this important problem and have always helped each other do better work. Special thanks to Alexandra Doronina, my undergraduate research assistant, whose dogged determination helped unearth many interesting sources. Thanks to Jean Como of the SEEK program at the College of Staten Island for providing me with such an excellent researcher. Special thanks to

Dr. H. H. Ting and Jack Chang in China. I am also pleased to acknowledge Thomas Tellefsen, chair of the Business Department at City University of New York—College of Staten Island, and my other colleagues in the department for their encouragement. Thanks also to my current and past students at the college who have shown consistent interest in the counterfeit goods problem.

Contents

1 **Introduction** 1
Overview 1
Definitions 2
Roadmap of the book 4

2 **The Global Growth of Counterfeit Trade** 7
Introduction 7
History of Counterfeiting 7
Measuring the Counterfeit Market 9
Negative Effects of Counterfeit Goods 11
The Growth of the Counterfeit Goods Market 14
Effects on the United States 16
Products Counterfeited 17
Large and Small Firms Affected 20
Reasons for the Growth of Counterfeit Goods 22
Low Cost High Technology = Low Investment, High Profits 22
Globalization and Lower Trade Barriers 24
Consumer Complicity 26
Expansion of Channels and Markets 26
Powerful Worldwide Brands 28
Weak International and National Enforcement 29
High Tariffs and Taxes 30
Conclusions 30

3 **The Supply of Counterfeit Trade: The Problem Countries** 33
Introduction 33
The Leading Sources of Counterfeit Goods 33
US Customs Seizures 36
Specific Countries 37
Russia 37
Argentina 39
Algeria 40

Canada 40
Chile 41
Egypt 41
India 42
Indonesia 43
Israel 43
Pakistan 44
Thailand 44
Turkey 45
Ukraine 45
Venezuela 46
Mexico 46
Brazil 46
Paraguay 48
Notorious Markets 48
Extra-country 50
Conclusions 51

4 Modeling the Intellectual Property Rights Environment 53
Introduction 53
Proposed Framework 53
Level of Consumer Complicity 54
Level of Pirate Activity 55
Level of Host Country Enforcement 56
IPR Actions Targeted at Consumers, Distribution Channels, Host Governments, International Organizations, and Pirates 57
The Model 58
The Research Study 58
Assessment of Managerial Perceptions 61
Examining the Role of Consumer Complicity 61
Evaluating the Effect of Indigenous Pirate Activity 63
Judging the Influence of Host Country IPR Enforcement 65
Managerial Insights Regarding the IPR Environment: Key Findings 68
Conclusions 69

5 The Demand for Counterfeit Trade: Consumer Complicity 71
Introduction 71
Consumer Drivers for Purchasing Counterfeit Goods 72
Conceptual Model of Consumer Complicity to Purchase Fake Goods 73
Marketing Variables That Influence Consumer Complicity 74
Demographics of Consumers 75
Attitude Towards Counterfeiting 76
Cultural Values 77
Ethical Perspective 78
Product Attributes 79

Shopping Experience 80
Demarketing Communications 81
Conclusions 82

6 The Use of Antipiracy Marketing Techniques to Educate the Consumer 85
Introduction 85
Overview of Social Marketing Concepts 86
Public Agenda 86
Media Agenda 88
Policy Agenda 89
Setting an Agenda to Change the Public Judgment of Counterfeit Trade 89
Anti-counterfeiting Advertisements 91
Previous Advertisements 92
Role Models 92
Peer Pressure 93
Education 96
Fear 98
Quality of the Product 99
Negative Association with Suppliers 100
Rewards Through Whistle Blowing 102
Blog Rebuttals to Advertisements 102
Conclusions 104

7 Changing Trade Policy: The EU and US Bolster Protection of Intellectual Property Rights 105
Introduction 105
U.S. IPR Enforcement Initiatives 105
Intellectual Property Enforcement Coordinator 107
America Invents Act 108
Strategy Targeting Organized Piracy 109
European Commission Taxation and Customs Union (TAXUD) 111
EU Patent Reform 113
IPR Enforcement Initiatives in the European Union 114
Retaliation: Understanding the Enforcement Directive in the EU to Pursue Counterfeiters 114
Seeking Retribution: The European Commission Develops Action Plans to Bolster IP 118
EU-US Action Strategy for the Enforcement of Intellectual Property Rights 119
Operation Infrastructure 121
EU Third-Country IPR Enforcement Strategy 122
Conclusions 123

8 Government and Industry Led Operations to Curb Counterfeit Trade ... 125
Introduction ... 125
Multilateral Organizations that Govern IPR ... 125
World Trade Organization: TRIPS ... 126
World Intellectual Property Organization (WIPO) ... 128
Organization for Economic Cooperation and Development ... 130
The International Criminal Police Organization (Interpol) ... 131
Industry Associations that Govern IPR ... 132
International AntiCounterfeiting Coalition ... 133
Business Software Alliance ... 134
Software Information Industry Association ... 135
Motion Picture Association of America ... 136
Recording Industry Association of America ... 136
International Federation of Phonographic Industry ... 138
Conclusions ... 139

9 The Special Case of China ... 141
Introduction ... 141
The Growth of the Chinese Economy ... 142
Estimating the Size of the Chinese Counterfeit Market ... 144
History of Intellectual Property in China ... 147
IPR Enforcement ... 150
Effective Firm Action in China ... 154
Recent Events ... 155
Information Sources ... 157
Conclusions ... 158

10 Internet Piracy: The Virtual Marketplace for Counterfeit Goods ... 159
Introduction ... 159
The Growth of Counterfeits in the Virtual Marketplace ... 159
Piracy in Selected Industries: Movies and Software ... 162
Ethical Perceptions of Internet Piracy ... 164
Pirates on the Virtual Sea ... 164
The Warez Scene ... 165
Internet Sites ... 166
Video Streaming ... 169
US Government: Led Sting Operations to Curb Internet Piracy ... 169
Operation Buccaneer ... 170
Operation Digital Gridlock ... 171
Operation Higher Education/Operation FastLink ... 172
Operation Site Down ... 172
Operation Strike Out ... 173

Enforcement Issues Related to Electronic Piracy 173
No Electronic Theft Act 174
Digital Millennium Copyright Act 174
Commercial Felony Streaming Act 176
Conclusions 177

11 Managerial Counterattack: Traditional and Novel Anticounterfeiting Strategies 179
Introduction 179
Firms Must Act to Protect their IP Rights 180
Suggestions from Researchers and Authors 180
Using Technology 181
The Role of Packaging 183
Developing a Plan 185
Summarizing the Existing Literature 185
Effectiveness of Recommended Actions 186
Frequency of Actions Used 186
Effectiveness of Actions 186
Organizing to Fight Counterfeit Product 188
Recommended Action Program 191
Conclusions 195

12 The Future: Will the Piracy Paradox Persist? 197
Introduction 197
The Growth of Counterfeit Trade 197
Source Countries 198
The IPR Environment 199
Consumer Complicity 199
Antipiracy Marketing Techniques 200
Actions by the EU and the US Governments 200
Government and Industry Led Operations 201
China 202
The Internet 202
Management Actions 203
Future Research 204
The Outlook 206

References 209

Chapter 1
Introduction

Overview

The desire to own a prestigious brand seems to have spread across the world. But multiple factors conspire to prevent most consumers from acquiring a real Prada handbag or Rolex watch. Many search for black-market vendors in places like Chinatown in New York City, venturing like Wendy Toth (2007) down dodgy alleys into dingy basements to find fakes at nearly unbelievable prices. Others find counterfeit look-alikes on the Internet when entering the words "replica watches" in Google yields more than 36 million hits and entering replica Louis Vuitton produces 39 million hits. (Replica is the code word on the Internet for counterfeit product.) On the web, it is easy to buy look-alike Prada handbags, Rolex watches, Armani sunglasses, Guerlain perfume, or the ubiquitous Vuitton products complete with phony logo.

The Internet sale of these pirated products created concern among IP holders but thus far has resulted in far different decisions by United States and foreign courts. In 2004 several major brands including Vuitton filed suit in Paris against eBay for trademark infringement. On June 30, 2008 the Tribunal de Commerce of Paris ruled against eBay and awarded the owners of the various brands €40 million ($63 million) for failing to prevent counterfeit products being sold over its website (Bufalino et al. 2010). This decision put the responsibility on eBay to enforce anti-counterfeiting measures. On the other hand, at nearly the same time, a New York court ruled against Tiffany & Co. in a similar case (Stone 2008). Here the burden is placed on Tiffany to warn eBay of any possible trademark infringement. On April 1, 2010 the Court of Appeals agreed with the original decision (Bufalino et al. 2010). These contradictory decisions reinforce the premise underlying this book that IP owners must be proactive in protecting their intellectual property in every market throughout the world.

But counterfeit products are not limited to designer perfumes, handbags, and other highly visible consumer items. Software, DVDs, and music are particularly vulnerable to copying or unauthorized use. Microsoft claims up to 40% of its software is pirated on a global basis (Anti-counterfeiting Amendments 2004). There is also a large market for phony pharmaceuticals and the results have been catastrophic in

P. Chaudhry and A. Zimmerman, *Protecting Your Intellectual Property Rights*, Management for Professionals, DOI 10.1007/978-1-4614-5568-4_1,

various countries. In 2007 the World Health Organization (WHO) estimated the sale of counterfeit drugs at approximately $40 billion per year and growing to $75 billion by 2010. In WHO's latest Fact Sheet (2010) medicines are now classified into a large catch-all collection which includes spurious/falsely labeled/falsified/counterfeit (SFFC) medicines. WHO states that less than 1% of drugs fall into this category in the more developed countries but that in Africa, parts of Asia and Latin America, and "countries in transition" a much higher percentage of SFFC drugs are for sale. The US Centers for Disease Control (2012) estimates counterfeit drugs at more than 10% in developing countries and says that in specific regions of Africa, Asia, and Latin America the chances of purchasing a counterfeit drug "maybe higher than 30%." WHO says categorically that more than 50% of medicines purchased over the Internet from illegal sites that conceal their address have found to be counterfeit.

The OECD (2007d) reports that more products than ever are being counterfeited and the types are expanding. Industrial products are not immune to piracy. Even military products have been widely counterfeited. The US Senate Armed Services Committee released a report after a 14-month investigation which found many counterfeit parts had been installed in US military equipment including thermal night vision sights, memory chips, and even a complete traffic alert and collision avoidance system (Capaccio 2012). Other studies have identified counterfeit auto parts, batteries, sewer pumps, aircraft bolts, and helicopter blades creating major problems for purchasers (UNODC 2010; Hopkins et al. 2003 and Naim 2005). The truth is any product may be subject to counterfeiting.

Product counterfeiting is a major problem for brand owners in nearly every country. Many stakeholders are injured by the widespread availability of pirated products. The beneficiaries of these products on the one hand are consumers who can show off their phony Rolex or Prada to their friends, even though the movement of counterfeits into nontraditional goods, such as pharmaceuticals, can place an unsuspecting consumer at risk. On the other hand beneficiaries also include some very nasty organized criminal groups and terrorists.

While there have been innumerable articles in the popular and business press focusing on counterfeit trade, there are only a handful of books and research articles published on the subject and far fewer that address the counterfeit predicament in a dispassionate, intellectual manner. This book examines the full scope of the problem. We believe the book fulfills a unique need for a thorough review of all aspects of the world intellectual property rights (IPR) situation and is the first work based on extensive research, both secondary and primary.

Definitions

According to the World Intellectual Property Organization (WIPO) intellectual property "refers to creations of the mind: inventions, literary and artistic works, and symbols, names, images, and designs used in commerce" (WIPO 2007). For clarity it is important to provide definitions of particular forms of IPR: copyrights, patents, and trademarks.

The US Department of State issued a glossary of intellectual property terms in January 2006. Following are the definitions provided in this glossary (USINFO 2006) and by WIPO (2007).

Copyright: "an exclusive right granted or conferred by the government on the creator of a work to exclude others from reproducing it, adapting it, distributing it to the public, performing it in public, or displaying it in public. Copyright does not protect an abstract idea; it protects only the concrete form of expression in a work. To be valid a copyrighted work must have originality and possess a modicum of creativity." WIPO (2007) details the kinds of endeavors covered by copyright: "literary works such as novels, poems, plays, reference works, newspapers and computer programs; databases; and films, musical compositions, and choreography; artistic works such as paintings, drawings, photographs and sculpture; architecture; and advertisements, maps and technical drawings."

Patent: "(in the United States) a grant by the federal government to an inventor of the right to exclude others from making, using, or selling the invention. There are three different kinds of patents in the United States: a utility patent on the functional aspects of products and processes; a design patent on the ornamental design of useful objects; and a plant patent on a new variety of living plant … . Once the patent expires, the public is entitled to make and use the invention and is entitled to a full and complete disclosure of how to do so." WIPO (2007) simply says: a patent is "an exclusive right granted for an invention, which is a product or a process that provides, in general, a new way of doing something, or offers a new technical solution to a problem." Their definition goes on to say that the protection for the invention to the owner of the patent is granted for a limited period, generally 20 years.

Trademark: The US Trademark Act (Title 15, US Code) gives a succinct legal definition, "the term 'trademark' includes any word, name, symbol, or device, or any combination thereof used by a person, or which a person has a bona fide intention to use in commerce … to identify and distinguish his or her goods, including a unique product, from those manufactured or sold by others and to indicate the source of the goods, even if that source is unknown."

The US Code also identifies trademark counterfeiting as the act of producing, selling, or distributing a product with "a spurious mark which is identical to or substantially indistinguishable from a registered mark." Also included as trademark counterfeiting is trademark infringement which means using marks "likely to cause confusion, or to cause mistake or to deceive" (Abbott and Sporn 2002; Trademark Act). The US State Department defines counterfeiting as "the act of producing or selling a product containing a sham mark that is an intentional and calculated reproduction of the genuine mark," and defines piracy as "the act of exact, unauthorized, and illegal reproduction on a commercial scale of a copyrighted work or of a trademarked product" (USINFO 2006).

In this book, the definition given by Cordell et al. (1996) will be used: "Any unauthorized manufacturing of goods whose special characteristics are protected as intellectual property rights (trademarks, patents, and copyrights) constitutes product counterfeiting."

A distinction between "knockoffs," gray goods and counterfeit goods must be made. Knockoff products may seem the same as branded products, but they do not abuse the copyrights, patents, or trademarks (intellectual property) of any manufacturer. Gray goods are products which are offered by the owner of the intellectual property. These products are genuine and legitimate, but have found their way into unintended markets through channel diversion. For instance in South Africa because the iPad was not released in the country for nearly a year after introduction in the US, local consumers bought unauthorized iPads through an online marketplace. It is estimated that 20,000 iPads were sold through the gray market or purchased on overseas trips (South Africa Web 2012). Gray markets are created because of product pricing differentials used by international marketers to meet the needs of particular markets or because of product shortages. When a product is shipped, without authorization from the manufacturer, from an authorized market to an unauthorized market, the gray goods problem rears its head. While gray goods are a distribution channel problem for international managers, they are not the subject of this book.

Roadmap of the book

Chapter 2 reviews the growth of counterfeit trade, beginning with the history of counterfeiting which stretches back 2,000 years or more to the development of early marks used to identify manufacturers. Next, the chapter identifies the stakeholders who are harmed by counterfeit product. Later on, an attempt is made to identify the actual size of the counterfeit product market. Numbers once developed have been repeated incessantly yet a careful examination shows that no estimate of the size of this problem can be made with confidence. Customs seizures of counterfeit product account for an extremely small percentage of the estimated market. A summary of the reasons for the growth in product counterfeiting follows.

Chapter 3 focuses on the main sources of counterfeit goods. While OECD (2009) data identifies more than 130 countries as sources for these products, a few nations provide most of the pirated products. China is by far the leading exporter while Hong Kong, India as well as some other Asian and Latin American nations are also offenders. The so-called BRIC countries (Brazil, Russia, India, and China) are often mentioned as the key countries for counterfeit product trade. In this chapter specific discussions about particular countries are provided based on findings from various information sources. Finally, notorious extra-country markets and those within countries are identified.

Chapter 4 offers a conceptual framework developed by the authors for the IPR environment. As determinant items it includes the level of consumer complicity, the level of pirate activity, and the level of host country enforcement. These major forces create the IPR environment in a particular market. Once a firm determines how risky that environment is, it can take action to combat IPR problems. These actions are directed at consumers, distribution channels, host governments, international organizations, and pirates. Some actions are also company internal. The remainder of this chapter describes and evaluates each of these potential actions and describes primary research, conducted by the authors, of the perceptions of managers related to the IPR environment in particular markets. Here we find that managers do not change their strategy in high vs. low complicity markets. On the other hand where managers perceived high levels of piracy and/or a low level of enforcement of IPR rights they changed their strategy. One very interesting finding from this chapter is that managers do not change their plans for future commitments in markets where the IPR environment is not ideal. The strategic importance of a particular country, not the IPR environment, is uppermost in their minds when making future investment plans for particular markets.

In Chapter 5 consumer complicity is examined in more depth. It is obvious that consumers' willingness to purchase counterfeit product is a critical factor in the growth of this illicit trade. The authors provide primary research describing intrinsic and extrinsic determinants affecting consumers' willingness to buy counterfeit product. A recent study of BRIC consumers by one of the authors found that the best predictors of consumer complicity to obtain counterfeits were perceived quality, a lower price, and a hedonic shopping experience. For example, the complicit consumer finds seeking counterfeits in both virtual and physical markets a "sense of adventure" or an enjoyable experience.

Chapter 6 uses social marketing concepts as a basis for examining anti-counterfeiting marketing techniques and provides several examples of the various approaches recommended in the demarketing literature adapted to educating consumers about pirated product. This chapter provides a number of illustrations of actual advertisements and also describes the blogs rebutting anti-counterfeiting advertising. It is not clear whether these anti-counterfeiting marketing techniques have a measurable effect on consumer attitudes toward counterfeit product. Previous research conducted by the authors reveals that managers tend to see educating the consumer as relatively ineffective. But, current research by one of the authors has found that some demarketing tactics targeted at even highly complicit consumers in BRIC and the United States may be effective, such as using a "fear" message in raising awareness about counterfeit pharmaceuticals.

Chapter 7 looks at IPR enforcement in the European Union (EU) and the United States. The complex array of US agencies involved in protecting IPR is described as well as the many directives established by the EU governing some aspect of IPR Changes in the governance of patents, such as the America Invents Act and the unitary patent protection in the EU are discussed. In addition, the recent creation of the Office of the US Intellectual Property Enforcement Coordinator (IPEC) is highlighted. The US program called STOPfakes is detailed and a diagram showing the major players in US IPR enforcement is incorporated. The nine EU directives are described in detail in this chapter as well. The relatively new US-EU action strategy for the enforcement of the IPR is explained to outline one of the new cosponsored strategic anti-counterfeiting measures. As described later in the book, the enforcement of strong anti-counterfeit legislation is seen by managers as the key to improving the IPR environment. It is not clear how effective these initiatives have been.

Chapter 8 describes the plethora of organizations focusing on some aspect of intellectual property rights. This is in essence a directory of the many multilateral organizations as well as business associations looking at the IPR problem. These institutions range from the World Trade Organization's TRIPs to the OECD to the IACC, the BSA, and the IFPI. Each of these agencies has some interest in IPR issues and this chapter describes the particular focus of each organization.

In Chap. 9 special attention is given to the People's Republic of China. As noted China is leading exporter of counterfeit product and the growth of these exports has kept pace with the rapid development of the Chinese economy. This chapter quickly reviews China's economic growth and estimates the size of the counterfeit product market in China. In discussing the history of IPR in this country, the chapter describes the reasons for the lack of Chinese consumer and business manager concern for the concept of intellectual property rights. While many laws have been written to protect patents, trademarks, and copyrights, enforcement is spotty at best. This chapter reveals the reasons for the poor enforcement and describes the actions taken by some firms to protect their own IPR in this hostile country environment.

The use of the Internet to distribute pirated products is the focus of Chap. 10. Here we see that the Internet has actually become one of the largest suppliers of counterfeit product, nearly equaling China as a source. As described in the opening of this chapter, eBay has provided a convenient venue for the sale of phony product and was called to task for its lack of policing the fake items sold at its site. Here again the problem of consumer complicity is critical since a large percentage of consumers do not see purchasing counterfeit product on Internet auction sites or downloading copied music or software as harmful. In addition, discussions of proposed legislation designed to deter pirates from videostreaming digital content, the Commercial Felony Streaming Act (Bill S. 978), as well as the overwhelming reaction to the Stop Online Piracy Act (SOPA) are provided. This chapter also describes several operations conducted by the US government which attempted to punish copyright infringement. Efforts to precisely measure the size of the Internet piracy market have not been successful. It appears that Internet piracy will continue to grow.

Chapter 11 strengthens the idea that IPR owners must enforce their own property rights. As we have seen, despite the best efforts of many government and nongovernment institutions, piracy continues to grow. This chapter reviews the multitude of advice given by various researchers and authors, nearly all of which is not based upon primary research with managers. A summary of all the earlier recommendations is given. Here a description of some of the most interesting technological approaches to fighting piracy is included. The chapter then reports results from primary research conducted by the authors describing managers' perceptions of the least effective and most effective actions used to fight pirates. Finally the chapter recommends a seven-point action program based upon this research that any firm can use to fight counterfeiting of its products.

The final chapter summarizes the earlier chapters and looks to the future of the counterfeit goods problem. This chapter reviews the thinking of some observers regarding the expected developments in the world IPR environment and closes with thoughts from the authors that include a succinct list of challenging research questions which remain to be addressed.

Chapter 2
The Global Growth of Counterfeit Trade

Introduction

Product counterfeiting is a well-known problem, one that has been with us for a very long time. Trademarks go back to ancient times and where there are trademarks counterfeiting soon follows. Recently more attention is being paid to fighting the problem. It would seem the first logical step would be to determine the size of the counterfeit market. But estimating the extent of this illicit trade is a difficult task. First, no direct measurement of counterfeit trade can be undertaken, since by definition this is an illegal activity. Customs seizures are such a small percentage of overall trade that it is impossible to draw conclusions from these statistics. Many organizations, including the US General Accountability Office (2010), have attempted to estimate the size of the counterfeit market and have described the major flaws in every method which tries to put a definite size on it. This chapter examines the history of counterfeiting, reviews the challenges of measurement, and describes the products most often counterfeited and the constituencies hurt by the practice. Finally the chapter describes the seven major drivers of the growth in counterfeit trade.

History of Counterfeiting

Counterfeiting is not a new business phenomenon and has been affecting trade for at least 2,000 years. Pliny the elder described counterfeit coins as popular collector's items for Romans (Barry 2007). The counterfeiting of coinage was part of the normal exchanges involving smuggling, minting privileges, alchemy, and foreign trade in Genoa in the sixteenth and seventeenth centuries. Goldsmiths, soldiers, bankers, convicts on galleys, and even priests were involved in developing counterfeit coinage. A famous example of counterfeiting occurred in Renaissance France when, over a 10-year period, supporters of the Pope directed parallel minting to

P. Chaudhry and A. Zimmerman, *Protecting Your Intellectual Property Rights*, Management for Professionals, DOI 10.1007/978-1-4614-5568-4_2,

undermine official coinage issued by a Protestant King. Since "official counterfeiting" was reserved for princes the penalties for doing this were rather severe and included being boiled alive (Grendi 1994; Gillard 1990).

But product counterfeiting may even be older. Babylonian and Egyptian priests placed inscriptions from earlier civilizations on monuments to increase their proceeds and legitimacy (Hopkins et al. 2003). The advent of trademarks used to identify manufacturers of particular products certainly created the opportunity for counterfeiting. Some form of trademark has probably been in use since ancient times. Marked pottery appeared in China four to five thousand years ago and Greek vases identified both the maker and also the wholesaler of the item. Merchant's marks appeared in about the tenth century. These were used to prove ownership of goods. In Japan lumber was marked when tied onto a raft before being sent down river (Ono 1999).

Roman builders indicated the maker of bricks and tiles by stamping an identifying mark on them. Marcus Sestius, a Roman wine merchant, apparently lost a large shipment of branded wine jars when his ship went down off the coast of Marseilles probably in about 230 BCE (Rokicki 1987). During the first three centuries of the Roman Empire oil lamps were made using the FORTIS brand name. Many artifacts with this name have been found which may indicate widespread product copying at the time (International Trademark Association 2007). Pliny also warned of counterfeit opals made of glass (Sidebotham 1986). While there is no record of legal enforcement of trademarks during Roman times it appears that the Romans punished abuses through their commercial institutions (Paster 1969).

During the Middle Ages guilds required craftsmen and merchants to affix marks which distinguished their products from low-quality imitations. The main function of these marks was to assign responsibility for inferior products (Ono 1999). By the thirteenth century trademarks were common in England. In fact a compulsory marking law required that a baker put his mark on every loaf of bread and goldsmiths were required to place marks on their work. During this time trademark infringement became a crime and in some cases rather draconian capital punishment was applied to abusers (Abbott and Sporn 2002). Stolte (1998) identifies the earliest trademark infringement action in England, Sandforth's Case, heard in 1584. The plaintiff had manufactured woolen clothing marked with the letters J. G. and a sign called a tucker's handle. The defendant had made similar clothing which were "ill, insufficient and unmerchantable; and deceitfully marked … J.G."

In the Aztec Empire some dishonest dealers sold counterfeit cacao beans. Honest sellers divided beans into piles according to their origin. But the counterfeiters used artificial coloring to sell inferior beans or even disguised worthless amaranth dough or avocado seeds with cacao hulls (Rust 1999). Fifteenth century Chinese painters accommodated forgeries by other artists (Alford 1995). In the seventeenth century Domingo Navarette, a Spanish priest, noted the Chinese ability to copy products. He complained that the Chinese had "imitated to perfection whatsoever they have seen brought out of Europe" (The Economist 2003).

Product counterfeiting came to the attention of the US government more than 100 years ago. William Eleroy Curtis (1889), reporting for the government, wrote "the superiority of American [cotton] goods is so great that the Manchester [England] mills send few goods to South America that do not bear forged American trademarks." In his report, Curtis quotes a member of the New York law firm of Smith, Hogg and Gardner as having recovered damages and costs in Manchester (UK) "although we have great difficulty in definitely locating the forgeries."

Of course the United States has not been innocent of piracy. It has been claimed with some accuracy that the Industrial Revolution in the United States began with significant help from an industrial spy, Samuel Slater. The English textile industry grew rapidly based on the invention of the water spinning frame by Richard Arkwright. The British wanted to be sure that this invention never reached America since it was the world's largest exporter of cotton but had no manufacturing industry of its own. By 1774 it was illegal for an English textile worker to share technological information or to leave the country. Slater, born in England in 1768, started as an apprentice in a cotton mill owned by a former partner of Arkwright and eventually became a supervisor. In America both state governments and entrepreneurs were offering rewards for machines like Arkwright's. After reading in a Philadelphia newspaper of a £100 bounty paid to the designer of an inferior cloth-making machine, Slater came to New York in 1789. He was able to reconstruct the entire English mill from memory and eventually, with the support of a Rhode Island merchant, built the first water-powered cotton spinning mill in America (BBC 2007; pbs.org 2007). Although creating a system of patents and copyrights was a priority for George Washington, the Patent Act of 1793 did not provide protection for foreign inventors. This meant that an American could copy any product patented in a foreign country and then apply for a US patent (Choate 2005). The same held true for copyright. In the country's infancy product copying and literary piracy were common. Charles Dickens, visiting the United States in 1842, was irate when he found many pirated copies of his novels in Boston bookstores. After Gilbert and Sullivan suffered a large loss of revenue when a number of successful pirated productions of *H.M.S. Pinafore* opened in the United States, they decided to premiere their next opera, *Pirates of Penzance*, at the Fifth Avenue Theatre in New York in order to be protected by the US copyright law (Gilbert and Sullivan 1960). In nineteenth century America it was common to find counterfeit foreign wines, gloves, and thread (Mihm 2007).

Measuring the Counterfeit Market

In 2008, the US government estimated the global market value of the counterfeit industry at $500 billion with a growth rate of 1,700% over the past 10 years (U.S. Customs and Border Protection 2008). The estimates for the size of the worldwide counterfeit goods market seem to have coalesced around $600 billion annually. In 2012, The IACC reports that "[c]ounterfeiting is a $600 billion a year problem. In fact, it's a problem that has grown over 10,000% in the past two decades, in part fueled by consumer demand." But searching behind this well-worn estimate reveals a serious problem with this "accepted wisdom." Estimates of the counterfeit goods market range from as low as $200–600 billion to as high as $1 trillion. Since there is little agreement on definitions and serious problems of measurement, it is not really clear what the right number is. Following is a brief examination of this problem.

Attempting to measure the global value of counterfeit products is excruciatingly difficult. This is understandable given the illegal nature of this activity. The only real data are surrogate indicators such as seizures of pirate product by police or Customs authorities. In addition, there is no agreement on factors that should be considered when calculating the scale of counterfeiting. Should the estimate include sales lost by specific brands and at what prices, damage to brand equity, total sales of counterfeits, or some combination of these factors? (Green and Smith 2002). The latest attempt to quantify the counterfeit goods market was completed by the US government's General Accountability Office (GAO). In developing their information the GAO interviewed government officials, representatives of industry associations, academic institutions, and firms and reviewed several existing documents and studies. The GAO concluded that counterfeit product is a significant problem but "quantifying the economic impact of counterfeit and pirated goods on the US economy is challenging primarily because of the lack of available data" (GAO 2010).

The GAO report focuses on two key assumptions in measuring counterfeit goods—substitution rate and value. The former is the rate at which the buyer is willing to switch from a fake good to the genuine product. If the rate is assumed to be one-to-one, it must be assumed that the fake is nearly identical to the real product, the buyer is paying full price for the fake, and the buyer is not aware of buying a fake. These assumptions are rarely all true at the same time. Value focuses on the level in the production chain at which the good is priced—production cost or retail price for instance.

The GAO found that commonly cited figures for counterfeit products are often attributed to the US government sources such as the Federal Bureau of Investigation (FBI) or the Customs and Border Protection Service (CBP). However, the FBI, when asked about their numbers by the GAO, claimed that they have "no record of source data or methodology" for their estimates and the CBP could not identify the origin of their figures and has informed its staff to discontinue their use (GAO 2010).

Several methods have been used to calculate the size of the counterfeit goods market including extrapolation from counterfeit goods seizures, survey of supply and demand, use of economic multipliers, and even the "rule of thumb." Each of these methods faces daunting challenges to accuracy and none of these methods can be relied upon.

Some economists even question the idea that there *are* losses associated with counterfeiting. The point is that consumers who buy fakes are a market segment that purchases counterfeit because of their inability to afford the genuine product. Therefore, buyers in that segment do not really represent lost sales. The argument centers on the idea that these consumers would not have bought the genuine product anyway.

The Organization for Economic Cooperation and Development (OECD 2007) states, after an in-depth look at the attempts to measure this market, "the overall degree to which products are being counterfeited and pirated is unknown, and there do not appear to be any methodologies that could be employed to develop an acceptable overall estimate."

Negative Effects of Counterfeit Goods

The existence of a large counterfeit market takes its toll in many ways. The harmed constituents are identified in Fig. 2.1. Obviously consumers may be harmed by using inferior products. This damage can be as minimal as the loss of a few dollars or disappointing product performance or as important as serious injury to physical well-being. The World Health Organization (WHO Fact Sheet No. 275) claims that a high percentage of medicines on sale in Africa, parts of Asia and Latin America may be what they call SFFC (Spurious/falsely labeled/falsified/counterfeit) medicines. The US Center for Disease Control states "Overall, global estimates of drug counterfeiting are ambiguous, depending on region, but proportions range from 1% of sales in developed countries to more than 10% in developing countries. In specific regions in Africa, Asia, and Latin America, chances of purchasing a counterfeit drug may be higher than 30%" (Green 2011). In 2010, the United Nations Office on Drugs and Crime cautions the growing concern about counterfeits encroaching on unsuspecting consumers as "[P]roduct counterfeiting is a form of consumer fraud:

Fig. 2.1 Damage from counterfeit goods market

a product is sold, purporting to be something that it is not. The practice is widespread—products destined for 140 countries were detected in 2008—and poses a serious global challenge. The branding of a product provides implicit quality assurance and a legal line of accountability that consumers have come to take for granted" (United Nations Office on Drugs and Crime 2010, p. 10).

In the past decade, bad news from China emphasized that the problem of counterfeit goods can be a matter of life and death. In less than a week cough syrup containing ethylene glycol was identified as responsible for the deaths of hundreds of people in Panama and the Dominican Republic, toothpaste tainted with the same chemical had been found on three continents (Castle 2007), and a cell phone exploded killing a 22-year-old man in western China. Phone manufacturers, Motorola and Nokia, blamed counterfeit batteries (Barboza 2007). These episodes followed the tainted pet food problem which surfaced in the United States in the spring and summer of 2007.

Overall, the problem of fakes is not just in luxury goods, but an array of illicit products ranging from counterfeit baby formula to fake auto parts have been reported in the media for the past decade. In 2011, *USA Today* claimed that even the US military is not immune to counterfeit goods and reports that "investigators found that counterfeit or suspect electronic parts were installed or delivered to the military for several weapons systems, including military aircraft such as the Air Force's C-17 and the Marine Corps' CH-46 helicopter, as well as the Army's Theatre High-Altitude Area Defence (THAAD) missile defense system." (*USA Today* 2011, p. 6).

According to the US Customs and Border Protection report for fiscal year 2010, more than $600,000 in counterfeit bearings was seized during the year. This represented a sevenfold increase in seizures in this product category. A 2010 report by the UN Office on Drugs and Crime mentions the obvious designer products as well as counterfeit auto parts and batteries. The US GAO (2010) also identifies electrical components, household cleaners, and other household goods as examples of counterfeit products which may harm consumers.

Home countries of firms suffering from imitated products lose exports, taxes, and other revenues as well as employment. Even host countries (here identified as the source of the counterfeit goods) while they may experience some short-term gains in consumer welfare will probably eventually suffer a reduction in foreign direct investment since firms may fear their products may be copied once they are manufactured or introduced into a particular market. In addition these host countries may experience a growth in the underground economy, less legitimate employment, more employment at substandard wages, and reduced competitiveness because of a heavy reliance on counterfeit products. There is some evidence that exports will be reduced from countries that are known for substandard goods particularly in pharmaceutical products (OECD 2007d). Host countries also incur a loss of tax revenues and additional costs for anticounterfeiting activities. In some cases corruption is more widespread with the growth of a large counterfeit market.

Both home and host countries may also suffer from environmental effects first from the waste of destroying pirated goods and second because substandard products may have negative effects. For instance, the use of counterfeit fertilizers caused serious damage and destruction of harvests in large areas in China, Russia, the Ukraine, and Italy (OECD 2007b). Various effects of pirated products can cause risks to public health and even loss of confidence in the governments themselves. In 2010, the United Nations Office on Drugs and Crime (UNODC) supports these concerns stating that "[U]naccountable [counterfeit] products are often dangerous products, and the damage is not just felt in the receiving countries: the producing countries also suffer. Even as the major brands work to improve labor standards and workplace safety at their outsourced manufacturing sites, counterfeit goods producers take advantage of global sweatshops. As licensed manufacturers try to improve their environmental impact standards, counterfeiters enjoy the cost savings of dirty production. In short, anywhere that the international community attempts to establish good practice standards for industry, counterfeiters undercut them" (UNODC 2010, p. 10).

For purposes of this book we will center on the losses to the owners of the intellectual property. Obviously these firms may suffer loss of revenues from royalties, sales, and profits as well as increased costs for policing and fighting pirates. These costs may reduce organizational growth. In addition they may suffer from declining customer loyalty through brand dilution. Because of widespread copying, some firms may cut their investments in research and development thereby decreasing innovation. Underwriters Laboratories (UL) summarizes the loss to genuine manufacturers as:

> Legitimate manufacturers invest in research and development, quality materials, and manufacturing processes, and they work to meet the conformity assessment schemes of their markets. They work to build brand recognition and to foster goodwill with their end users. The counterfeiters that are their direct competition rely on stealing their brand names and profiting from their goodwill and reputations resulting in the following:
>
> - Direct loss of sales.
> - Loss of goodwill.
> - Irreparable damage to corporate brand/reputation.
> - Trademark dilution.
> - Costs of protecting and enforcing their intellectual property rights (IPR). ("The Impact of Counterfeiting," 2012, pp. 4–5).

Smaller firms face displacement of management time from growing the business to fighting the counterfeiters. Legitimate wholesalers and retailers are also harmed by counterfeit goods. First they lose revenue to the fakes. But these channel members may also be put in a difficult position when consumers ask for repairs or replacement of counterfeit products. The end result may be a loss of confidence in these middlemen and ultimately in the brand.

One additional cost must be considered. Counterfeiting is a major funding source for organized crime and terrorist organizations. The EU Organised Crime Threat Assessment (Europol 2011) identifies Chinese organized crime groups as particularly active in the production and distribution of "counterfeit cigarettes, shoes, toys, and pharmaceuticals." Other groups identified as the beneficiaries of counterfeit products are the Real Irish Republican Army (Real IRA), the Kurdistan Workers'

Party (PKK), Hezbollah, Hamas, and al Qaeda and those who perpetrated the Madrid train bombings in 2004 (US Department of Homeland Security 2008; "Counterfeit goods linked" 2007; Anti-Counterfeiting Amendments 2004; Willson 2009). The first report on transnational crime conducted by the UNODC (2010) claims that, "[M]ost organized crime problems today [2010] seem to be less a matter of a group of individuals who are involved in a range of illicit activities, and more a matter of a group of illicit activities in which some individuals and groups are presently involved: strategies aimed at the groups will not stop the illicit activities if the dynamic of the market remain unaddressed" (p. 5).

Thus, either criminal organizations or individuals can provide a portfolio of products and services that range from human trafficking and narcotics to counterfeit goods. Indeed, UNODC (2010) provides separate analyses on trafficking in persons; smuggling of migrants; cocaine; heroin; firearms; environmental resources (e.g., wildlife taken from Africa); counterfeit products; maritime piracy; and cybercrime. Overall, illicit traders can diversify activities and can ultimately reinvest profits from one of their illicit business units, such as counterfeit goods, to fund another such as human trafficking.

The Economist (2008) advised brand holders to "look for the silver lining" of piracy. Companies can find out which songs are most popular by determining those most often shared on peer-to-peer networks. Or a software firm may establish itself as the standard since the initially used pirated software creates a future market for the real thing. But even this article advises that IPR owners should fight for their rights despite the fact that sometimes they can use the counterfeit product to their advantage.

The Growth of the Counterfeit Goods Market

There is no doubt the counterfeit market is growing but it is not clear what the real magnitude is. In 1982 the International Trade Commission estimated the worldwide sales of counterfeit goods at $5.5 billion (Abbott and Sporn 2002). Since that time many estimates of world counterfeit goods markets have been made. In 1984 the International Anti-Counterfeiting Coalition estimated the worldwide market at $25–30 billion (Stern 1985). By 1996 the *Economist* even found a source that gauged the market at $1 trillion. In 2001 the International Chamber of Commerce estimated that 5–7% of world trade was in counterfeit goods and that the counterfeit market was worth $350 billion. This 5–7% figure initially was used by the Chamber in 1997 which even then called the percentage only a "general assumption" (Bialik 2007). As the OECD report (2007c) politely puts it "the metrics underlying the ICC estimates are not clear." The OECD report says that the ICC estimates "reflect judgments that are not supported by clear data." In 2006, the US government estimated the global market value of the counterfeit industry at $500 billion with a growth rate of 1,700% over the past 10 years (Intellectual Property Rights, 2006). As we have seen, most estimates seem to agree on the $500–600 billion range (IACC 2007;

Punch 2005). It is assumed that this estimate includes all forms of IPR violations involving both products and services and sales within and across country borders.

The OECD (2007c) put the worldwide volume of tangible counterfeit *products* at about $200 billion, an amount larger than the GDPs of 150 countries. However even the OECD estimates are based on incomplete information. The OECD (2007d) itself says, "available information on counterfeiting and piracy falls far short of what is needed for robust analysis and policymaking" and the organization makes a series of detailed recommendations for the improvement of data collection. According to Bialik (2007) the OECD's estimate was originally extrapolated from Customs seizures based on reports from 45 countries who responded to requests for data with enough information to be useful for analysis. A recent attempt to quantify the counterfeit goods market was completed by Frontier Economics. They estimate value of the worldwide counterfeit product market at $465–650 billion in 2008 (Frontier Economics 2011). Their approach is based on Customs seizure ratios developed by the OECD. But that approach raises many questions.

The amount of counterfeit product intercepted by Customs services around the world is a tiny percentage of the overall estimate of the worldwide counterfeit goods market. The OECD (2007c) gives the value of seizures by Customs services in 35 countries reporting this particular data at about $769 million in 2005, representing 0.01% of total imports for these countries. Nevertheless, the received data were extrapolated to the non-responding countries. Researchers used a factor of 5% for frequently pirated goods in countries where there are a large number of pirates. Using this factor, researchers calculated a total of $100 billion then doubled that number to account for "statistical variability in their model" (Bialik 2007). The OECD (2009) updated their work at the end of 2009 claiming that the total had reached $250 million and accounted for 1.95% of world trade in 2007. The update uses the same methodology but adjusts for increasing world trade. Yet searching "OECD counterfeit goods report" on Google results in about 70,000 hits, most of which are unquestioningly repeating either the earlier $200 billion or the later $250 billion figure.

Another example of this may be found in information provided by Havocscope. This organization puts forth an extremely precise global estimate for counterfeit and piracy of $657.76 billion (Havocscope 2012) and estimates the total availability of counterfeit products in the United States at $225 billion. However even a cursory review of this organization's website reveals problems with the numbers. Estimates are developed from published resources such as newspapers and government studies. The organization also states that "the manner in which the original source determined the figure is not always available" and "the numbers will include a high level of uncertainty. A majority of the figures will be based on estimates and will be difficult to verify."

In Canada the cost of counterfeiting was estimated at $30 billion annually. This figure, used repeatedly by many, including the US Ambassador David Wilkins in a March 2007 speech, originated with the Royal Canadian Mounted Police (RCMP) in 2005. Careful research by Geist (2007), Chair of Internet and E-Commerce Law on the University of Ottawa Law Faculty, revealed that the $30 billion number was derived from two main sources: an IACC claim that 20% of the Canadian market is made up of counterfeit product and an estimate that 3–4% of Canadian two-way trade consists of counterfeit product given by the chief economist for the Canadian Manufacturing and Exporters Association in 2005. Geist (2012) recently repeated his doubts about this number. The recent OECD estimate placing the total for global counterfeiting at $250 billion certainly calls into doubt the formerly accepted $30 billion Canadian figure since Canadian trade accounts for less than 3% of world trade (Geist 2012).

Researching the size of the counterfeit market reveals that the same numbers from very few sources are repeated over and over. In truth it is virtually impossible to determine the real size of the worldwide counterfeit product market. But despite the uncertainty of measurement methods, it appears that product counterfeiting is significant and growing (GAO 2010; OECD 2009; Croxon 2007; UNECE 2007; ICE 2007; IACC 2007; EC-europa 2009).

Effects on the United States

There is some confusion as to the true effect of counterfeit product upon US firms. As long ago as 1994 estimates of the US losses stood at $200 billion per year (Nill and Shultz 1996). The US Customs Service estimated that the US economy was losing between $200 and $250 billion per year and a total of 750,000 American jobs because of product counterfeiting (ICE 2007). It is not clear whether these figures are meant to refer to lost sales on a worldwide or domestic basis. Since many US firms achieve up to 50% of their sales in overseas markets, it seems reasonable to believe that this figure most likely includes all worldwide sales. Certainly in order to agree with the latest OECD estimate of $250 billion on a worldwide basis, the effect on the US markets would have to be far smaller.

Over the years the US Customs has generally increased the number of counterfeit product seizures. The graph below shows the dollar volume of seizures made from 1997 through 2011 (Fig. 2.2).

In 1997 the US Customs stopped about $38 million worth of counterfeit products. Seizures increased to $99 million in 1999 and then declined in 2000 and 2001 only recovering to $99 million once again in 2002. Customs made counterfeit product seizures in 2006 valued at about $155 million. The dollar amount of seizures had continued to increase, moving up to nearly $200 million in 2007, over $273 million in 2008 but slipping to about $178 million in 2011 (US Customs and Border Protection 2011).

The growth in the number of counterfeit product seizures is certainly commendable but an earlier study by the GAO (2007) suggests that the percentage of the US market accounted for by counterfeit product may be much smaller than has been previously thought. Inspecting 287,000 randomly selected shipments from 2000 to 2005 the GAO found counterfeiting violations in only 0.06%. The GAO also stated that Customs seizures in 2005 amounted to only 0.0017% of the value of goods in

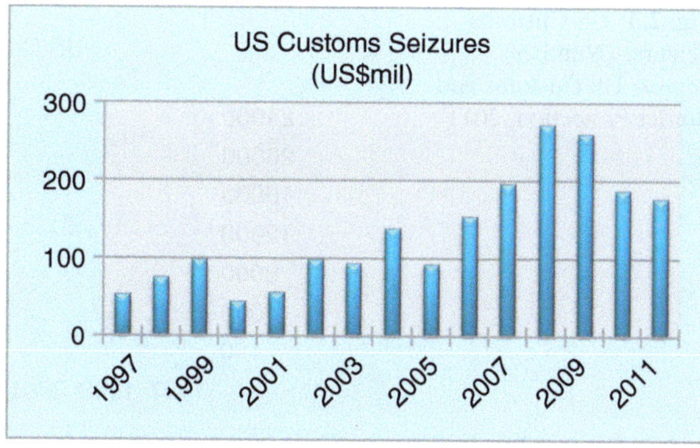

Fig. 2.2 US Customs Seizures (US$ million). *Source*: US Customs and Border Protection (2011)

product categories likely to be subject to counterfeit. The GAO analyzed all products imported into the United States and developed a list of IP-related product categories. For 2005 imports of these products totaled approximately $555 billion. This list was based on products where IP-related seizures had been made over the last 5 years. It hardly seems possible that the US level of counterfeit goods would reach nearly 40% of all imported IP-related products which would be the case if the $200 billion figure for U.S. losses from counterfeits is used.

Recently, the *number* of seizures has been increasing (US Customs and Border Protection 2011). In 1997 Customs stopped 1,943 shipments of pirated goods. This increased to more than 3,000 in 1998 and moved steadily up to over 8,000 in 2005. The number of shipments intercepted held steady in the 14–15,000 range from 2006 to 2009 and then increased to about 20,000 in 2010 and nearly 25,000 in 2011. This can clearly be seen in the graph below. Since the total dollar value of seizures has decreased while the number of shipments intercepted has increased, it is obvious that the average value of an IPR seizure dropped significantly, from $17,566 in 2009 to $7,180 in 2011 (Fig. 2.3).

The earlier GAO study raises questions about the usability of the Customs seizure data as an indicator of the size and growth of the counterfeit market. First it appears that enforcement varies widely between ports with some ports finding 100 times the amount of counterfeit products as other ports. Only ten ports accounted for a quarter of seizure value and 84% of penalty cases since 2001. The pressure to move products through ports and airports is very high especially since imports had grown from about $1.2 trillion in 2001 to about $1.7 trillion in 2005, and shipments filed with Customs up about 25% over the same period.

Products Counterfeited

Products that are most vulnerable to product counterfeiting fall into four categories according to Jacobs et al. (2001):

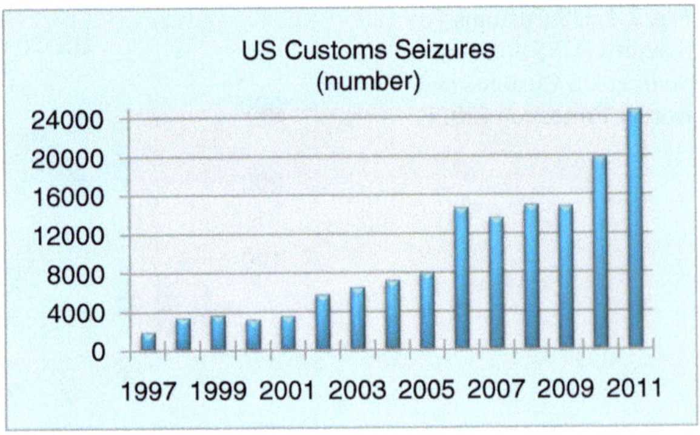

Fig. 2.3 US Customs Seizures (Number). *Source*: US Customs and Border Protection, 2011

- Highly visible, high volume, low tech products with a well-known brand names such as toothpaste and chocolate.
- High-priced, high-tech products such as computer games, CDs, DVDs, auto and airplane parts.
- Exclusive prestige products such as clothing, apparel, and perfume.
- Intensive R&D, high-tech products such as pharmaceuticals and some industrial products.

More contemporary research indicates that the types of products being counterfeited are expanding. The OECD (2007) found a shift from high-value luxury items to common products and an expansion of the range of pirated luxury products. Their list of products subject to intellectual property infringement includes all the product types identified by Jacobs et al. but also chemicals and pesticides, electrical components, food and drink and agricultural products, tobacco products, furniture, sporting goods, and a variety of other items including qualification certificates. In the OECD study (2007d) 13 countries reported that the scope of products counterfeited was expanding rapidly and 16 other countries said the range was expanding steadily.

Naim (2005) also supplies an exhaustive list. He identifies the Chery QQ, made in China, as an automobile which has the look and feel of the Chevrolet Spark. He also describes forgeries of American-made sewer pumps and Italian valves. Hopkins et al. (2003) tell of counterfeit aircraft bolts as well as helicopter blades.

In the United States, types of products seized vary from year to year but wearing apparel and footwear have often topped the list since 1982. Pirate optical media, computers, and pharmaceuticals are nearly always among the most frequently seized products. The total value of confiscated cigarettes has appeared in the top ten for the past 2 years. The table below describes the latest US government seizures by value (Table 2.1).

Recent data from the European Union show similar product patterns. EU Customs reported the value of seized product (designated as "detentions" by the European Commission) at €1,110,052,402 for 79,112 cases. Seizures included over €200 million in clothing and accessories, €166 million in various types of shoes, approximately €100 million in bags, wallets and purses, €94 million in watches, and €76

Table 2.1 FY 2011 top IPR commodities seized

Commodity	Domestic value ($)	% of total
Consumer electronics	38,992,613	22
Footwear	25,562,613	14
Pharmaceuticals	16,848,192	9
Optical media	15,567,059	9
Wearing apparel	14,755,599	8
Perfume/cologne	9,456,208	5
Watches/parts	8,435,256	5
Cigarettes	8,183,993	5
Computers/hardware	7,814,457	4
Toys/electronic games	7,597,367	4
All other commodities	25,419,276	14
Total FY 2011 domestic value	178,322,633	
Number of seizures	24,792	

Source: US Customs and Border Protection

million in mobile phones and accessories. Nearly €125 million in counterfeit cigarettes was seized in 2010 (European Commission 2011a, 2011b, 2011c, 2011d).

Software is particularly vulnerable to copying. According to the most recent Business Software Alliance (BSA) study more than 40% of software used worldwide is pirated. Such widespread copying amounts to $59 billion in annual losses from counterfeiting according to the software industry (BSA/IDC 2011e). In a recent case Microsoft, working with the US and Chinese authorities, built the "largest [software] counterfeiting case in history" against a criminal ring believed to have accounted for more than $2 billion in counterfeit Microsoft product from 2003 to 2008. Eleven members of the ring were convicted, receiving prison terms of 1½–6½ years (Microsoft 2010).

The growth of counterfeit pharmaceuticals, the so-called SFFC drugs, has taken a heavy toll. Almost one decade ago, a healthy 22-year-old Argentinean woman was given iron injections to cure her mild anemia. In December 2004 she died of liver failure. It was determined that she had been given a toxic counterfeit but the authorities were unable to determine the source of the product because of falsified paperwork. A recall was begun but the fragmented distribution system made it impossible to take the entire harmful product off the market.

In 2008, the blood thinner Heparin was found to have counterfeit active ingredients sourced from Changzhou SPL in China. In this case, this ingredient was replaced by a substitute, eventually resulting in as many as 81 deaths. Baxter, the firm which sold the drug in the US, faced 740 lawsuits and eventually sold the division that produced the drug. In 2009, a Chinese antidiabetic medicine containing six times the normal active ingredient was blamed for the deaths of two people. In 2012, *The Wall Street Journal* reported the problem of a counterfeit cancer-treating drug, Avastin®, distributed by way of Canadian Internet pharmacies on a trade route that, "illustrated the circuitous path that pharmaceuticals can take before reaching consumers. Wherever the counterfeit Avastin® was manufactured—possibly China—investigators are examining a zigzagging route that may have taken the product through Turkey and Egypt before it was sold to Swiss and Danish wholesalers and then to Mr. Haughton's [a Canadian citizen] UK wholesaler, River East Supplies Ltd" (Weaver et al. 2012, p. 9). The myriad of distribution points (both physical and virtual) used in the recent case is illustrated in Fig. 2.4.

Large and Small Firms Affected

Both large and small firms are fighting against unauthorized copying of their products. An example on the smaller end is ABRO, a private branding auto-parts distributor. The firm has built its sales to $180 million and offers more than 600 products under the ABRO brand name. Peter Baranay, president and chief executive of the firm, is aggressive in fighting against counterfeiters, spending about $1 million per year to do so. They claim success in fighting counterfeiters in China, Pakistan, India, and Saudi Arabia (Morton 2011). Another small firm that faced counterfeiting was Heelys, a manufacturer of sneakers that incorporate wheels in the heel. When first introduced the product took off with sales increasing over 250% to about $188 million by first quarter 2007. At the time, Heelys employed less than 50 people, and had arranged for manufacture of their products in South Korea and China. As a result one Korean firm was selling a one-wheel roller shoe called "Heatys" (Phillips 2007; Heelys, Inc 2007a, 2007b). Since 2002 Heelys has been fighting counterfeits in China. Despite a ruling from the Chinese government that two factories were violating Heelys' patents, a year passed before the government took action. Moreover, this delay was followed by minimal corrective action, amounting to confiscation of just a few cases of counterfeit shoes and a promise not to make any more copies (Yung 2006).

At the other end of the scale is Starbucks, a firm with more than $12.2 billion in sales and nearly 150,000 employees (NY Times 2012). Starbucks has been fighting to protect its trademark around the world. In Russia the firm regained its right to use its brand after a favorable ruling against a "trademark squatter." Anyone visiting Shanghai will see not only a number of Starbucks locations, but also copycats of every kind. One Shanghai coffee house was using the name Xingbake, a clever knockoff of the Starbucks name. In Pinyin "xing" means star, and "bake," pronounced bah-kuh, sounds like bucks. Thus, the coffee house name replicated the Starbucks brand name using a combination of Chinese characters and sound. Starbucks sued in 2003, asserting that its trademark had been registered in China since 1996. In early 2006, a Shanghai court ordered Xingbake Café to discontinue the use of their version of the Starbucks name, and required that it pay Starbuck's 500,000 Yuan, equivalent to about $62,000, in damages. This was the first ruling of its kind under a 2001 Chinese law (Noon 2006). Few firms have been successful in legal proceedings in China. The Walt Disney Co. was the first to receive damages when a Beijing Court ruled in 1999 against Chinese companies for their production of children's books based on Disney's animated films. Disney received a $77,000

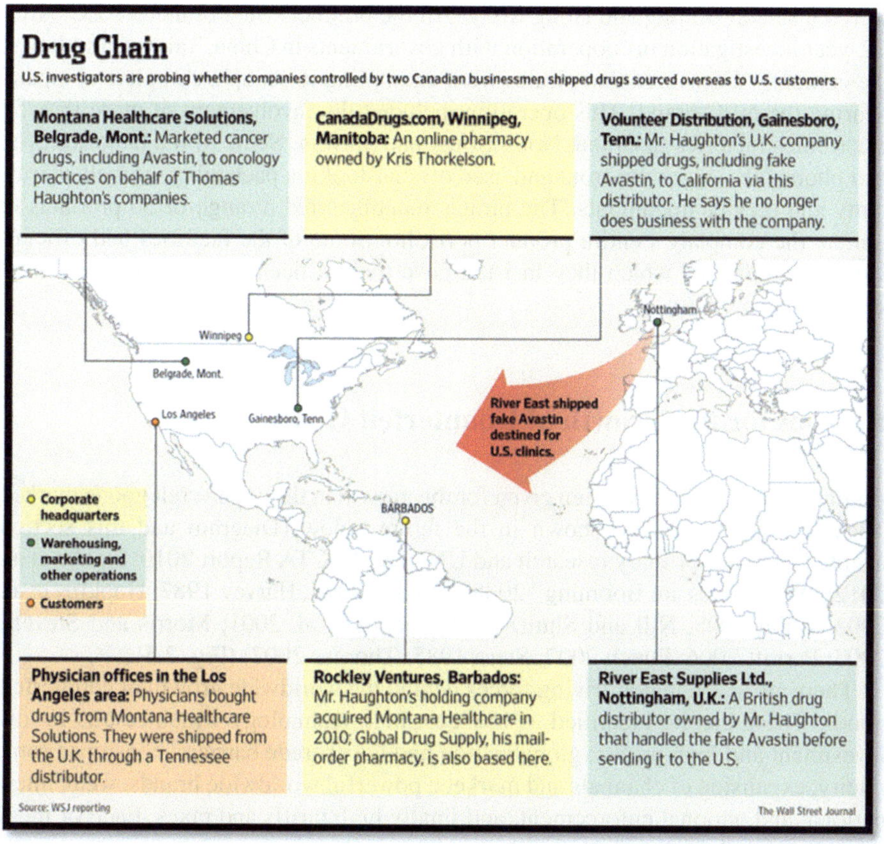

Fig. 2.4 Estimated trade routes of fake Avastin®. *Source*: Weaver, C., Whalen, J., & Faucon, B. (March 7, 2012). Drug distributor is tied to imports of fakes. *The Wall Street Journal*

judgment (Faison 1995). Nike, a $30 billion firm, has also been fighting counterfeits for years. A few years ago, the German Customs Department seized what could have been the largest cache of counterfeit goods—one million pairs of phony Nike sneakers, in a total of 117 shipping containers worth nearly $500 million ("Counterfeit Sneakers" 2006). After breaking up a large counterfeit market for their products in the Ukraine, Procter & Gamble found that 43% of hair care products and 23% of laundry products branded with their name were actually counterfeit (UNECE 2007).

A particularly brazen case of counterfeiting was discovered in Summer, 2011 (BBC 2011). An American visiting Kunming, China found three fake Apple stores. The décor and staff mimicked the genuine stores and the workers even believed they were working in one. After launching an investigation, Chinese authorities eventually found 22 of these unauthorized stores.

Apparently this is a common occurrence in the PRC. A few years ago, managers at the Tokyo headquarters of NEC learned that pirated keyboards, CDs, and DVDs were on sale in Beijing and Hong Kong. All the products were branded NEC. After a 2-year investigation in cooperation with governments in China, Taiwan, and Japan, the company discovered that pirates were attempting to set up a complete company bearing the NEC brand. This operation included the involvement of more than 50 electronics factories in China, Hong Kong, and Taiwan. Some of the factories even had phony NEC signs out front and used official-looking packaging, as well as warranty and service documents. The pirates manufactured a range of 50 products to imitate the company's entire product portfolio. Some of the factories had official-looking documents which they insisted gave them a license to manufacture NEC goods (Lague 2006).

Reasons for the Growth of Counterfeit Goods

A number of reasons have been given for the growth in the counterfeit goods market. These driving forces are shown in the figure below (Diagram and this section adapted from our primary research and UNODC TOCTA Report 2010; Staake et al. 2012; "Why Fakes are Booming" 2008; OECD 2007d; Harvey 1987; Hopkins et al. 2003; Naim 2005; Nill and Shultz 1996; Jacobs et al. 2001; Morris and Stevens 2007; Parloff 2006; Punch 2007; Stern 1985; Thomas 2007) (Fig. 2.5).

There are seven major driving forces behind the worldwide growth of counterfeit goods. These can be identified as low cost high technology which results in low investment and high profits; globalization and lower trade barriers; consumer complicity; expansion of channels and markets; powerful worldwide brands; weak international and national enforcement, and finally high tariffs and taxes. Each of these is explored in the following sections.

Low Cost High Technology = Low Investment, High Profits

Pirates avoid all the usual costs related to creating and marketing a product, including research and development, advertising, and warranty service. They also avoid the costs of meeting health and safety, quality control, and minimum wage regulations. Staake et al. (2012) point out that some counterfeiters experience high costs licit manufacturers do not face. According to their analysis product seizures are the major costs impacting these pirates. Nevertheless, without the start-up and overhead costs of legitimate manufacturers counterfeiting may be vastly profitable. These researchers estimate counterfeiters experience margins two-thirds higher than licit manufacturers with no tax burden applied to the profits.

Many products can be manufactured with easily purchased high technology equipment that is widely available at reasonable prices. And technological developments in modeling, printing, and scanning make it easy to make convincing copies through reverse engineering. According to *Fortune*, manufacturers themselves have

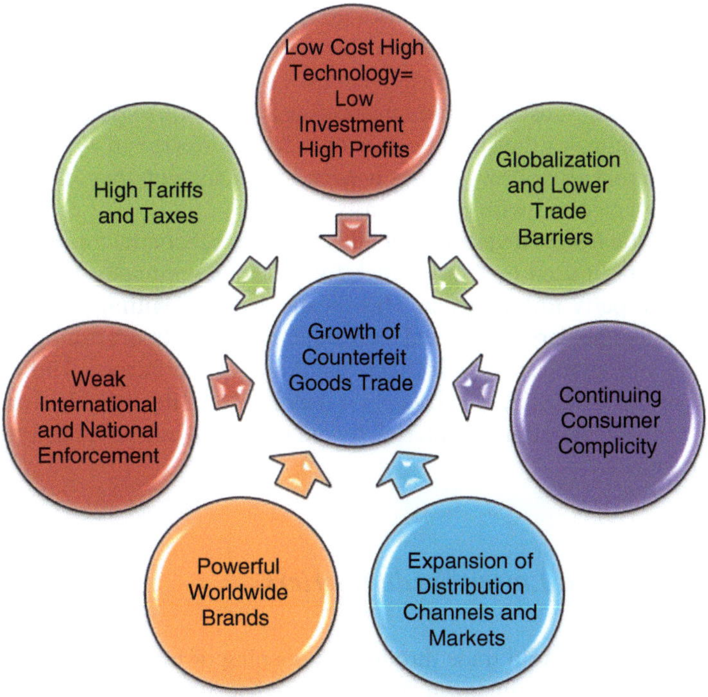

Fig 2.5 Reasons for the growth of counterfeit goods trade

shared technology and know-how including designs, molds, specifications, and trade secrets with various subsidiaries, licensees, contractors, and subcontractors in markets all across the world and therefore "it's extremely hard to police global supply chains, and IP is leaking out through 1,000 cracks." In the fashion industry pirates can buy one copy of a genuine product, take it apart and using scanning equipment, develop patterns which allow them to make almost perfect fakes (Parloff 2006). Dr. Frederick Mostert (2008), past president of the International Trademark Association, describing digital fakes in a *Financial Times* supplement says, "every product known to mankind can, and is, being perfectly copied." He describes personally witnessing software and scanners which allowed reverse engineering of highly complicated watches.

One example of the rapid reduction in cost for technology is computer equipment, which formerly was priced out of the grasp of most pirates, and is now available at a fraction of the cost. Doms (2003) shows the cost of computer equipment declining between 14 and 17% annually from 1991 to 2000. This makes copying of DVDs and CDs quite simple and inexpensive. This computer equipment, combined with high quality digital printers, also makes it easy to imitate genuine trademarks and packaging. Counterfeiters have also improved their ability to reproduce holograms and other sophisticated genuine identifying marks. Searching the Internet will give a pirate many sources for manufacturing equipment. Purchasing software to help in manufacturing is also easy with some of it even available on the counterfeit market. Since manufacturing is driven by software, getting the right CD allows pirates to make a clone that looks right but uses lower grade materials.

The decline in the cost of communications is also a boon to pirates. For instance, Doms (2003) estimates the cost of cell phones fell an average of 17% from 1983 to 1997. The Internet also allows pirates to keep in contact with their distribution outlets at very low cost and with high security.

Of course, the lowest investment of all is faced by subcontractors who engage in "split runs," a term used by Chris Israel, former US Coordinator for International Intellectual Property Enforcement. This means making legitimate products under contract to brand holders by day and then either high quality overruns or poor quality imitations by night after the official shutdown of the factory. These so-called third shift products (USITC 2011), even if they are indistinguishable from genuine products, are most definitely counterfeit by our definition and have been found to be so in some courts.

Globalization and Lower Trade Barriers

The rapid growth of world trade through the opening of markets, coupled with the reduction of barriers to financial and merchandise flows, has certainly opened opportunities for product pirates. The sheer volume of imports in many countries makes it almost impossible for Customs Services to interdict phony products. According to Deutsche Bank Research (2011) more than 25 million containers flowed through each of the ports of Shanghai and Singapore, ten million through Rotterdam and more than five million through Los Angeles in 2009. Between 1990 and 2008 total container throughput grew at an average annual rate of 10%. In 2011, Maersk, a leading shipper with an estimated 14.4% of container-fleet capacity, predicted more than an 8% growth in the global container market (Leach 2011).

The advent of NAFTA and the closer cooperation within the European Union means fewer checks on products flowing across borders. Just since 1999, according to the World Trade Organization (2012), annual world trade in goods and services has doubled from less than $6 trillion to about $19 trillion in 2010 (Fig. 2.6).

During the same time, the average tariff applied to imports by developing countries declined from 16.5% in 1996 to less than 10% in 2011, and in the most developed countries the average tariff declined from 5.3 to 2.7% over the same period (World Bank 2011).

Free-trade zones can serve as safe havens for counterfeiters. There are now about 3,000 in about 135 countries (Shah 2010). The OECD (2007e) reports that free trade zones and free ports are used by counterfeiters in three different ways. First, products are shipped into the free-trade areas and then re-exported. This allows the pirates to engage in "origin laundering" whereby the true origin of these products is obscured or erased by moving them through a number of ports and sometimes altering the documentation accompanying the shipments. Second, unfinished products

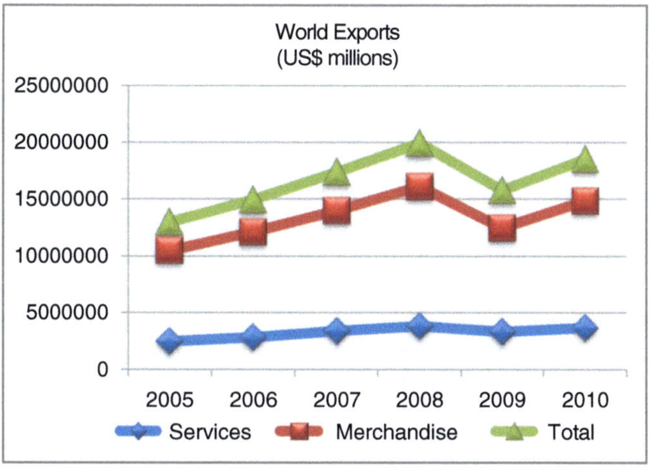

Fig. 2.6 Annual world trade. *Source*: World Trade Organization

may be shipped to these free-trade areas for further processing including adding counterfeit trademarks or labels or repackaging. Finally, free-trade areas are used for manufacturing pirate goods.

An important seizure revealed that large amounts of counterfeit drugs were supplied through a complex arrangement using a free-trade zone known as Jebel Ali in Dubai, United Arab Emirates (UAE). This free-trade zone, the oldest in the Emirates, handles 11 million containers each month (Shah 2010). The drugs were originally manufactured in China, sent through Hong Kong to the free-trade zone in Dubai to Britain then the Bahamas and finally back to Britain where the products were mailed to customers with UK postage. They were sold on an Internet site which made American customers believe they were buying medicines from a Canadian website. The sheer size of Jebel Ali makes it extremely difficult to track down counterfeit product. In addition there is a "murky line of authority" for rooting out counterfeits there (Bogdanich 2007).

The free flow of financial resources has also been helpful to counterfeiters since it is relatively easy for them to launder profits from pirate operations and to move investment and therefore production from one country to another. Exchange controls have been reduced or eliminated in most countries. The growing wire transfer industry including Western Union and even the expanding use of ATM cards make it easier for counterfeiters to move their funds to the most advantageous markets. Chaudhry and Stumpf (2010) assert that, "[A] key issue that has been ignored by most anti-counterfeiting studies is money: how to stop the cross-border flow of funds needed to make this illicit trade solvent. The trade in fakes requires massive amounts of funds that are facilitated across borders. Middlemen involved in the money supply chain are potential targets to choke the flow of illicit goods." (pp. 311–312).

Consumer Complicity

There is a great deal of evidence to suggest that consumers are all too willing to purchase counterfeit products even when they know the products are fake. Cultural differences can account for the popularity of counterfeiting. In a study of consumer willingness to obtain fake pharmaceutical and/or movies in Brazil, Russia, India, China, or the United States, we found varying levels of complicity for movies and pharmaceuticals (Chaudhry et al. 2011a, b). For example, Russian consumers had an 80 and 11% willingness to obtain illicit movies and pharmaceuticals respectively. Some years ago the *Journal of Commerce* (1999) reported that IPR is a Western concept and IPR infringement is not seen as morally wrong in China. This will be explored in more detail in Chap. 9.

In an early study, Tom et al. (1998) found that consumers are willing to purchase counterfeit goods for a variety of reasons, including a perception of the counterfeit to be as good as the authentic version; support of the counterfeit market as a means of expressing anti-big-business sentiment; and lax attitudes about the legal protection of intellectual property. Many analysts have attempted to generate a descriptive profile of a consumer who knowingly engages in illicit trade. Variables such as gender, age, ethnicity, occupation, and level of income have been assessed for decades with inconsistent results. For example, Eisend and Schuchert-Güler (2006) found that both demographic (e.g., age, education, income) and psychographic variables (e.g., willingness to take risks) identify consumers that were more receptive to fake goods. However, in one of our recent studies (Chaudhry et al. 2011a, b) we found that antecedents with the greatest impact on consumer attitudes towards and decisions/intentions to obtain fakes are product (i.e., price and quality) and purchase situation/mood. In contrast, demographics and national origin were poor predictors of complicity (p. 235).

Research completed by the authors revealed that, in markets where a firm was experiencing the most difficult counterfeit problems, over two-thirds of managers interviewed believed that consumers were willing to purchase a counterfeit good. We asked managers to rate the importance of specific product attributes that might be used by a consumer to determine whether a good was counterfeit or legitimate.

According to the managers we surveyed, consumers are fairly sophisticated. They can tell by price and by where they purchase the product whether it is legitimate or counterfeit. In any event consumers are quite willing to purchase counterfeits (Table 2.2).

This important subject is reviewed in depth in Chap. 5.

Expansion of Channels and Markets

With the growth of world trade, manufacturers have penetrated many markets which they were unable to serve only a few years ago. The emergence of an affluent class in Brazil, Russia, India, and China (BRIC countries) offers huge new markets for

Table 2.2 Product attributes used to determine authenticity

Product attribute	Importance in determining product authenticity (% choosing)
Price	88
Point of purchase	88
Slight difference in brand name	75
Packaging	56
Quality	50
Warranty	38
Anticounterfeiting label	31

Sources: Adapted from Chaudhry, P., Peters, J., Zimmerman, A., & Cordell, V. (2008). Evidence of managerial response to the level of consumer complicity, pirate activity, and host country enforcement of counterfeit goods: An exploratory study. *Multinational Business Review*, *17*(4), 32

products with well-known global brands. Counterfeiters have three major distribution outlets to customers: established retail shops, informal channels such as "flea markets," sidewalk vendors and clandestine shops, and of course the Internet.

While it is difficult for pirates to gain any real market share in well-established retail outlets, research suggests that the sale of counterfeit product through this channel is increasing. Although a British Home Office survey found that 44% of the businesses in three high-crime areas had been offered counterfeit goods in the year prior to the survey, generally it is most likely that legitimate retailers selling counterfeit products are not aware that the products are illegitimate (UNODC 2010).

A more common distribution method for fake products is through informal channels. A walk along Canal Street in New York City, Santee Alley in Los Angeles or Nanjing Lu in Shanghai will reveal a number of street vendors selling every kind of pirated product. Flea markets around the world feature branded products at impossible prices. On a recent trip to Shanghai one of the authors was able to spot fake Calloway golf clubs right next to counterfeit Docker shorts, being sold openly all in the same market. Toth (2007) describes a harrowing experience searching for counterfeit handbags in New York's Chinatown, being admitted to back room and basement "retail outlets." In the case of auto or aircraft parts, health and beauty aids, pharmaceuticals and even wearing apparel, the sheer complexity of distribution makes it easy for counterfeiters to intervene at some step to substitute copies for the real thing.

The Internet has provided an irresistible opportunity for pirated product. This channel allows a producer of counterfeit products to reach a nearly unlimited worldwide audience with his offers. Although it is extremely difficult to measure the size of this market *The Economist* estimated (2003) $25 billion in counterfeit goods was traded online annually. Virtually every type of product is now sold across the Internet and consumers have gained more confidence when using this channel. *Internet World Stats* (IWS) estimates that as of December 2011 there were more than two billion Internet consumers in the world with a global penetration rate of nearly 33% (Internet World Stats 2011). One brazen site claiming to sell "replicas" is called cannnyouseethedifference.com. It features knock-off Rolex watches, Gucci handbags, and Tiffany earrings. Photos of the real products are positioned next to the fakes with the question posed by the site itself: "can you see the difference?"

The OECD (2007) gives five major reasons for pirates' attraction to the Internet:

- *Anonymity*—it is easy for counterfeiters to conceal their true identities and lower the risk of detection.
- *Flexibility*—pirates can easily establish an online site then take it down or move it within 24–48 h to markets where IPR enforcement is weak.
- *Market size*—the sheer number of e-commerce sites and listings makes it very difficult for IPR owners and enforcement agencies to find and take action against pirates.
- *Market reach*—the Internet allows sellers to reach a huge global audience at low cost 24 h a day.
- *Deception*—widely available software and images on the Internet make it easy for pirates to create "clone" websites that look almost exactly like the brand holders' official sites.

Auction sites like eBay are popular venues for counterfeit product. Although there is some controversy related to the actual number, one source claims eBay is now host to more than 150 million listings at any given time (Power Sellers 2012). By some estimates eBay accounts for about 15% of Internet fraud which results in an estimated $32 million in annual losses (Berntsen 2010). One way to measure this is to look at the number of designer items for sale on sites like eBay. The truth is major designers rarely sell their products across the Internet nor do they license others to sell online. The inability of buyers to look carefully at these items makes it easy to sell fakes. Tiffany & Co. filed suit against eBay claiming that only 5% of Tiffany items for sale on the auction site were genuine (Punch 2005). Tiffany also claimed that eBay had a financial interest in looking the other way when it comes to counterfeit products sold on their site. The US courts did not agree with Tiffany, finding that eBay was not liable for trademark infringement that occurred on their site (Leu 2011).

Counterfeit drugs are an especially troubling aspect of Internet sales. Some Internet pharmacies are legitimate but there are many which provide prescription drugs just for the asking. In many cases these drugs are counterfeit. They may not produce the curative effects of the real thing or in the worst case they may do untold harm.

Powerful Worldwide Brands

Globalization has made it possible to develop truly global brands. Brands such as Coca-Cola, Apple, Chanel, and Google are recognized all over the world and have become hugely valuable assets. For instance, the world's most valuable brand is Coca-Cola and is worth about $72 billion. IBM's brand is valued at about $70 billion and not far behind are Microsoft and Google each of which is worth over $50 billion. Each of these brands and many others have been subject to extensive counterfeiting ("Best Global Brands" 2011). One 2009 study looking at the impact of counterfeiting on consumers' brand relationships in India and Thailand stated that "consumers are drawn to premium brands in part because of the exclusivity and connotation of prestige associated with them. These characteristics are also the reason such brands are attractive targets of counterfeiting" (Commuri 2009).

Consumers in Shanghai, London, Mumbai, and Moscow are now completely familiar with these brands. As described above these consumers want these brands but many cannot afford to purchase the legitimate items. This has given rise to suppliers who fill the need for products with famous brands at much lower prices.

Weak International and National Enforcement

The risk of starting a counterfeit products business is rather low in many countries for one very good reason: weak enforcement of intellectual property regulations.

US laws such as the Tariff Act of 1930, the Lanham Act, the Trademark Counterfeiting Act of 1984, and the Stop Counterfeiting in Manufactured Goods Act of 2006 are all designed to provide some form of legal recourse for the owners of intellectual property through civil and criminal law penalties in the United States. In addition, the NAFTA treaty, The Agreement on Trade-Related Aspects of Intellectual Property Rights (TRIPS) in the World Trade Organization (WTO), and the Scrivener regulations of the European Union are international measures implemented to encourage protection of intellectual property rights. For a detailed discussion of these multilateral trade agreements, see Chaudhry and Walsh (1995, 1996).

Although there are a number of national laws and international agreements designed to protect intellectual property rights, according to Chaudhry and Walsh (1996), "legal remedies available to the victims of counterfeited or pirated goods historically have been inadequate." Recent attempts to strengthen anti-pirating activities on the Internet have resulted in widespread public criticism. The proposed US laws Stop Online Piracy Act (SOPA) and the Protect Intellectual Property Act (PIPA) were so widely disliked that the US Congress decided not to go ahead with a vote on either. A similar international measure the Anti-Counterfeiting Trade Agreement (ACTA) is also facing worldwide protests (Jolly 2012).

A recent example of the relationship between penalties and profits was revealed when three men were arrested for selling phony Procrit, a very expensive drug which is a clear liquid. The men simply filled vials with water, then packaged them using genuine-looking boxes, labels, and inserts. Although the men were convicted, their sentences were less than they would have received for selling illegal narcotics (A Crime with Huge Profits 2012).

Naim (2005) attributes the lack of enforcement to government fiscal restraint imposed by the demands of the global capital markets. Since investors are "turned off" by large government deficits, these governments have had to cut funding to law enforcement. In addition these governments cannot compensate their civil servants adequately leaving them no alternative but to accept bribes from counterfeiters and to limit their enforcement activities. The extreme example of this is the so-called failed state, where criminal elements can capture the government. The recent world-wide financial crisis has only increased the strain on government budgets and has probably necessitated reductions in anticounterfeiting activities.

The descriptions in an earlier part of this chapter of the problems faced by ABRO, Heelys, Disney, and Starbucks in China and the paltry fines levied on the pirates reinforce the idea that the rewards of counterfeiting far outweigh the potential penalties.

High Tariffs and Taxes

We have seen how lowering trade barriers has increased trade, creating opportunities for counterfeit product to be made in one country and exported to others. At the same time, while it may seem counterintuitive, high tariffs and taxes can create opportunities for counterfeiters as well. These extra costs price consumers out of certain markets especially in less developed countries. In the case of disease-curing drugs, consumers may be aware that products are available and they are obviously highly motivated to get these products. Where governments have placed artificial price controls or import duties on these drugs counterfeiters may step in to supply the demand, offering far less effective or even dangerous products at affordable prices. According to Morris and Stevens (2007) combined total duties and taxes on retail medicines in 11 developing countries in 2003 ranged from 24% in Mexico to 55% in India. Many high-tariff countries have a serious problem with counterfeit medicines and the authors state "it is unlikely that this is entirely coincidental."

Highly taxed products such as alcohol and cigarettes often show a direct relationship between the level of taxation and the extent of counterfeit product available. In Ireland, where cigarette excise taxes were raised sharply between 2000 and 2009, the inflow of contraband products increased to 25% of the market over the same period (ITIC 2011).

The same logic may be applied to branded luxury goods where extensive advertising and highly visible retail outlets create demand but high prices deter most consumers from purchasing the products. This umbrella is one counterfeiters will most happily step under where investment and potential penalties are limited and rewards are significant.

Conclusions

Although product counterfeiting is certainly not a new phenomenon, much more attention is being paid to it in recent years. As we have seen counterfeit products may go back more than 2,000 years and punishment for infringement at least 700 years. Products which can be classified as counterfeit are those made without authorization from the owners of IPR (trademarks and patents and copyrights) associated with those products.

The measurement of the counterfeit market is fraught with difficulty. Given the illegal nature of the activity no direct measurement is possible. Compounding the problem is defining what exactly is being measured. Is it sales lost and should it be calculated based on current retail prices? Or should damage to brand equity be added? Those making the estimates, such as the OECD and the International Trade Commission, readily admit their methodologies leave much to be desired. Nevertheless the global value of counterfeit products at $600 billion seems to have gained acceptance. Some see the number as much higher and claim that 5–7% of world trade is in counterfeit. Since the actual seizures by Customs agencies around the world represent approximately 1/10 of 1% of total imports, one must say the true number is not known with any confidence today.

Products counterfeited at one time were limited to high-priced, high-tech, highly visible branded and intensive R&D products. But today nearly every consumer and industrial product is subject to counterfeiting. The existence of a counterfeit goods market damages consumers as well as home and host countries, the owners of the intellectual property both large and small, and their associated wholesalers and retailers. There is evidence that organized crime and terrorist organizations are using the proceeds from counterfeit products to finance their activities. As we have seen, counterfeit drugs exact a tragic toll upon the often uneducated users. There are seven main drivers of the growth of counterfeit goods, many associated with the reduction in the cost of high technology and the increasing openness provided by globalization. The Internet has afforded counterfeiters a nearly unlimited market, low-cost communications, and the means for avoiding detection. Weak enforcement of both national and international intellectual property protections has made counterfeiting a low-risk market entry strategy.

Chapter 3
The Supply of Counterfeit Trade: The Problem Countries

Introduction

The supply of counterfeit product seems almost inexhaustible. Nearly every nation has a piracy problem since, according to OECD studies, counterfeit product has been shipped from more than 130 countries. Without doubt China is the world's largest supplier of counterfeit products. Statistics from both the EU and the United States make this abundantly clear. It is such an important source we have devoted a special chapter to it later in the book. The United States Trade Representative (USTR) is responsible for developing an annual review of various countries' intellectual property environments. The latest report identifies 40 countries for special attention, special markets within these countries and areas where no government has sway such as Ciudad Del Este at the border of Brazil, Paraguay, and Argentina. This chapter identifies the most important sources for counterfeit product and details the IPR environments in these countries.

The Leading Sources of Counterfeit Goods

According to the OECD's (2009) latest update counterfeiting is taking place in just about all economies. Their data show counterfeit products intercepted from more than 130 economies including 27 of the OECD's 34 member countries.

The OECD (2007d) looked at the sources of counterfeit product in two different ways: first by summarizing reports of interceptions of fake product and second, reviewing reports by industry sectors. On the first list China is cited most often, followed by Hong Kong and Thailand. By sector, China again leads, mentioned as a source for counterfeit product in all 12 industry sectors reviewed. Second was Russia mentioned in eight of the sectors followed by India (7), Thailand (7), Taiwan (6), Turkey (6), and the Ukraine (6). The OECD update (2009) presents a "general trade related index of counterfeiting and piracy." This index shows the intensity of counterfeit exports for each country among the 134 reviewed. Among major economies China exhibits the

P. Chaudhry and A. Zimmerman, *Protecting Your Intellectual Property Rights*, Management for Professionals, DOI 10.1007/978-1-4614-5568-4_3,

highest intensity for counterfeit exports. Other countries with high levels of intensity include many smaller economies—Afghanistan, Cyprus, Kyrgyzstan, Uzbekistan, Lebanon, Thailand, Laos, Vietnam, and the United Arab Emirates as well as larger economies such as Malaysia and Pakistan. The government of Canada (RCMP 2010) says China is its most common source for counterfeit goods. Naim (2005) also identifies China as the world's biggest exporter of counterfeit products. He names Taiwan, Vietnam, the Philippines, Malaysia, Russia, and the former Soviet republics as other leading sources of counterfeit product. Hopkins et al. (2003) also cite China as well as Taiwan, Korea, and Thailand as sources for many counterfeit branded goods. Naim points out that some countries have developed counterfeit good specialties such as optical discs in the Ukraine, software in Russia, and cigarettes in Paraguay.

Each year the US Trade Representative (USTR) is required to develop a report detailing the adequacy and effectiveness of IPR protection in about 80 countries. The USTR must "identify those countries that deny adequate and effective protection for IPR or deny fair and equitable market access for persons that rely on intellectual property protection" (USTR 2012).

Some have questioned the USTR methodology. The introduction of the 1998 Annual Review and the required unilateral retaliatory trade action violates international law according to Rosenthal (1998). The organization has a small staff of about 200 plus about two dozen "temporary detailees" yet is asked to coordinate and implement US trade policy, leading 19 federal agencies and offices in complex regional and bilateral negotiations as well as the multilateral negotiations with the World Trade Organization (GAO 2005). According to interviews conducted by Mertha (2005, p. 56), this small staff necessarily, and in fact by statute, relies upon submissions from US commercial interests, especially trade associations, who feel most affected by IPR violations. He concludes "this approach is suboptimal at best and unbiased information is often difficult to obtain." The USTR and therefore US trade policy responds to "the squeaky wheel." This is reflected as we shall see in the heavy influence of large pharmaceutical firms in the country assessments below.

The USTR has three list levels: Priority Watch List, Watch List, and Section 306 Monitoring. For 2012, the countries listed in Table 3.1 have been placed on the Priority Watch List. These countries are given special focus concerning particular problem areas (USTR 2012).

The European Union has also identified the most important sources for counterfeit according to the number of cases brought to their attention in 2010 (Fig. 3.1).

China leads by a wide margin as the most important source for IPR violations with 85% of the articles seized. Other source countries by this measure include Hong Kong, India, Moldova, Turkey, Greece, and the United Arab Emirates. China also is the most important source country when measured by the value of seized products at 73%. Second by value is Hong Kong at about 8% followed by India at only about 3%, and by very small percentages from the UAE, Greece, Turkey, Moldova, and Thailand. Reviewing EU statistics by product category paints the same picture. Of 36 product categories examined in the EU data, China is the major source for counterfeit product in 32 of them and in another Hong Kong and China combined account for about 98% of seizures.

Table 3.1 USTR priority watch list

Priority watch list 2012	
China	Russia
Argentina	Chile
Algeria	India
Israel	Pakistan
Thailand	Venezuela
Ukraine	Indonesia
Canada	

Source: US Trade Representative Section 301 report

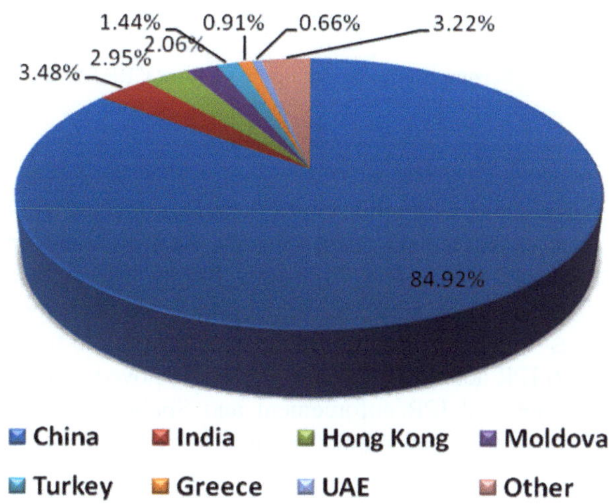

Fig. 3.1 EU seizures by country of origin in 2010 (% of seizures). *Source*: European Commission—Taxation and Customs Union

In research conducted by the authors, respondents were asked to identify two countries where their firms experienced the highest level of product counterfeiting. The top markets named were Brazil, China, Germany, Japan, Mexico, the Philippines, South Korea, Taiwan, Thailand, Turkey, the United States, and Venezuela. The managerial responses compiled from our study also identified four countries where consumers are particularly willing to *purchase* counterfeit products: China, Taiwan, the United States, and Mexico. We discuss this study in greater detail in Chap. 4.

While these managers selected several countries which appear on the Priority Watch List and on the EU List, they also pinpoint some countries that do not, reemphasizing the widespread nature of this problem.

One country is designated by the USTR to receive special attention: Paraguay. In past years Paraguay was designated as a Priority Foreign Country. Today the special attention is called Section 306 Monitoring. An additional 26 countries have been placed on a lower category list, called the Watch List, indicating less egregious product piracy problems, by the USTR (2012): Belarus, Bolivia, Brazil, Brunei

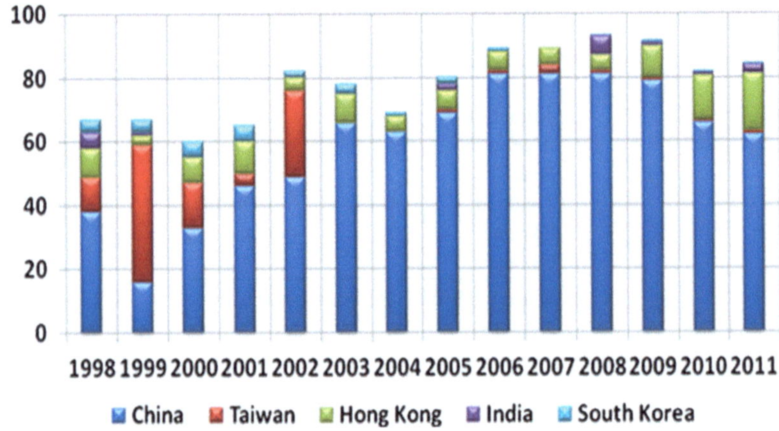

Fig. 3.2 Seizures by country of origin. *Source*: CBP FY (2011) seizure statistics

Darussalam, Colombia, Costa Rica, Dominican Republic, Ecuador, Egypt, Finland, Greece, Guatemala, Italy, Jamaica, Kuwait, Lebanon, Mexico, Norway, Peru, the Philippines, Romania, Tajikistan, Turkey, Turkmenistan, Uzbekistan, and Vietnam.

For 2012 the USTR added Ukraine to the Priority Watch List from the less strenuous Watch List because the government failed to meet its commitments from the 2010 IPR action plan. Malaysia was removed from the Watch List mainly because of improved IPR enforcement and Spain was removed from the list especially because of its new regulations to combat piracy over the Internet.

US Customs Seizures

Although US Customs seizure statistics fluctuate, there is one consistency in the data. Since 1998, China has accounted for the largest percentage of counterfeit products seized, ranging from a low of 16% in fiscal year 1999 to a high of 81% in fiscal years 2006–2008 and continuing at 62% for 2011 (CBP 2012) (Fig. 3.2).

Taiwan which had accounted for more than 40% of seizures in 1999 has had its share decline considerably to only about 1% for 2011. Hong Kong has been a consistent source of counterfeit product with the share of fakes confiscated from this country ranging from 10% in fiscal 2001 to as low as 3% in 1999. Recently Hong Kong's share has increased from 5% in 2008 to 18% in 2011. It seems logical to assume that some counterfeit product produced in China is now being transshipped through Hong Kong. Adding the most recent Hong Kong and Chinese percentages would bring the total back to about 80%, the historical level of Chinese sourcing for counterfeit products since 2006.

Table 3.2 Top trading partners for IPR seizures, FY (2011)

Trading partner	Domestic value ($)	Percent of total
China	109,996,380	62
Hong Kong	32,155,987	18
India	4,535,478	3
Pakistan	3,954,932	2
Taiwan	2,287,596	1
Switzerland	1,407,426	1
Malaysia	1,285,547	1
Korea	714,424	<1
United Kingdom	703,721	<1
Mexico	654,941	<1
All others	20,626,201	12
Total	178,322,633	

Source: CBP FY (2011) seizure statistics

The table below shows the most important sources for counterfeit product for the latest full year according to the US Customs Service (Table 3.2).

Many countries seem to have major problems in the IPR area. In the next sections we will examine particular locations.

Specific Countries

The most important source for counterfeit products is the People's Republic of China, according to every governmental organization and researcher who has studied the problem. In Chap. 9, we have devoted a separate discussion to the special case of China. The OECD (2007e) examined 15 country's intellectual property situations looking at the legal and regulatory framework, enforcement, program evaluation, international cooperation, awareness, and recent policy developments. While the report does not provide an assessment of the IPR environment in any particular market, it does address a number of the countries where problems have been identified including Brazil, China, India, Israel, and Russia.

Russia

Russia has been on the Priority Watch List since 1997 (IIPA 2012a, b) and continues on the list for 2012. According to the Russian Department of economic security 37% of branded clothing was counterfeit and 15–30% of perfumes, cosmetics, clothing, household and food products were not genuine. Illegal software reached 80%. Official estimates claim the counterfeit product market in Russia amounts to

Fig. 3.3 Falsified Russian Nike product

over 100 billion rubles per year. Russia is a destination country for many counterfeit products and also the leading producer of pirate alcohol, audio and video products, medicines, and dietary supplements (Salnik 2011).

While the USTR (2012) says Russia made important progress to improve IPR protection and enforcement, the US government continues to have concerns with counterfeit products sold over the Internet and further improving enforcement. According to the US Department of Commerce, "conducting business may be impeded by: burdensome regulatory regimes; inadequate IPR protection and enforcement; extensive corruption and inadequate rule of law; inconsistent application of laws and regulations" (Export.gov. 2011).

An EU report cites widespread availability of counterfeit trademarked products, software, music, and films. They also identify the lack of deterrent level sanctions and enforcement hampered by corruption and insufficient resources (trade.ec 2009). In 2006 Pletneva estimated that Russia ranked second only to China as a counterfeit producer. The total of industry losses from counterfeit production was estimated at 708 billion rubles in 2005. Fifty-three percent of Russians purchased counterfeit goods during that year. Russian consumers believed food products, medicines, clothing, and alcohol products were most frequently falsified. Morris and Stevens (2007) claimed that counterfeit medicines make up 5–10% of the total Russian market (Fig. 3.3).

One major problem had been optical discs which are copied and exported. Recently law enforcement made significant raids against pirate optical disc distributors making the largest known seizure in Russia of two million optical discs (USTR 2012).

A sore point mentioned by the USTR is the misuse of music by social networking site vKontakte—often called the "Facebook of Russia" (http://vk.com/club200). In May 2012 the Russian appeals court confirmed that the site was liable for copyright infringement (IFPI 2012).

Large crop protection manufacturers developed an alliance to fight counterfeit products. According to DuPont (2007) trade in fake crop protection products had been expanding causing approximately €40–50 million in damage to agricultural products.

As part of the accession process to joining the WTO, Russia enacted four new IPR laws. The US government is concerned with Russia's complete compliance with the provisions of the TRIPS agreements. The publishing, software, and motion picture industries are of major concern. The USTR (2012) is urging Russia to increase the number of IPR-related investigations and improve the resources to law enforcement organizations. The number of raids related to intellectual property had decreased significantly in 2011 and the police force had been reduced by 20%.

The "IPR Toolkit" for Russia may be found at http://moscow.usembassy.gov/ipr-toolkit.html. This link provides an overview of IP issues in Russia, and specific links to copyright, patents, trademarks, enforcement options, and market-entry planning. The overview contains the link for the Russian Federal Service for Intellectual Property, Patents and Trademarks (Rospatent) at http://www.fips.ru/rospatent/index.htm. The site is in Russian but can usually be translated using the Google service.

Copyright is regulated by the Russian Authors' Association at http://rao.ru/orao/ and the site is in Russian. For a quick synopsis of the laws that govern copyright, such as Article 7.1, the Law on Copyright and Neighboring Rights of 1993, consult the US Embassy at http://moscow.usembassy.gov/ipr-copyright.html. The Russian government provides criminal, civil, or administrative penalties against IP infringement, but, again the problem centers on enforcement. According the US government, the main drawbacks to prosecution in Russia focus on obtaining evidence, slow court decisions, proving damages, and executing a judgment in civil cases (http://moscow.usembassy.gov/ipr-enforcement.html). US Country Commercial Guides offer practical advice on "Protecting Your Intellectual Property" and recommend seeking assistance from these Russian agencies (to name just a few): the Russian Anti-Piracy Organization (RAPO), the Russian Anti-Software Piracy Association, and the Association of Branded Goods Manufacturers in Russia (RusBrand).

A final noteworthy anti-piracy site is the Nordic-Russian project, dedicated to "enhancing intellectual property rights competence and cooperation in St. Petersburg, Finland, Denmark and Sweden," established by the Nordic Council of Ministers (www.norden.ru).

Argentina

Argentina has been a focus of the USTR since 1997, when the US government, reacting to the country's pharmaceutical patent law, suspended half the benefits to Argentina under the general system of preferences (Benson 2004). In 1999 the United States filed a case with the WTO related to Argentine regulations for pharmaceutical products, agricultural chemicals, and certain matters related to patents. Although progress was made in joint meetings between the United States and Argentina, the country continued on the Priority Watch List in 2002 (USTR 2002). At that time the USTR claimed that counterfeit products were available virtually everywhere and unlicensed software was widely used in business and even in government. Enforcement against IPR violators was weak and penalties were inconsistently applied. Argentina has been on the Priority Watch List every year but one since 1993 (IIPA 2012a).

Argentina remains on the Priority Watch List in 2012 despite some improvements in intellectual property protection. Specific improvements cited by the US government include civil and criminal actions the Argentine government took against illegal distribution of content over the Internet. The USTR (2012) continued to have concerns with patent issues related to pharmaceuticals. Piracy over the Internet appears to be growing. The EU also cites Argentina as a country where protection of intellectual property is problematic, although they note several improvements have taken place recently. A continued large backlog in the Argentinean patent office, almost unchanged since their earlier 2006 report, is a major concern. The EU authorities specifically cite ineffective criminal procedures, the lack of a specialized IP court, and the low level of sanctions as problem areas (trade.ec 2009).

The IIPA (2012b) reported that "the nature and scope of piracy in Argentina remained unchanged" from 2011 to 2012. Illegally manufactured DVDs and other products are available in many cities of the country. Digital piracy is a key problem and the recording industry reported that 99% of the music market in country was covered by piracy.

Algeria

Algeria appeared on the Watch List in 2008 and has been on the Priority Watch List for 2009–2011 (IIPA 2012a). The main reason for Algeria's inclusion is a law that keeps a number of imported pharmaceuticals and medical devices out of the country in favor of local items. The USTR (2012) uses the same language the agency uses for many countries, pointing to "lack of protection against the unfair commercial use, as well as unauthorized disclosure, of test or other data generated to obtain marketing approval for pharmaceutical products, and to provide an effective system to address patent issues expeditiously in connection with applications to market pharmaceutical products."

Canada

Canada has appeared on the Priority Watch List for 4 years starting in 2009 (IIPA 2012a). The USTR (2012) recommends that Canada fully implement the WIPO Internet treaties and completely address Internet piracy problems. The USTR is also concerned about procedures for approval of pharmaceutical products and limitations in Canada's trademark process. The government of Canada is to enact new copyright legislation which the US government wishes to see. The EU also lists

Canada as a country whose "IPR system features several significant shortcomings" (trade.ec 2009). The EU report cites poor implementation of existing legislation and the lack of reform legislation as concerns, especially from a developed country. The report also points out that proposed amendments to Canadian copyright law include more lenient provisions related to Internet service providers' liability.

Chile

Chile was placed on the USTR's Priority Watch List after an "out of cycle" review in January 2007 and it has remained on the list through 2011 (IIPA 2012a). The USTR (2012) sees similar problems in Chile and Argentina, namely inadequate protection for data used to obtain marketing approvals for pharmaceuticals. The USTR sees some welcome progress in administrative and judicial procedures. The EU no longer mentions Chile as a Priority Country (trade.ec 2009). According to the US Department of Commerce, Chile has made legislative changes to strengthen its IPR laws to bring them in line with international commitments, such as the US-Chile Free Trade Agreement. But the US government continues to see deficiencies in Chile's IPR laws and enforcement procedures. Concerns center on pharmaceuticals and copyright piracy of movies, music, and software (Export.gov. 2011). The IIPA claims that 50% of the market for optical disks is in counterfeiter's hands and 90% of music is illegally copied (IIPA 2012b).

Egypt

Egypt had appeared on the USTR Priority Watch List from 1997 to 2007 with the exception of 2003. Since then the country has appeared on the Watch List each year (IIPA 2012a). The EU does not include Egypt as a target country (trade.ec 2009). Although the government had made some improvements in its IP protection and enforcement, there are a number of actions the USTR (2012) suggests including ratifying and implementing the WIPO Internet treaties, a recommendation the USTR has been making since 2007. Some trademark rights holders mention that the Egyptian government is registering invalid trademarks. Here again the USTR recommends Egypt insure that courts impose sentences which will deter copyright and trademark infringement and also provide better training for enforcement officials. The US government uses essentially the same language to express concern about unauthorized disclosure of pharmaceutical data used to obtain marketing approval for medicines (USTR 2012). The IIPA (2012b) identifies software, games, movies, and music as particular areas with widespread IPR violations. Obviously the political turmoil following the January 2011 revolution has put IPR protection on a lower priority for the present time.

India

Although India is a signatory country to the Paris Convention, the Berne Convention, Patent Cooperation Treaty, the TRIPS accord in the WTO and a member of the WIPO, India has been on the USTR Priority Watch List since 1994 (IIPA 2012b). The country remains on this list for 2012 because of a week legal framework and enforcement system (USTR 2012). India was the third-largest source for counterfeit goods seized by the US Customs and Border Protection in 2011 (CBP 2012). One main concern of the USTR is the lack of progress on implementation of the WIPO Internet treaties as well as other reforms. As in the other BRIC countries, there is large-scale infringement in such sectors as software and optical media. The USTR recognized some improvement in enforcement and copyrights and work against pirated movies and music.

India is a center for counterfeit pharmaceuticals (Morris and Stevens 2007). A study conducted by one researcher (Bate 2010) found 12% of tested pills in Delhi to be substandard, as were 5% in Chennai. He found, "About 2% of the pills contained no active ingredient. The others did but it had degraded, probably because the pills had expired and been repackaged with new labels; some may have degraded through poor storage." In this study, of all tested samples 7% were substandard and 3.6% were likely counterfeit.

Naim (2005) describes India's generic pharmaceutical manufacturers' ability to reverse-engineer drugs patented in other countries. Until the end of 2004 India's patent regulations related only to processes not to products. This created the opportunity for rapid expansion of generic drug manufacturers (TRIPS 2007). India's pharmaceutical industry ranks fourth in the world by volume but 13th by value, indicating the predominance of generics in the market (The Economist 2007 "Few Indian firms are creating drugs"). With their accession to the WTO and as a signatory to TRIPS, India was given a 5-year transition to help the country conform to TRIPS. This ended on 1 Jan 2005 and India passed new laws to come into compliance with the WTO (TRIPS 2007). Because India is the primary supplier of cheap generic drugs to the rest of the world, many organizations including Doctors Without Borders applauded an Indian court decision which went against Novartis related to granting patents for incremental developments (Silverman 2007). Indian patent legislation does not allow "evergreening," slightly modifying drugs whose patents are about to expire in order to extend their patent monopoly (Gentleman 2007). At issue is how much leeway WTO members have in deciding whether an invention is patentable or not. There are many parties who will continue to be interested in what the future holds for the Indian pharmaceutical industry. Naim (2005) believes generic drugmakers' experience with knockoffs allowed these firms to develop scientific skills and they are now "warming to patent protection." The EU (trade.ec 2009), while noting progress in the IPR situation, points out the need for further strengthening of IPR enforcement, speed up of proceedings, and better training for officials. The EU report specifically cites the high percentage of counterfeit pharmaceuticals seized at EU borders. Following the lead of Thailand, India is also issuing a compulsory license (CL) to a patented cancer drug allowing a local drug manufacturer to provide generic copies, much to the chagrin of pharmaceutical patent holders (Bajaj and Pollack 2012). The EU report also says that “India is generally defensive regarding IPR and often opposes plurilateral and multilateral efforts to fight piracy and counterfeiting in *fora* such as the WTO, the WCL and the WIPO.”

The US Country Commercial Guide reinforces the idea that the current legal system in India does not adequately protect IP and enforcement is a problem. This report says “piracy of copyrighted materials is widespread (Export.gov 2011).” The report also points out that while the central government passes laws related to copyright, it is the responsibility of state, municipal, or local police forces, who are largely untrained in these matters, to enforce these IPR laws.

The US Embassy IPR toolkit for India is at http://newdelhi.usembassy.gov/ipr.html and gives very general information on copyright protection, market entry planning, infringements and enforcement mechanisms, and the like. The Indian agencies suggested are its Copyright Office (http://copyright.gov.in/) and the Central Board of Excise and Customs (www.cbec.gov.in). Both of these websites provide an English version to navigate for possible resources. For example, copyright studies that focus on movies, sound recordings, software, and literary works are provided at the Copyright Office site. A guidebook to the copyright act and general copyright information is also available. The site is designed to educate practitioners about the IP environment in India. Links to related industries, such as the Indian Music Industry (a counterpart to the RIAA) are provided in English. A very interactive website for the Indian Performing Rights Society Limited (www.iprs.org) is a noteworthy source for copyright issues in this sector in India.

Indonesia

Indonesia has appeared on the Priority Watch List every year with one exception since 1996 (IIPA 2012a). According to the USTR (2012) in Indonesia there is “rampant piracy and counterfeiting … and widespread availability of counterfeit pharmaceutical products.” The USTR sees problems in prosecutions and the judicial system and sentences which are too lenient for IPR violations. This report also uses the language related to pharmaceuticals seen in many other country descriptions. The EU (trade.ec 2009) complements the government of Indonesia for forming a National Coordination Team on IPR reporting directly to the president. Their report claims 92% of the video market is in the hands of pirates and also cites weaknesses in court actions and a lack of implementation of certain TRIPS requirements.

Israel

Israel has appeared on the USTR Priority Watch List since 1997 and is on the Priority Watch List for 2012 (IIPA 2012a; USTR 2012). The main complaint continues to be protection of confidential pharmaceutical test data and patent term extension.

The USTR is also encouraging Israel to ratify the WIPO Internet treaties. Both the USTR and the EU (trade.ec 2009) cite problems regarding compensation for use of television programs by local cable operators. Both organizations also criticize the country for procedures related to granting pharmaceutical patents including a long period during which patents remain unpublished and therefore unprotected. This allows local generic manufacturers to produce these products but offers no basis for legitimate patent owners to claim damages. The USTR mentions favorably Israel's intention to change its laws and expects to remove the country from the Watch Lists once the required legislation is enacted and implemented.

Pakistan

Pakistan has appeared on the Priority Watch List since 2004 with the exception of one year (IIPA 2012a). The country remains on the Priority Watch List for 2012 (USTR 2012) because of "widespread counterfeiting and piracy, particularly book and optical disc piracy." The USTR urges Pakistan to reform its copyright law and repeats the language related to pharmaceuticals used in many other country descriptions. Pakistan provided the fourth-largest amount of counterfeit material in seizures made by the US Customs and Border Protection service in 2011 (CPB 2012).

Thailand

Thailand was placed on the Priority Watch List in 2007 and has remained there through 2012 (IIPA 2012a). According to Hopkins et al. (2003), "Thailand has long been a haven for piracy in Southeast Asia." Although the USTR saw some encouraging signs in IPR protection from the new government, the USTR is concerned with Thailand's inability to follow through on initiatives begun over the past years. The USTR is urging the government to take action against the growing problem of IPR infringement on the Internet, to improve enforcement efforts and provide sentences which will deter counterfeiters. The US government continues to be concerned with Thailand's use of test data related to pharmaceuticals while addressing the country's public health problems. The EU (trade.ec 2009) sees Thailand has one of the five highest priority countries where deficiencies exist in IPR protections. Their report also identifies weak enforcement, difficulties in bringing civil and criminal actions to successful conclusions as key problems in addition to corruption.

According to the World Health Organization (WHO 2003), in Thailand approximately 8.5% of the total pharmaceutical market is accounted for by substandard medicines. But the case is somewhat more complicated regarding pharmaceuticals. The Ministry of Public Health had issued Compulsory Licenses (CLs) on HIV and heart disease drugs believing they were within their rights under the WTO to allow copies of the medicines even though the patents are held by American firms (Bangkok

Post 2007). A CL is a government license that allows someone other than the patent holder to copy patented or copyrighted products. In the case of a severe health emergency, CLs are allowed and royalties do not have to be paid to the original patent holder (TRIPS 2007). The USTR (2007a, b, c) cited the issuance of these CLs as "further indications of a weakening of respect for patents." The EU also mentions its concerns of the use of CLs in Thailand (trade.ec 2009). Thailand has been a leader in granting compulsory licenses. It was the first to grant a CL to a cancer drug (Bajaj and Pollack 2012). It was believed in Thailand that since the country is relatively small and does not have the leverage of China or India, the USTR's 2007 action expresses the revenge of large US pharmaceutical companies (Bangkok Post 2007).

Turkey

Turkey had been on the USTR Priority Watch List from 2004 to 2007 (IIPA 2012a) but has been on the less strenuous Watch List since 2008 (USTR 2012). According to the USTR "piracy and counterfeiting remain widespread in Turkey including increasing levels of piracy over the Internet." Here again the USTR recommends full implementation of the WIPO Internet treaties as well as better enforcement efforts and includes the same language regarding the use of pharmaceutical data used to gain marketing approval. The EU (trade.ec 2009) identifies Turkey as one of its five priority countries. Their report also mentions poor enforcement of IPR regulations as well as a need for better dialogue between rights holders and the government. EU customs data shows Turkey to be one of the most important sources for counterfeit products seized at EU borders (trade.ec 2009).

Ukraine

Ukraine had been upgraded to the Priority Watch List in 2006 from the Priority Foreign Country List on which it had been placed in 2001. At that time the United States withdrew Ukraine's benefits under GSP and imposed sanctions on their exports valued at $75 million in January 2002. After 4 years on the Watch List the country was again placed on the Priority Watch List for 2012 (USTR 2012). This is because the US government has seen "minimal progress" from Ukraine in implementing its 2010 commitments. In fact there has been some evidence of moving in the wrong direction. One example cited by the USTR is that days after the country's largest website infringing IPR was taken down it was allowed to reopen. The number of IP inspectors has been significantly reduced and enforcement efforts are ineffective against "widespread availability of counterfeit and pirated products, many of which are transshipped through Ukraine to third countries." For the EU (trade.ec 2009) Ukraine is a third level problem country. They see improvements in commitment at the government level and application by enforcement authorities of available laws. On the negative side, some seized goods have been placed back on the market.

Venezuela

Venezuela, the last country on the USTR's (2012) Priority Watch List, has been on this list since 2012 (IIPA 2012a). USTR says that Venezuela has made "some progress, notably through its seizure of a larger number of counterfeit and pirated products than in previous years." Venezuela withdrew from the Andean Community in 2006 and reinstated an old (1955) industrial property law which created uncertainty for protection of trademarks registered under the Andean Community law. According to the USTR there is widespread piracy and counterfeiting. The same language is used regarding pharmaceuticals in this country report as well—Venezuela does not protect against unfair commercial use of data used to gain drug marketing approval. Venezuela is not mentioned by the EU as a priority country (trade.ec 2009).

Mexico

Mexico is classified on a lower level by the USTR (2012)—the Watch List. The country has been on this list since 2003 (IIPA 2012a). One major problem in this country is counterfeit pharmaceuticals. Morris and Stevens (2007) claimed that Mexico "is a major global source of counterfeit medicines" with sales of $650 million per year or about 10% of drug sales in the country. Since the prices for pharmaceuticals are between 72 and 104% higher in the United States than in Mexico, it is not surprising that many US citizens patronize *farmacias* just over the border either personally or through the Internet (Hopkins et al. 2003). This is an ideal place for distributing genuine as well as counterfeit medicines. Factories in Mexico get raw materials from India in order to make and package diluted medicines which can look like the real thing. They sell these counterfeits primarily to Americans (Naim 2005).

The USTR sees some improvements in IPR enforcement by Mexican authorities but once again points out problems with the ability of firms to gain access to pharmaceutical data used to obtain approvals for drugs. Though Mexico established the Mexican Institute of Industrial Property in 1994 to fight counterfeiting and to comply with NAFTA, the country is still seen as one of the largest pirate markets in the world. The Ford Motor Co. found counterfeit autoparts makers in Mexico in 2001 (Hopkins et al. 2003). The USTR (2012) wants to see improved coordination between federal, state and municipal officials, increased resources for IPR prosecutions and an increased number of them and the need for higher level penalties against infringers as well as legislation to fully implement the WIPO Internet treaties.

Brazil

Brazil continues to be listed by the USTR on its Watch List for IP infringement as it has since 2007 (IIPA 2012a). Brazil is a signatory country to the Paris, Bern, and Universal Copyright conventions, the TRIPS agreement in the WTO, and the Patent

Fig. 3.4 Anti-piracy slogan in Brazil. *Source*: Originalidade: piratatofora (2012)

Cooperation Treaty. Brazil is also a member state of WIPO. Thus, in terms of supranational protection and recent national legislation, Brazil is an advocate of IP protections. However, once again, the key issue is enforcement of IPR in the Brazilian marketplace. The US commercial service advises that firms in the country face "a lengthy process for enforcing IPR and commercial law (Export.gov 2011)."

One practitioner-oriented website that will give a manager a synopsis of the IPR environment for Brazil is called the "IPR Toolkit" and is located at http://www.embaixada-americana.org.br/. This US Embassy site provides a succinct overview of the places to register patents, trademarks, and copyrights. The web page also summarizes current IP legislation in Brazil, such as biosecurity that will govern genetically modified organisms. In addition to US and International agencies listed at this site (such as the USTR and WTO), links to Brazilian non-government organizations and Brazilian author's associations are given.

The Brazil Against Piracy Council (under the Brazilian Ministry of Justice) has developed a website (www.mj.gov.br/combatepirataria) that is replete with IP information in Portuguese. A quick click on the website "*Pirata: tô fora!*" (Originalidade: piratatofora 2012) and the following anti-piracy message (Fig. 3.4) is revealed with rap-like music chanting the slogan—*Pirata: tô fora! Só uso original* (*Piracy*: Count me out! I only use originals). This campaign continues to be used and was seen at the Carnival in Recife and Olinda, and Pernambuco (Fig. 3.4).

Brazil's Institute of Industrial Property (INPI) oversees industrial property rights, such as trademark registration, and is governed by the Ministry of Development, Industry, and Commerce. The agency's website in Portuguese is at http://www.inpi.gov.br/. There is also a provision for an English translation.

Paraguay

Paraguay is a unique case. It has been a USTR Priority Foreign Country since January 1998 (IFPI 2012) and now is listed for "Section 306 Monitoring." This level requires more attention from the USTR than the Priority Watch List. It should be noted that at this point there is only one country on that list (USTR 2012). Although the EU (trade. ec 2006) had called Paraguay "a notorious entry point for IPR infringing goods into Latin America," the current EU report (trade.ec 2009) does not include Paraguay as one of its priority countries. As described in Sect. 3.5 below, Paraguay is the home of the infamous Ciudad del Este, a kind of Wild West for counterfeit product. A comprehensive memorandum of understanding (MOU) on the protection of intellectual property was signed by the US and Paraguayan governments in 1998 and the country has been under special monitoring since. This MOU expires during 2012 and the US government is focused on its renegotiation. Although the USTR notes some efforts to improve the IPR environment, the country has major problems in providing effective IPR protection. The report states "piracy and counterfeiting remain rampant in the country and enforcement efforts internally and at the border have been insufficient to address this problem." Once again the country is cited for unfair use of data generated to obtain marketing approval for pharmaceuticals.

Notorious Markets

Within specific countries particular marketplaces have been identified as centers for counterfeit product. The most infamous are detailed below (USTR 2011a, b).

- *Beijing's Silk Street Market*—also known as Xiushui Market, has been described as the third best-known tourist destination in Beijing after the Forbidden City and the Great Wall (Zhu 2005). It has also been called the single biggest symbol of China's IP enforcement problems (USTR 2007c). It was established in 1985 near foreign embassies and luxury hotels. Local authorities never promised to close down this market as they did Shanghai's Xiangyang. In mid-2005 Gucci, Chanel, Burberry, Prada, and Louis Vuitton sued the landlord, Beijing Xiushui Haosen Clothing Company Ltd., for selling counterfeit products.
- *Harco Glodok*—located in Jakarta, one of the largest markets for fake product, specifically pirated optical discs. Organized criminal gangs keep IPR enforcement at a low level.
- *La Salada*—located in Buenos Aires, Argentina, it is the largest illegal market in Latin America, selling approximately $9 million in merchandise per day. It is one of more than 40 markets in the city, nearly all dedicated to selling pirated goods. Approximately 6,000 vendors sell products to 20,000 customers everyday. Hundreds of buses arrive every week from remote areas in Buenos Aires province or even from neighboring countries. Because of organized gangs there is little IPR enforcement. According to Sardon (2007) various law enforcement

groups pass the responsibility to each other and political will is lacking to do something about the trade in illegal goods.

- *Mexican markets*—seven locations are identified by the USTR in Mexico: Tepito, Plaza Meave, Eje Central, Lomas Verdes, and Pericoapa Bazaar in Mexico City; Tepito is the main warehousing and distribution center for counterfeit products sold in many smaller markets throughout the country. Despite actions which resulted in large seizures pirate activity continues.
- *Quiapo Shopping District*—in Manila, this is just one of many locations dealing in counterfeit and pirated goods especially clothing, shoes, watches, handbags, and software.
- *Yiwu*—both Hopkins et al. (2003) and the USTR identify Yiwu, a city about 5 h from Shanghai as a key counterfeit market. In fact Hopkins et al. call this "counterfeit central," where customers can buy fake Gillette razor blades, Safeguard soap, Skippy peanut butter, Budweiser beer, Duracell batteries, Marlboro cigarettes, and Tide detergent just to name a few. According to the USTR (2007c) there are more than 400,000 different items for sale at this market, mostly in the form of bulk quantities of small consumer goods.
- *Bahia Market*—located in Guayaquil, Ecuador, this expansive market sells large quantities of counterfeit goods, including clothing and shoes, pirated DVDs, CDs, and software.
- *Lo Wu Commercial Center*—in Shenzhen, China, on the border between Shenzhen and Guangzhou provinces, and Hong Kong. Includes dozens of markets offering counterfeit product. As the USTR (2011a, b) understates it, "the display of signs prohibiting the sale of such goods has reportedly not served as an effective deterrent."
- *Nehru Place*—in New Delhi, one of the many markets in major cities throughout India known for offering large volumes of pirated software, pirated optical media containing movies and music, and counterfeit goods.
- *PC Malls, China*—The Buynow PC Mall is a very large personal computer mall chain in China, operating 22 stores across the country. It is known for selling computers with illegal operating systems and other unlawfully preinstalled software.
- *Petrivka Market*—in Kyiv, Ukraine, an open air market reportedly including about 300 stands that sell pirated goods, including music, films, games, software, clothing, and shoes.
- *Red Zones in Thailand*—Thai authorities have designated the Panthip Plaza, Klong Thom, Saphan Lek, and Baan Mor shopping areas, among others, as targets for enforcement against piracy and counterfeiting.
- *San Andresitos*—in Colombia, these consist of marketplaces of varying sizes scattered throughout Colombia which are notorious for unauthorized reproduction of music, video games, and movies, and for the unauthorized distribution of pirated and counterfeit goods.
- *Urdu Bazaars*—in Karachi and Lahore, Pakistan, these remain the main sources of pirated books in the country, though book piracy is widespread.

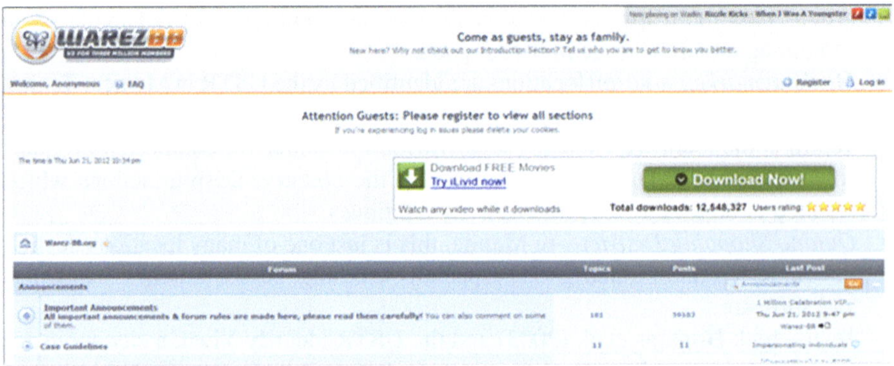

Fig. 3.5 Homepage of Warez-bb. *Source*: http://www.warez-bb.org/index.php

The USTR (2011a, b) also identifies virtual markets for counterfeit product. These include online services involved in "deep linking" to other sites such as Sogou MP3 and Gougou. Some B2B and B2C sites they mention are Taobao, based in China and Modchip.ca and Consolesource, based in Canada. Some sites are bit torrent indexing sites. These include ThePirate Bay, IsoHunt, BtJunkie, Kat.ph, and torrentz.eu. Some bit torrent trackers they mention are Rutracker from Russia, Demonoid located in Ukraine, and zamunda, based in Bulgaria. A well-known forum also chosen as a notorious market is Warez-bb, reportedly based in Luxembourg, Switzerland and Sweden. Figure 3.5 is a screen shot of their website (Fig. 3.5).

Extra-country

Ciudad del Este, a city at the border of Brazil, Paraguay, and Argentina is said to be the largest illicit market in the Western Hemisphere. Some have compared it to the famous Cantina at Mos Eisley seen in Star Wars IV, where shady characters of every description are in evidence. The USTR (2007c) identified this tri-border region as a "hotbed of piracy and counterfeiting of all kinds of products," with a total trade of approximately $12 billion per year. Naim (2005) calls Ciudad del Este "a crossroads for virtually every illicit trade, including counterfeit software and electronics, smuggled imported goods and reportedly weapons." The city is located just over the Brazilian–Paraguayan border and goods are smuggled out of Paraguay into Brazil, Argentina, and eventually the United States over a single bridge crossed by 25,000 people each day. With widespread corruption in the government, no immigration or customs checks take place.

CBS News found one seller offering a thousand copies of Microsoft Windows XP priced at $15 and pirated CDs for one dollar each. An investigator for Motorola found fake cellphone parts including batteries which may overheat and explode. The city's 55 banks serve to recycle profits not only from counterfeit products but also from illicit drugs. Investigators are concerned that a large number of Middle Eastern immigrants in the area are sending vast sums to terrorist organizations like Hamas and Hezbollah. Hezbollah is not considered a terrorist organization in Paraguay so no action against this has been taken by the local government (CBS News 2006; CNBC.com 2007).

Conclusions

Counterfeit product is produced in nearly every country in the world. The OECD identified pirated product shipments from nearly 130 nations. Looking at many sources including the USTR, the EU, the US Foreign and Commercial Service, and the International Intellectual Property Alliance as well as a number of researchers on the problem, it is possible to identify the most important sources for these products. The primary source in nearly every product category continues to be the People's Republic of China which accounted for 62% of US Customs seizures of IPR-violating product in 2011.

Other leading countries housing producers of fakes are Russia, Algeria, Argentina, Chile, India, Indonesia, Israel, Pakistan, Thailand, Ukraine, Venezuela, Brazil, Paraguay, and Mexico. Research conducted by the authors confirms these markets as leading problem areas. The United States is a primary consumer of counterfeit product but a smaller center for production.

Major problem areas include CDs and DVDs, cigarettes, software, and pharmaceuticals as well as books, clothing, footwear, and jewelry. Some controversy centers on generic copies of important drugs. The USTR identifies ready access by others to test data required for approvals from pharmaceutical patent holders as an important problem in nearly every country on the Priority Watch List. Some health authorities believe they are able to produce generics without violating their international obligations but it is apparent that large pharmaceutical companies do not agree.

Some particular areas within these countries have been identified as hotbeds of counterfeit product. These range from Yiwu and Beijing's Silk Street Market in China to markets in Indonesia, Mexico, and the Philippines, Ecuador, Ukraine, Thailand, Pakistan, and Columbia as well as the infamous La Salada in Buenos Aires. Perhaps the most notorious center for counterfeit product is Ciudad del Este, on the border of Brazil, Paraguay, and Argentina. Paraguay in fact has held a special place for monitoring by the USTR since 1998. The addition of websites to the Notorious Markets List shows the USTR's recognition of Internet piracy as a key problem. A list of the various types of sites is included in this chapter.

The specific reviews of each of these major havens for pirates reinforces the conclusion that weak enforcement, sometimes abetted by corruption, allows counterfeiters to flourish in particular areas. The ability to sell and ship product throughout the world facilitated by globalization means producers can locate in the most accommodating markets anywhere in the world. The lesson for international managers is clear—evaluation of the IP environment should be a critical consideration in making sourcing decisions.

Chapter 4
Modeling the Intellectual Property Rights Environment

Introduction

The study of the global protection of intellectual property rights environment is an important issue, but the need to develop a theoretical framework is acute. Several descriptive studies of the business problem have been conducted, but, few offer a conceptual framework that tests a model by way of managerial perceptions. In this chapter, a detailed discussion of the results of the research of Chaudhry, Zimmerman, Peters, and Cordell (2009) is given to present a framework and statistical measures to accept (or reject) the proposed model of the IPR environment. First, general research questions and a model of the intellectual property rights environment are given. Second, a synopsis of the variables used in the model, such as the level of consumer complicity, pirate activity, and host country enforcement of intellectual property rights. Third, a brief discussion of the study design to capture managerial perceptions to test this model follows. Fourth, an in-depth discussion of managerial assessment of the variables presented in the model is given with detailed statistical results that either support (or refute) the model proposed in Fig. 4.1. Several of the topics presented in this model are further discussed in other chapters of the book. In Chap. 3 an outline of the source countries of counterfeit trade and the problem of enforcement of intellectual property rights was given. In Chaps. 5 and 6, consumer complicity to purchase counterfeits and plausible social marketing anti-counterfeiting measures is debated. In Chap. 11, detailed recommendations for managers to combat this illicit trade are addressed.

Proposed Framework

Chaudhry et al. (2009) assert that the three distinct areas that shape a country's IPR environment are the level of consumer complicity to use counterfeit goods, the indigenous pirate activity to supply the fake products, and the host country enforcement measures.

P. Chaudhry and A. Zimmerman, *Protecting Your Intellectual Property Rights*, Management for Professionals, DOI 10.1007/978-1-4614-5568-4_4,

This IPR environment then stimulates the anti-piracy actions that companies employ to target consumers, distribution channels, host governments, international organizations, and pirates. A succinct review of the three key areas that determine the IPR environment follows.

Level of Consumer Complicity

It is apparent that the willingness of the consumer to purchase a counterfeit product/service is a major factor of the intellectual property rights environment. In initial work on consumer complicity, Tom et al. (1998) found that consumers are willing to purchase counterfeit goods for a variety of reasons, including a perception of the counterfeit to be as good as the authentic version; support of the counterfeit market as a means of expressing "anti-big-business" sentiment; and "lax attitudes" about the legal protection of intellectual property. Later work by several researchers studies the intention to obtain counterfeits through surveys, experiments, and qualitative research (Bian and Veloutsou 2007; Chaudhry et al. 2011a, b; Commuri 2009; Nunes et al. 2004; Penz and Stöttinger 2008; Wilcox et al. 2009). The overall acceptance of nondeceptive purchases of counterfeit goods will significantly affect the intellectual property environment and the subsequent level of future investment. Chaudhry et al. (2010) expected managers to decrease their level of market commitment in terms of future investments and increase the frequency of anti-counterfeiting tactics in highly complicit markets.

Muncy and Vitell were leaders in developing a scale that measures consumer ethics (see Muncy and Vitell 1992; Vitell and Muncy 1992) regarding their dubious behavior resulting in a four-dimensional belief: (1) actively benefiting from illegal activities, (2) passively benefiting, (3) actively benefiting from deceptive (or questionable, but legal) practices, and (4) no harm/no foul activities. The literature yields various studies that investigate a segment of the intellectual property rights dilemma facing managers. Later, Vitell and Muncy (2005) expanded their consumer ethics scale to include three new items: downloading/buying counterfeit goods, recycling/environment, and doing the right thing/do good. In this study, the researchers looked at respondents' belief about whether "downloading music from the Internet instead of buying it" and "buying counterfeit goods instead of buying the original manufactured brands" were unethical.

The level of consumer complicity towards counterfeit product usage has been examined in an ethical framework (e.g., moral judgment) and is usually product-specific (e.g., software piracy) (see Al-Rafee and Cronan 2006; Chaudhry and Stumpf 2011; Chiu et al. 2008; Cronan and Al-Rafee 2008; Goles et al. 2008; Gupta et al. 2004; Kini et al. 2004; Wee et al. 1995). Al-Rafee and Cronan (2006) model that attitude of a person who engage in digital piracy is a function of his or her moral judgment, individual attributes, affective beliefs, cognitive beliefs, perceived importance, and subjective norms. Cronan and Al-Rafee (2008) later refined their model to investigate intention to pirate (the dependent variable) if a function of attitude, subjective norms, perceived behavioral control, past piracy behavior, and moral obligation.

Goles et al. (2008) examine the determinants of a consumer attitude towards softlifting (software piracy) and modeled intention to softlift (the dependent variable) is a function of attitude towards softlifting (past behavior, perceived usefulness, awareness of the law, personal moral obligation, risk-taking personal identify, legal personal identify, and technical personal identity). Gupta et al. (2004) speculated that the decision to pirate (or not to pirate) was based on ethical considerations, economic issues (e.g., perception of industry loss due to piracy), legal implications, consumer behavior (e.g., frequency of soflifting), accessibility, and demographics.

Chaudhry and Stumpf (2011) suggest that consumer complicity for counterfeit usage is a result of demographics, espoused values (relativism, idealism, collectivism), attitudes towards counterfeits (ethical concerns, quality of the counterfeit, previous use of counterfeits), actions to reduce product counterfeiting (product and social marketing anti-piracy tactics), and the shopping experience (e.g., hedonic behavior resulting from engaging in an illicit act).

Overall, the literature is addressing the specific role of consumer complicity but does not offer a holistic perspective of the IPR environment.

Level of Pirate Activity

Recent research and current events reveal problems that companies may experience with organized crime and/or legitimate dealers in the distribution channel. Initially, the counterfeit market evokes the image of a person selling fake Prada handbags on Canal Street in New York City or the savvy Chinese hawking look-alike North Face jackets in the infamous New Xiushui Market ("silk alley") of Beijing. The report on *Intellectual Property Rights Violations: A Report on Threats to United States Interests at Home and Abroad* (2011) gives a more accurate description of the counterfeiters involved as an array of offenders that engage in IPR violations at various stages of the manufacture, distribution, and sales of counterfeit product. These pirates include "individuals and small groups; members of general criminal enterprises, as well as their subset organized crime groups; supporters of terrorist organizations; members of gangs; foreign government actors; and members of warez groups" (p. 3).

As acknowledged by the United Nations Office on Drugs and Crime (UNODC) and the World Health Organization (WHO), several different grades of imitation are often available for any popular product (Counterfeit Medicines 2006; UNODC 2010). Different price points exist to reflect such variance in the level of sophistication. On the one side of the spectrum, there are high-quality "replicas" and "Grade-A merchandise," which may have been manufactured in the factories licensed to produce the authentic goods and, therefore, are virtually indistinguishable from their genuine counterparts since these goods use the same infrastructure as the legitimate producers (OECD 2007). On the other side of the spectrum are low-quality counterfeits that would deceive only inexperienced consumers. In between the two extremes are products of lesser grades diverted from factories or produced in dedicated workshops using lower-grade materials.

Table 4.1 Seizure of potentially harmful products (FY2010-FY2011)

FY 2011	Domestic value (US$)	% of total
Pharmaceuticals	$16,848,192	28
Electrical articles	$10,277,849	17
Perfume/cologne	$9,245,642	15
Cigarettes	$8,183,993	14
Health/personal care	$4,118,168	7
Toys/electronic games	$2,975,421	5
Eyewear/parts	$2,566,197	4
Critical technology components	$2,397,208	4
Batteries	$1,301,295	2
All other commodities	$2,149,389	4
Total FY 2011 value	$60,063,354	
Number of seizures	4,369	

Source: US Customs and Border Protection, *Intellectual Property Rights FY 2011 Seizure Statistics*, p. 24

While most of these fake products are harmless, some can inflict great damage. An alarming trend in recent years has been the spread of illicit trade into products that are potentially dangerous. Seizure figures in Table 4.1 by the US Customs and Border Projection (CBP) show the extent to which a variety of "potentially harmful products" are supplied by counterfeiters.

While it is difficult to determine the precise "level of illicit trade activity," it is clear that this is a huge problem and that both counterfeiters and smugglers continue to infiltrate many markets around the world. There have been few studies that actually attempt to determine the "level of pirate activity" facing managers in the IPR environment. It is obvious that there exist both domestic and international pirates that infiltrate a country's market in order to distribute counterfeit goods in both the physical and virtual marketplace. However, actually attempting to measure the activities of this illicit trade is problematic and was discussed in Chap. 2.

Overall, the level of organized pirate activity in the country market where a firm is experiencing the most significant piracy should shape the IPR environment. In addition, one would anticipate that the firm would increase the number of anti-counterfeiting tactics targeted within this country market as a result of formidable competition from the organized pirates.

Level of Host Country Enforcement

US laws such as the Tariff Act of 1930, the Lanham Act, the Trademark Counterfeiting Act of 1984, and the Stop Counterfeiting in Manufactured Goods Act of 2006 are all designed to provide some form of legal recourse for the firm through civil and criminal law penalties in the United States. In addition, the NAFTA treaty,

The Agreement on Trade-Related Aspects of Intellectual Property Rights (TRIPS) in the World Trade Organization (WTO), and the Scrivener regulations of the European Union are international measures implemented to encourage protection of intellectual property rights.

Although there are a number of national laws and international agreements designed to protect intellectual property rights, many believe that the legal remedies available to the victims of counterfeited or pirated goods historically have been inadequate.

The Index of Economic Freedom (IF) is another metric used to rank countries based on ten economic freedoms, such as trade freedom, investment freedom, and property rights that yield an overall score from 0 to 100 (Index of Economic Freedom, 2010). The top ten countries based on the IF for 2010 were Hong Kong (89.9), Singapore (87.5), Australia (83.1), New Zealand (82.1), Switzerland (81.1), Canada (79.9), Chile (78.3), Mauritius (77.0), Ireland (76.9), and the United States (76.3).

Overall, one would expect to find a positive correlation between the level of host country enforcement of intellectual property rights and the IPR environment. This should also lead to a reduced number of anti-counterfeiting measures employed in markets where host country enforcement is on the rise.

IPR Actions Targeted at Consumers, Distribution Channels, Host Governments, International Organizations, and Pirates

Because of the inability of governments to protect IPR throughout the world, many firms are becoming independently proactive. Many measures have been proposed to counter the growing problem of counterfeiting, and research has offered various recommendations to firms, ranging from the development of better relations with the distribution channel, encouraging consumer distinction between a genuine product and its fake counterpart, and emphasizing the truly prestigious image portrayed by purchasing a genuine product while stressing potential embarrassment associated with owning a counterfeit product (Chaudhry and Stumpf 2011; Commuri 2009; Wee et al. 1995). Sophisticated packaging and marking of products include special spouts which discourage refilling of bottles, the use of holograms, covert chemical fingerprints, "invisible" printing, Radio-Frequency Identification ("RFID"), or various types of "taggants" which may be chemical or biological and are read only when aided by special detectors, In fact, there are a number of firms which sell product identification technologies and the software used to track sales to contractors and through retailers.

These technologies, such as holograms, security inks, watermarks, and micro-printing, are designed to verify authenticity of products for consumers or IP owners. Anti-counterfeit packaging technology can be used by manufacturers on both the demand-side (by consumers and resellers) as well as by the supply-side (Berman 2008). On the demand side, consumers can—in some cases—make use of more "covert" cues and look for signs of counterfeiting, such as "packaging with blurred lettering or labeling; misspelling of words or altered product names; no placement of legal notices on the product or packaging … products or packaging without manufacturer's codes, trademarks and/or copyrights …"(Battersby 2011). Tamper-evident packaging also enables consumers to evaluate the authenticity of a product (Allen 2010; Perkins 2009a, b). As a result, manufacturers are constantly looking for new authentication technologies that are harder for counterfeiters to replicate (Berman 2008; Kwok et al. 2010; Stumpf and Chaudhry 2010). Lobbying host government and international organizations for increased protection of IPR is another tactic. A concise discussion of anti-counterfeiting strategies targeted at consumers is given in both Chaps. 5 and 6. Insight into both traditional and novel anti-counterfeiting tactics that target other stakeholders, such as the company's distribution channel and its adversary—the pirates are found in Chap. 11. A succinct discussion of the international organizations that safeguard IPR is found in Chap. 8.

The Model

Chaudhry, Peters, Zimmerman, and Cordell (2009) developed a comprehensive model and subsequent research inquiries to provide a framework for debate regarding the following questions:

1. How does the level of consumer complicity, pirate activity, and host country enforcement affect the perceived risk of the intellectual property rights environment?
2. Based on this managerial perception of IPR environment, how does this moderate the company's anti-counterfeiting actions targeted at consumers, distribution channels, host governments, international organizations, and pirates?
3. Finally, how does this affect a firm's future market commitment?

Figure 4.1 illustrates the conceptual framework developed to provide a holistic view of an IPR environment that is shaped by the "level of consumer complicity," the "level of organized pirates," and the "level of host country enforcement." This managerial perception of the IPR environment in each country will influence and elicit a strategic response in terms of the frequency of company actions targeted at consumers, distribution channels, host governments, international organizations, and pirates.

The Research Study

The research conducted by Chaudhry, Zimmerman, Peters, and Cordell (2009) was an exploratory study of managerial perceptions of the perceived risk of the intellectual property rights environment, obtained through assessing the use of anti-counterfeiting tactics in response to the level of consumer complicity, the degree of

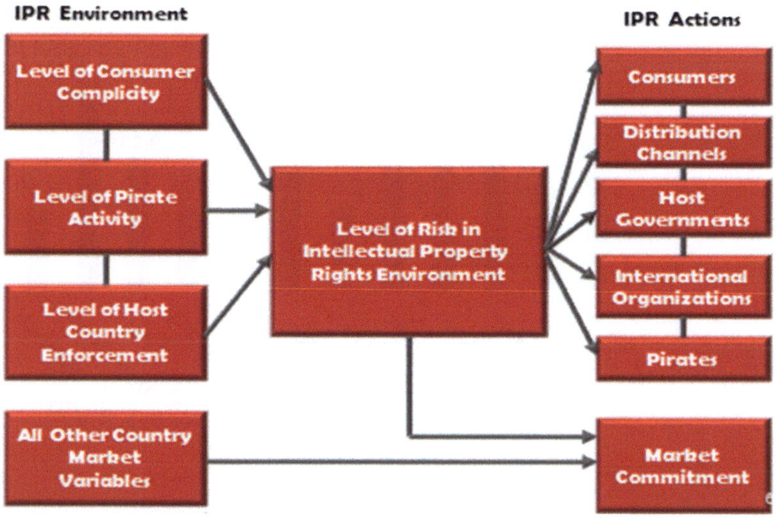

Fig. 4.1 Conceptual framework of the IPR environment. *Source*: Adapted from Chaudhry, P., Peters, J., Zimmerman, A., and Cordell, V., "Evidence of Managerial Response to the Level of Consumer Complicity, Pirate Activity, and Host Country Enforcement of Counterfeit Goods: An Exploratory Study," Multinational Business Review, 2009, 17(4), p. 25

organized pirates, and host country enforcement. Overall, the researchers had wanted to test through statistical measures whether our preconceived expectations of managerial perceptions concerning the future level of market commitment in counterfeiting markets, and the effectiveness of anti-counterfeiting tactics in a country where a firm experiences a high level of counterfeit activity. This study sought to confirm the credibility of our assumptions regarding the intellectual property rights environment through the analysis of panel data from a variety of firms in different industries. This is an appropriate method of data collection for investigating the perceptions of managers regarding a future event, such as the perceived risk of investments in markets with high piracy rates (e.g., see the literature on "scenario analysis" beginning with Leidecker and Bruno 1984).

The panel data consists of 29 managerial reports from executives located in the United States. Securing managers to participate in an in-depth interview on country conditions for this panel data was an arduous process. Based on this experience, we can attest that the lack of empirical analysis on anti-counterfeiting strategies results in part from a lack of cooperation, since many firms that we contacted were not willing to disclose their strategic vision, since they considered their anti-counterfeiting tactics proprietary information. Therefore, this panel data is used to create and explore a conceptual framework by defining the variables that constitute the intellectual property rights environment [that is, level of consumer complicity, pirate activity, and host country enforcement], how these variables affect the perceived risk of market commitment, and the firm's subsequent anti-counterfeiting action.

Table 4.2 Intellectual property protection in selected countries

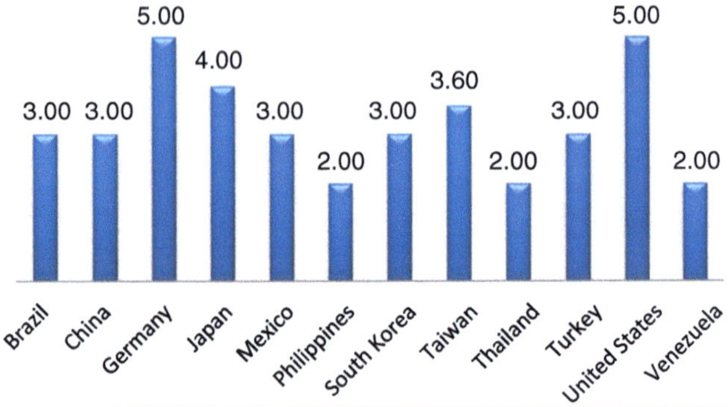

Source: *The Economist Intelligence Unit* 2012, www.eiu.com

The literature is replete with models and information on what factors influence the market commitment of the firm, such as economic conditions, political risk, currency fluctuations, trade barriers, and the like. However, this exploratory research will establish whether a high-risk intellectual property rights environment significantly affects the firm's market commitment.

Although time-consuming and typically involving very few participants, panel data captures the prevalent managerial perceptions of a phenomenon, such as whether a firm's anti-counterfeiting tactics directed at consumers have decreased the level of consumer complicity to purchase fake goods. Given the lack of statistical analysis on managerial perception of the growing counterfeiting problem, we believe that this study, as an initial exploratory analysis, is a substantial contributor to a critical global business topic.

The managers interviewed in this study had several years of relevant work experience and the majority of the respondents had worked for more than 10 years in international business. Thirteen of the managers had worked for a company that had sold its product outside of the United States for more than 12 years, the average sales outside of the United States by these companies at 30%. The majority of the firms reported annual sales of less than $1 billion per year, while a few companies were in the $1—5 billion range. One participant reported annual sales over $5 billion. The managers represent a cross-section of various industries which encompass battery manufacturing; apparel; contact lens solution; computers; sunglasses, videos, and CDs.

The respondents were asked to identify two countries where their firms experienced the highest level of product counterfeiting. The top markets for counterfeit goods were reportedly Brazil, China, Germany, Japan, Mexico, the Philippines, South Korea, Taiwan, Thailand, Turkey, the United States, and Venezuela. *The Economist Intelligence Unit* (2012) ranks countries on their level of intellectual property rights protection (5 = highest degree of protection; 1 = lowest) and Table 4.2 illustrates these countries overall ratings.

Table 4.3 Comparison of the level of consumer complicity to the level of market commitment and strategic importance

Group	Market commitment	Strategic importance
High consumer complicit markets	3.500	3.857
Low consumer complicit markets	1.833	3.333
F-statistic/p-value	10.328/p=0.005*	0.592/p=0.452

*$p<0.01$

Assessment of Managerial Perceptions

Examining the Role of Consumer Complicity

The four main country markets that managers rated highly regarding level of consumer complicity were China, Taiwan, the United States, and Mexico. Over two-thirds of managers interviewed perceived that, in the market where the firm was experiencing the most difficult counterfeit problem, consumers were willing to purchase a counterfeit good. In addition, each manager rated the perceived influence of select consumer product attributes in determining whether a good is counterfeit or legitimate. The managers rated price (85%), point of purchase (85%), and quality of the product (76%) as the top three attributed used to determine the authenticity of a product.

To test our research question, an analysis of variance (ANOVA) was conducted to measure the extent to which a high level of consumer complicity to purchase counterfeits in a given country market deters a firm from future investment in that market. Again, the expectation was to discover that in high consumer complicit markets like China, firms would be unwilling to expand their current level of market commitment with future investment engagements. Respondents were asked to rate the "level of consumer complicity" on a scale of 1 (very unwilling to purchase counterfeits) to 5 (very willing to purchase counterfeits) for the main country that they experienced counterfeits. We correlated this response with the respondents view of future investment decisions in this country on a scale of 5 (very high future investments) to 1 (very low future investments), and the perceived strategic importance of this country market on a scale of 5 (very important) to 1 (very unimportant). Table 4.3 reveals the results of the ANOVA below:

Testing the null hypothesis that the level of market commitment is the same for the two groups at a 1% level of significance, Table 4.1 shows that one can reject the hypothesis that firms in both high- and low- complicit markets will make the same investment decisions. Thus, our assumption that firms will avoid markets with a high level of consumer complicity to purchase counterfeits is *not* supported and the ANOVA implies that managers plan to make significantly more future investments in markets where there is a higher level of consumer complicity. Table 4.3 indicates that the higher the number, the more future investment planned. Thus, it appears that the managers of companies operating in a highly complicit market, such as China, feel that the strategic importance of this market outweighs the intellectual property

Table 4.4 Comparison of means on frequency of use of anti-counterfeiting tactics between firms operating in complicit vs. non-complicit foreign markets

Anti-counterfeiting tactic	High-complicit vs. low-complicit consumer markets	Mean	F-statistic/*p*-value
Actions directed at consumers	High-complicit	2.929	0.688/p=0.418
	Low-complicit	2.167	
Actions directed at channel members	High-complicit	3.143	0.336/p=0.569
	Low-complicit	2.667	
Lobbying the US government	High-complicit	2.615	0.061/p=0.807
	Low-complicit	2.833	
Lobbying the foreign government	High-complicit	2.154	0.169/p=0.686
	Low-complicit	1.833	
Participating in international organizations	High-complicit	3.538	0.1246/p=0.280
	Low-complicit	2.667	
Actions directed at pirates	High-complicit	3.583	1.098/p=0.310
	Low-complicit	2.500	
Actions directed at educating employees	High-complicit	3.077	0.007/p=0.936
	Low-complicit	3.000	

*p>0.10 for all items

rights infringements, and will continue to invest in the market. This idea is further supported by the fact that the managers rated both high- and low-complicit markets relatively the same in terms of the strategic importance of each country market and that the counterfeit problem does not outweigh the future significance of maintaining a presence in one of these foreign markets.

The managers were asked to rate the frequency of anti-counterfeiting actions implemented in attempt to reduce counterfeiting of their product in the foreign market. The specific tactics designated in the survey included the use of special packaging; educating channel members; lobbying for more effective intellectual property laws in the United States; lobbying for more effective laws in the foreign country; participating in organizations, such as the IACC; creating a company enforcement team to pursue pirates; and developing internal company strategies, such as educating employees on the product counterfeiting problem.

To test whether the degree of anti-counterfeiting actions changed in foreign markets, an ANOVA analysis was conducted to see if the "frequency of anti-counterfeiting actions" varied as a function of whether the market was complicit or non-complicit. To analyze this inquiry, a composite score of all of the seven anti-counterfeiting tactics listed in the survey was developed (see Table 4.4). Thus, a company with a high frequency (scale item = 5) of all of these seven strategies would have a score of 35 (7×5). Then, a comparison between complicit and non-complicit consumer markets in terms of frequency of use of these distinct strategies was analyzed. Table 4.5 illustrates that, using a composite score; there are no visibly tactical differences between firms operating in a complicit vs. non-complicit market.

Table 4.5 Comparison of complicit vs. non-complicit consumer markets and frequency of anti-counterfeiting tactics used in the foreign market

	Mean of actions
High-complicit markets	19.400
Low-complicit markets	17.667
F-statistic/p-value	0.187/$p = 0.672$*

*$p > 0.10$

There is simply no statistical evidence that supports that firms use more anti-counterfeiting tactics in highly complicit markets. However, each anti-counterfeiting tactic was examined to see if there was a strong correlation between the implementation of any one strategy, such as using special advertising or labeling, to deter the purchase of counterfeits, and market complicity.

As indicated in Table 4.5, the managers responses did not indicate any statistical significance of anti-counterfeiting efforts as a variable dependent on market complicity (tested at the $p = 10\%$). So, overall, contrary to our expectations, the level of market complicity does not affect the frequency of the company's anti-counterfeiting efforts in that market. It is evident from this analysis that firms are employing various anti-counterfeiting tactics regardless of whether the managers perceive a high degree of consumer complicity in their most important markets. Overall, the firms are using a uniform, standardized strategy to protect intellectual property in the global marketplace. It is interesting to note that they are not varying the level of "actions directed at consumers" in highly complicit markets.

In Chap. 5, a more detailed discussion of consumer complicity is given. In Chap. 6, an in-depth review of anti-counterfeiting strategies to decrease demand for fake goods, specifically whether companies can use novel demarketing techniques to change the consumer behavior towards purchasing illicit products is provided.

Evaluating the Effect of Indigenous Pirate Activity

As suggested previously, we expected the level of pirate activity to negatively impact the level of market commitment and/or increase the use of anti-counterfeiting strategies employed by the firm in a particular country market. An ANOVA [analysis of variance] was conducted to test these expectations and respondents were asked to rate the "level of counterfeiting activity" on a scale of 1 (very insignificant) to 5 (very significant) for the country in which the firm primarily experienced counterfeits. We correlated this response with the respondents view of future investment decisions in this country on a scale of 5 (very high future investments) to 1 (very low future investments), and the perceived strategic importance of this country market on a scale of 5 (very important) to 1 (very unimportant). Again, we expected to find that markets with a formidable level of pirate activity, such as China, would lower the willingness to further expand market commitment through future investment in

Table 4.6 Analysis of variance for level of piracy in foreign market compared to the level of market commitment and strategic importance

Group	Market commitment	Strategic importance
High-piracy markets	3.222	3.778
Low-piracy markets	3.000	3.182
F-statistic/p-value	0.112/0.742	0.807/0.381*

*$p > 0.10$

Table 4.7 Comparison of high- vs. low-piracy markets and frequency of anti-counterfeiting tactics used in the foreign market

Group	Mean of actions
High-piracy markets	22.4286
Low-piracy markets	11.7273
F-statistic/p-value	17.500/0.001*

*$p < 0.01$

that market. We also wanted to see if there existed a correlation between the strategic importance of the market and the incidence of indigenous pirates in the foreign market. Table 4.6 reveals the results of the ANOVA:

The results in Table 4.6 indicate that the managers did not vary the level of firm commitment nor the perceived ranking of strategic importance of the foreign market based on the expected level of pirate activities in the host country market, thus negating our expectations. However, a test of the frequency of counterfeiting tactics related to the level of piracy in the foreign market was conducted to discern whether the frequency of anti-counterfeiting actions varied between markets with a large number of indigenous pirates and low-piracy markets. A composite score of all of the seven anti-counterfeiting tactics listed in the survey was developed, thus, a company with a high frequency (scale item = 5) of all of these seven strategies would have a score of 35 (7×5). Then, a comparison of the difference between high-piracy and low-piracy markets in terms of frequency of use of these distinct strategies was analyzed. Table 4.7 indicates that there is a difference between the two groups at the 1% level of confidence in terms of the number of actions employed in a high-piracy environment.

To further understand the alleged difference in tactical maneuvers in markets with a high level of indigenous pirates, we conducted an ANOVA for each tactic. As indicated in Table 4.6, three stratagems, actions directed at the US and the foreign governments, and local pirates, are significantly different at the 1% level of significance between the two groups of high- vs. low-piracy markets. If we expand our level of significance to the 5 and 10% level, we can add two more strategies, participating in international organizations, such as the International Anti-Counterfeiting Coalition (IACC), and educating the company's employees to deter the pirates. In sharp contrast to the analysis of consumer complicit markets, there is a proven statistical difference between the two groups, that is, high- vs. low-piracy markets, regarding "actions directed at pirates" (Table 4.8).

Table 4.8 Comparison of means on frequency of use of anti-counterfeiting tactics between firms operating in high-piracy vs. low-piracy foreign environments

Anti-counterfeiting tactic	High- vs. low-piracy environment	Mean	F-statistic/*p*-value
Actions directed at consumers	High-piracy	2.556	0.337/0.569
	Low-piracy	2.091	
Actions directed at channel members	High-piracy	3.444	0.674/0.422
	Low-piracy	2.818	
Lobbying the US government	High-piracy	3.250	12.538/0.003***
	Low-piracy	0.818	
Lobbying the foreign government	High-piracy	2.750	17.216/0.001***
	Low-piracy	0.545	
Participating in international organizations	High-piracy	3.889	6.278/0.022**
	Low-piracy	2.273	
Actions directed at pirates	High-piracy	4.125	19.183/0.000***
	Low-piracy	1.091	
Actions directed at educating Employees	High-piracy	3.444	3.072/0.097*
	Low-piracy	2.091	

$^{*}p<0.10$; $^{**}p<0.05$; $^{***}p<0.01$

Judging the Influence of Host Country IPR Enforcement

The lack of legal enforcement of intellectual property rights has been well cited in the literature (e.g., see Chaudhry and Walsh 1995, 1996). However, the empirical measurement of managerial perceptions of this enforcement issue rarely goes beyond descriptive statistics of the types of strategies used by firms to combat counterfeits. In this study, an assessment of the influence of the degree of intellectual property rights enforcement on a manager's decision to increase the firm's level of market commitment and effectively employ anti-counterfeiting tactics was conducted.

In the interview, the mangers were asked two questions related to the level of host country enforcement of IPR: (1) How protective are the laws that cover intellectual property rights in this country? (2) How effective do you feel the enforcement of intellectual property rights laws are in this country? The scale used for the first question ranged from 5 = very protective to 1 = very unprotective. The scale for the second question ranged from 5 = very effective to 1 = very ineffective. The logic behind these questions was to correlate the legislation in a foreign market with the effectiveness of such legislation to enforce a company's intellectual property rights. A composite score of both of these questions was conducted by way of ANOVA to determine whether a low level of intellectual property rights enforcement in a foreign market would deter the firm's future investments or perceived level of strategic importance of the host country. Table 4.9 reveals that both the company's investment

Table 4.9 Analysis of variance for level of enforcement of IPR compared to the level of market commitment and strategic importance

Group	Market commitment	Strategic importance
High level of enforcement of IPR	3.400	3.700
Low level of enforcement of IPR	2.889	2.700
F-statistic/p-value	0.771/$p=0.392$	2.356/$p=0.142$*

*$p>0.10$

strategy and its rating of the host country's strategic importance were not influenced by the level of enforcement of IPR. In fact, one can draw an analogy between the findings related to consumer complicity and enforcement of IPR. In both cases, our findings were contrary to our expected results. The firms were still willing to expand their level of market commitment in highly complicit markets and markets with a low level of intellectual property rights protection. Again, this emphasizes the fact that strategic importance of the markets in this study outweighs potential negatives associated with counterfeit products.

Finally, a test was done to see if the number of anti-counterfeiting tactics implemented in the market where the firm was experiencing the highest level of counterfeits varied as a function of perceived level of legal enforcement of intellectual property rights. An ANOVA was conducted to further understand how the legal framework governing the protection of IPR in a host country environment affects the frequency of anti-counterfeiting strategies directed at consumers, pirates, channel members, and the like. In order to test this assumption through statistical analysis, a composite score of all seven of the categories of company actions, such as "actions directed at consumers," was calculated, and a comparison of the use of these strategies in environments of high vs. low level of legal protection was conducted.

Table 4.10 illustrates that there is a noteworthy difference between countries of high vs. low level of IPR protection, in terms of the company's frequency of use of anti-counterfeiting strategies at the 1% level of significance. However, the research finding is exactly the *opposite* of what we had expected and the frequency of anti-counterfeiting actions was greater in a country where the level of local law enforcement was higher, *not* lower. The researchers assume that a manager will use more actions when he or she perceives a legal environment that will enforce the company's anti-counterfeiting campaign. On the contrary, the firm will use fewer tactics in an environment where the manager does not foresee the legal support to enforce its anti-piracy stratagems.

Given our unexpected statistical results for this research question, the importance of each individual tactic was further investigated through the ANOVA in Table 4.11. There was an important finding in terms of actions directed at consumers and pirates at the 1% level of significance. To reinforce our previous assertion, managers will aggressively pursue the counterfeiters and consumers in a supportive legal environment. There was nominal support for actions directed at lobbying foreign governments and educating the company's employees at the 10% level of significance.

Table 4.10 Analysis of variance for level of enforcement of IPR and company actions taken against counterfeit goods

Group	Composite actions mean
High IPR protection in local laws	22.750
Low IPR protection in local laws	13.111
F-statistic/p-value	9.334/p=0.008*

*p<0.01

Table 4.11 Comparison of means on frequency of use of anti-counterfeiting tactics between firms operating in high-legal protection vs. low-legal protection foreign environments

Anti-counterfeiting tactic	High- vs. low-legal protection in the legal environment	Mean	F-statistic/p-value
Actions directed at consumers	High-legal Protection Low-legal Protection	3.700 1.100	20.979/0.000**
Actions directed at channel members	High-legal Protection Low-legal Protection	3.900 3.300	1.200/0.288
Lobbying the US government	High-legal Protection Low-legal Protection	2.556 1.300	2.426/0.138
Lobbying the foreign government	High-legal Protection Low-legal Protection	2.444 1.100	3.720/0.071*
Participating in international organizations	High-legal Protection Low-legal Protection	3.222 3.300	0.015/0.903
Actions directed at pirates	High-legal Protection Low-legal Protection	4.333 1.778	11.888/0.003**
Actions directed at educating employees	High-legal Protection Low-legal Protection	3.700 2.100	3.095/0.064*

*p<0.10; **p<0.01

Managerial Insights Regarding the IPR Environment: Key Findings

One of the major findings of the work-in-progress presented in this Chapter (Chaudhry, Zimmerman, Peters, and Cordell 2009) was that managerial implementation of anti-counterfeiting strategies targeted at the consumer of fake goods was not influenced by market complicity. Overall, the test results found that there were no tactical differences between firms operating in a complicit vs. a non-complicit market. The researchers had anticipated that firms would employ a multi-domestic anti-counterfeiting strategy approach to curtail the consumer purchase of counterfeit goods in highly complicit markets and expected to find more consumer-directed tactics used in these markets, such as special advertising and labeling techniques like holograms. However, we found no statistical evidence that would support this assertion and discovered that none of the seven tactics designed to bolster the protection of intellectual property rights were significantly different in markets of high vs. low complicity. The researchers conclude that companies are using various anti-counterfeiting tactics in foreign markets, regardless of whether the managers perceive a high degree of consumer complicity. Firms are using a uniform, standardized strategy to protect intellectual property in the global marketplace in terms of special packaging/advertising, warning channel members, devising actions against pirates, and the like.

In sharp contrast to the analysis of consumer complicit markets, there was a difference in anti-counterfeiting stratagems directed at pirates in terms of the level of counterfeiting activity in the country where the firm was experiencing the highest level of illicit trade. In markets where managers perceived a high level of piracy, firms were more likely to employ tailor-made actions designed to combat the pirates in that foreign market. In addition, the companies were more likely to use lobbying tactics targeted at both the foreign government and the US government to alleviate the problem of this type of crime. In addition, the firm was more likely to participate in an international organization, such as the WTO. This topic is further addressed in both Chaps. 8 and 11.

Overall, the study discussed in this chapter revealed a strong indication that managers do not perceive curbing the demand side—consumer complicity—as an effective way to remedy the problem. That is, consumer complicity is not regarded as an actionable item warranting significant management behavior. However, the managers did view deterring the pirates to be an actionable item warranting proactive behavior. Overall, the respondents were more likely to use the following tactics: lobbying the US government, lobbying the host country government, participating with international organizations, using company enforcement teams to curtail indigenous pirates, and educating their employees about the counterfeit problem.

We compared the use of anti-counterfeiting tactics in markets where managers perceived a high vs. low level of legal protection in the host country to analyze whether there was a difference between these two distinct types of markets. The researchers expected to see a higher number of tactics used in markets where there was a low level of enforcement of the company's intellectual property rights. However, contrary to their prediction, the study results supported that the managers employed more anti-counterfeiting stratagems in a country where the level of local law enforcement was higher, *not* lower. Thus, the researchers conclude that a manager believes employing several anti-counterfeiting measures in a country with a low level of enforcement is futile. Firms anticipate the detriment of weak international litigation in an unprotective legal environment to yield a negative outcome.

In the model (refer to Fig. 4.2) the researchers expected that the level of consumer complicity, level of pirate activity, and the level of host country enforcement would influence the future level of market commitment made by the firm in the country where the company was experiencing the highest degree of counterfeit activity. For example, in 2011, the *Business Software Alliance* estimated that highest software piracy rates were in countries like Georgia, Zimbabwe, and Bangladesh at 93%, 91%, and 90%, respectively (Business Software Alliance 2011d, p.3). Thus, one would question whether firms such as Microsoft would increase the level of market commitment in this type of marketplace.

The findings were mixed in terms of supporting this of assumption about a firm's behavior in markets that have a high degree of counterfeit trade. First, the study results support that in markets where there is a higher level of consumer complicity, the managers planned to make significantly more investments in the future. Conversely, the presence of a high degree of pirates did not change the level of the company's commitment to future investments, nor its perception of the country's ranking of strategic importance. Likewise, the investment strategy of the firm was not altered based on whether the manager faced a high or low level of enforcement of its intellectual property rights in a given market. Thus, the suggested negative linkage between the IPR environment and the level of market commitment could not be statistically supported in this study. In fact, the results are just the opposite. Managers were willing to increase their investments in markets where they experienced a high level of consumer complicity, pirate activity, and a low level of intellectual property rights enforcement. Consequently, this study shows that despite a weak IPR environment, a market may be perceived as strategically important and a market deserving of future commitment and investment.

Conclusions

In this chapter, a concise summary of the results of an exploratory analysis based on 29 managerial reports of the IPR model (refer back to Fig. 4.2) was given. Given the small sample size, the researchers cannot support or refute the proposed framework (Fig. 4.2)—this is the task of future work using a larger number of respondents. However, the valid contribution of this exploratory study centers on the fact that many of the results of this study were not expected and several of the researchers' assumptions were not supported. Thus, future studies must be conducted to build on this initial empirical analysis of managerial response to the IPR environment. First, it is possible that other factors in addition to the level of consumer complicity, pirate activity, and host country enforcement determine the intellectual property rights environment of a particular country market. The exact relationships between the IPR environment, the level of the firm's market commitment and subsequent IPR actions targeted at consumers, distribution channels, host country government, international organizations, and pirates are all fertile areas that need to be explored across country marketing using a larger number of managerial respondents to determine the validity of the model proposed in this chapter. In Chap. 5, an overview of research that attempts to capture the essence of consumer complicity to purchase fake goods is debated. Chap. 6 draws from the demarketing literature to provide a unique discussion of plausible anti-counterfeiting techniques targeted to change a consumer's behavior, such as using a "fear of prosecution" in advertisement to diminish demand for counterfeits. Finally, Chap. 11 extends the initial discussion of anti-counterfeiting tactics presented in this chapter through an overview of both traditional and novel anti-counterfeiting stratagems for firms to employ in the global marketplace.

Chapter 5
The Demand for Counterfeit Trade: Consumer Complicity

Introduction

There is a need for business managers, policymakers, and other constituents to start focusing on the demand side of the counterfeit problem. The academic literature, business, and trade publications have addressed various anticounterfeiting tactics, the types of organized piracy activities, and the level of international and host country enforcement used to protect a company's IPR. Little research has been conducted measuring the "demand side" of the problem, i.e., the willingness of consumers to purchase counterfeit goods. The current research has relied on convenience samples of consumers within single country markets, such as Germany or Hong Kong. Very few empirical studies have been conducted to explain this consumer behavior across country markets. Imagine the insights we might gain by examining consumer attitudes and purchase behavior for counterfeit goods.

In this chapter, we propose a conceptual framework to better understand the various components that affect a consumer's willingness to purchase counterfeit goods. We assert that consumer complicity to purchase counterfeit goods is a function of both *intrinsic* (demographics, attitude towards counterfeits, cultural values, and ethical perspective) and *extrinsic* (product attributes, shopping experience, and demarketing communications) determinants. These are all key variables that drive the global demand for counterfeit goods. Most of the measurement of consumer demand has been conducted in the software and music industry and there is a heavy reliance on data provided by both the Business Software Alliance and the Motion Picture Association to highlight global piracy rates. In Chap. 6, we highlight various anti-piracy marketing techniques designed to reduce this demand for illicit goods. In Chap. 10, we provide a detailed discussion of Internet piracy to further underscore consumer complicity to acquire counterfeit goods through this virtual distribution channel.

P. Chaudhry and A. Zimmerman, *Protecting Your Intellectual Property Rights*, Management for Professionals, DOI 10.1007/978-1-4614-5568-4_5,

Consumer Drivers for Purchasing Counterfeit Goods

Most studies have addressed the supply side of counterfeits by assessing the level of pirate activity (e.g., Green and Smith 2002; UNODC 2010), and the level of international and host country enforcement of intellectual property rights (e.g., Chaudhry 2006; Chaudhry et al. 2005; Chaudhry and Walsh 1995, 1996). Wee et al. (1995) looked at the non-price determinants of intention to purchase counterfeit consumer goods and described the lack of demand side research as a major problem and suggested that more consumer behavior concepts need to be investigated in order to better understand what motivates a consumer to purchase illicit goods beyond the low-price incentive. The Business Action to Stop Counterfeiting and Piracy (BASCAP) echoes this concern and conducted its own comprehensive study, *Research Report on Consumer Attitudes and Perceptions on Counterfeiting and Piracy* (BASCAP 2009) to provide better insight into consumer complicity. These researchers emphasized that global consumer complicity is widespread:

> You will find that this report clearly shows that from Mumbai to Moscow, from Central London to the suburbs of Mexico City, counterfeiting and piracy represent a widely tolerated and unspoken social plague. The consequences of participating in this illicit trade are poorly understood by consumers, and the associated risks are insufficiently demonstrated by traditional authorities. In short, it seems that, "hear no evil, speak no evil" has become the norm which it comes to counterfeiting and piracy.

The 2009 BASCAP study included consumers in Mexico, Russia, the U.K., India, and South Korea using focus groups and quantitative surveys to better understand consumer complicity. This research concluded that the predominant drivers of counterfeit purchases were the following (BASCAP 2009, p. 8):

- Low price and increasingly better quality create temptation.
- Low risk and penalty equates to a license to buy.
- Availability, quality, price, and low risk generate an overall sense of social acceptability.

In 2012, the Business Software Alliance reported the results of a complicity survey of 15,000 computer users in 33 countries that comprise 82% of the global PC market. The respondents were asked, "How often do you acquire pirated software that is not fully licensed—all the time, most of the time, occasionally, rarely, or never?" Figure 5.1 illustrates that a significant portion of these consumers (57%) concede to some level of piracy. The BSA also segmented the respondents by the level of economic development of the country in which they reside and stated, "[E]ven more striking is the difference in behavior between users in emerging economies and users in the developed world. Frequent pirates in emerging economies install nearly four times as many programs of all sorts per new PC as do frequent pirates in mature markets" (Business Software Alliance 2012, p. 2).

Prior to the 2008 Beijing Summer Olympics, *The Wall Street Journal* reported that in conjunction with severe penalties for selling a counterfeit 2008 Olympic product in China, the consumer in China was less likely to purchase a fake

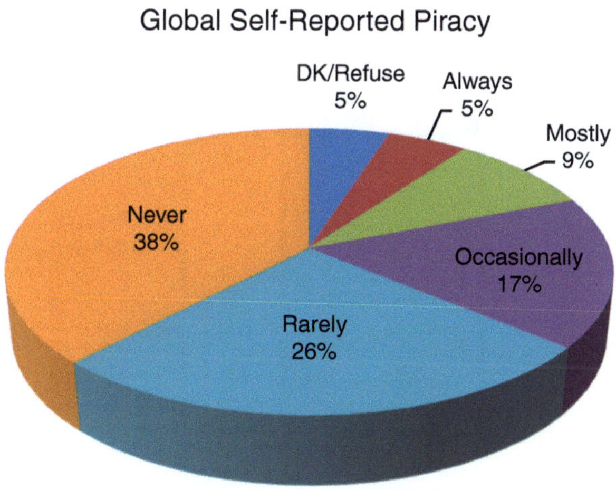

Fig. 5.1 Top 10 economies in commercial value of pirated PC software, 2011. *Source*: Adapted from *Shadow Market*, 2011 BSA Global Software Piracy Study, Ninth edition, May 2012, p. 1

Olympic item due to nationalistic pride—the feeling that his or her country owns the 2008 Olympic logo (Solomon 2005). Thus, both government policymakers and managers need to work together to change the attitudes of consumers, developing a negative connotation for the purchase of counterfeit goods that will decrease the demand for these products.

Conceptual Model of Consumer Complicity to Purchase Fake Goods

Chaudhry and Stumpf (2011) have developed a conceptual model to represent the factors that influence the demand side of the counterfeit goods problem, i.e., the willingness of consumers to *knowingly* buy counterfeit goods. As hypothesized by these researchers, consumer complicity to purchase counterfeit goods is a function of both *intrinsic* (demographics, attitude towards counterfeits, cultural values, and ethical perspective) and *extrinsic* (social marketing communications, shopping experience, and product attributes) determinants. This model is depicted in Fig. 5.2.

The acceptance of nondeceptive purchases of counterfeit goods on the part of consumers significantly affects the intellectual property environment. Gaining a better understanding of the factors underlying this acceptance and how these factors vary from country to country will help managers deal more effectively with the global problem of counterfeiting.

Fig. 5.2 Conceptual model of consumer complicity. *Source*: Adapted from Chaudhry and Stumpf (2011)

Marketing Variables That Influence Consumer Complicity

Table 5.1 below lists the variables included in the conceptual framework that influence the consumers' complicity to buy fake goods (Chaudhry and Stumpf 2011). Each dimension is fully explained in the pages that follow. Applicable findings from previous research studies are also provided.

Demographics of Consumers

A few studies have addressed whether demographic variables influence consumer complicity to buy fake goods. Nia and Zaichkowsky (2000) examined gender, age,

Table 5.1 Variables that induce consumer complicity to purchase counterfeit goods

Intrinsic determinants	Extrinsic determinants
Demographics of consumer	Product attributes
Age, income, level of education, gender, and the like	Image/perceived fashion content
High vs. low spenders on counterfeit goods	Price, quality, performance
Level of disposable income	Investment-at-risk
Other psychographic variables [e.g., risk-taker]	Purpose [personal use vs. gift]
Attitude towards counterfeiting	Shopping experience
Anti-big business sentiment	Location [e.g., Internet, flea market]
Social benefit of dissemination	Situation [e.g., holiday trip in China]
Attitude of counterfeits in a product category [movies vs. pharmaceuticals]	Ease of accessing counterfeits [e.g., Internet downloads]
Cultural values	Demarketing communications
Individualism vs. collectivism	Effectiveness of anti-piracy ads
Ethical perspective	
Attitude towards morality and lawfulness	
Idealism vs. relativism	

Source: Adapted from Chaudhry and Stumpf (2011)

ethnicity, occupation, level of income, and previous ownership of counterfeits to discern whether counterfeits devalue the ownership of luxury brands. Prendergast et al. (2002) examined similar demographics, but also addressed "high" vs. "low" spenders and any differences between these two segments. Overall, their findings from a decade ago suggested that compared to low spenders, high spenders on pirated VCDs (Video CD) place greater importance on quality and large supply in their purchasing decisions. However, both groups are similarly indifferent when it comes to the ethical and legal issues involved in purchasing fake goods.

Wee et al. (1995) included age, household income, and education, and they expected to find that the frequency to buy counterfeit goods would vary across respondents in terms of age, level of education, and income. Overall, the researchers felt that wisdom comes with age, judgment with more education, and the higher purchasing power related to increased income would covariate with other non-price determinants of consumer complicity to buy fake products. However, in this study the researchers reveal that only "attitude towards counterfeiting" appeared in the majority of their models as an explanatory variable in terms of predicting a willingness to purchase counterfeit, and "age" could not be used as a segmentation variable. For one product, purchasing pirated software, one demographic variable, "educational attainment," was determined to be a significant factor. The other important variables explaining intentions to purchase counterfeit software were product quality, attitude towards counterfeiting, and purpose of the purchase. In summary, the authors concluded that the higher the level of education for the respondents, the higher the likelihood of purchasing counterfeit software.

In our recent web survey examining consumer complicity in four emerging markets, Brazil, Russia, India and China, and the United States, we did not find a strong correlation between the respondents' demographics and national origin to predict a

Table 5.2 Consumer complicity index segmentation

Complicity group	Brazil	Russia	India	China	USA	Total
High complicity	131 (33%)	187 (47%)	107 (27%)	206 (52%)	43 (11%)	674 (34%)
Some complicity	139 (35%)	168 (42%)	128 (32%)	114 (29%)	103 (26%)	652 (33%)
Not complicit	129 (32%)	45 (11%)	167 (42%)	79 (20%)	258 (64%)	678 (34%)
Total	399	400	402	399	404	2,004

Source: Chaudhry and Stumpf (2012)

willingness to obtain fakes (Chaudhry et al. 2011a, b, p. 223). In fact, using this sample of 2,004 respondents, we developed a "consumer complicity index" that combines decision/intention to buy counterfeits with their actual acquisition thereby profiling a consumer based on his/her actual behavior. As illustrated in Table 5.2, this allowed us to segment consumers based on their level of complicity across country markets. The objective of this segmentation was to identify complicit consumers and look at them specifically, leaving non-complicit consumers out of the analyses. Consumers were grouped into three mutually exclusive and exhaustive categories: no complicity, some complicity, and high complicity. Percentages for each category across country-of-origin were examined, revealing significant differences (Chi-square = 346.7, $p < 0.000$) across nation states (see Table 5.2). Over 50% of Chinese and nearly 50% of Russian consumers are in the high complicity group based on self-reported decision/intentions as well as previous acquisition of counterfeit products. Only 27% of Indian and 11% of US consumers reported high complicity, while Brazilian consumers were equally divided in each category.

Attitude Towards Counterfeiting

Previous studies have supported the fact that consumers generally see purchasing a counterfeit good as a victimless crime. Tom et al. (1998) supported that consumers are willing to purchase counterfeit goods for a variety of reasons that include perceiving the counterfeit to be as good as the authentic good; expressing an "anti-big-business" sentiment; and holding "lax attitudes" about the legal protection of intellectual property. In the Tom et al. study, the researchers developed a list of attitude statements to determine consumer demand for pirated goods. Statements given included "counterfeit products do not hurt the US economy," "people who buy counterfeit products are committing a crime," and "I buy counterfeit products because the prices of designer products are unfair and gouge." In the study's major findings, the researchers discovered a halo/horn effect that discriminated between the mind-set of consumers who had previously purchased a fake product and those who had never bought a counterfeit good. One of their key findings was that consumers believe that the quality of a fake is similar to the genuine product.

In a study addressing the cultural determinants of intentions to purchase counterfeits, Schuchert-Güler and Martin (2003) verified that German consumers

Fig. 5.3 Counterfeit and/or pirated product purchaser profiles. *Source*: Adapted from the *Research Report on Consumer Attitudes and Perceptions on Counterfeiting and Piracy*, BASCAP, 2009, p. 10

"on holiday" were more than willing to purchase counterfeits as gifts. In fact, they make the point that the "mood" of the consumer on holiday, such as sense of adventure, does increase their willingness to purchase fakes as souvenirs.

In the previously mentioned BASCAP survey of consumers in India, U.K., Russia, Mexico, and South Korea, the researchers summarized an array of five "attitudinal profiles cutting across cultural, demographic and social categories" as defined in Fig. 5.3. These profiles were derived from 20 focus groups ($n=200$ participants) to better understand the perceptions of consumers towards counterfeit products (C/P in Fig. 5.3). The researchers at BASCAP described their qualitative research as follows (*Research Report on Consumer Attitudes and Perceptions on Counterfeiting and Piracy*, p. 9):

> [W]e encountered an amazing diversity of profiles, buying power and lifestyles: we talked with struggling consumers and upper-middle-class executives, we met single moms and business owners. All had regular or casual experience of buying counterfeit or pirated products. For each we tried to identify the nature and dimensions of their relationship to such products: what and how they bought, the drivers behind the practice and the deterrents that might stop them.

Cultural Values

Cultural differences in attitudes and values also contribute to consumer complicity. Several years ago, the *Journal of Commerce* (1999) reported that intellectual property rights are a Western concept and in China intellectual property infringement is not seen as morally wrong. In India, counterfeit pharmaceutical makers claim that the government believes it is more important to save lives than provide profits to the inventors of drugs (McNeil 2000). The concept of collectivism has been shown in recent studies to provide an explanatory cultural variable of the distinction between eastern and western cultures regarding a consumer's willingness to purchase of fakes. Husted (2000) and Marron and Steel (2000) identified that a collectivist culture plays a major role in the ethical decision-making used in the purchase of a counterfeit good.

Moores (2008) investigated the wealth of a country (per capita national income) and Hofstede's cultural variables to gauge the effect of both wealth and culture on reducing a country's software piracy rates (as reported by the Business Software Alliance) using secondary data for 57 countries. Moores (2008) used all four of Hofstede's national cultural dimensions (i.e., power distance, individualism/collectivism, masculinity/femininity, and uncertainty avoidance) to infer causality between increased wealth and reduced software piracy rates. This study found strong support for cultural variables, such as individualism and collectivism and piracy as determinants of consumer complicity. Moores summarized that there is a reciprocal relationship where individualism reinforces wealth, and future prosperity supports individualism and diminishes software piracy (2008, p. 46).

In earlier studies, such as Swinyard et al. (1990), the cultural roots of collectivism have a significant impact on the attitudes toward, and purchasing decisions for, counterfeit software. Wang et al. (2005) use the Chinese proverb, "He that shares is to be rewarded; he that does not, condemned," to illustrate how cultural beliefs can shape the individual's attitude toward buying counterfeit software. In summary the cultural variable of collectivism is the strongest explanatory variable driving the purchase of counterfeit products.

Ethical Perspective

In 1980, Donelson Forsyth in his "Taxonomy of Ethical Ideologies," developed an Ethics Perception Questionnaire (EPQ) that consists of ten statements designed to measure the assumption that desirable results can be obtained if the right action is taken, that is *idealism*. For example, one of the statements is "[A] person should make certain that their actions never intentionally harm another even to a small degree." The other part of the EPQ questionnaire is *relativism*, that measures "the degree to which a person's moral philosophy assumes that the proprietary of actions should be judged on the basis of the context of time, culture, and place rather than some set of universal moral rules" (Bruner et al. 2001, p. 233). One of the ten statements used to judge the degree of relativism is "[W]hat is ethical varies from one situation and society to another." This dichotomy of ethical perspectives, that is, idealism vs. relativism, may be a useful way to discern whether this type of intrinsic value influences consumer complicity.

The influence of an ethical perspective on whether a consumer will obtain a counterfeit product has been addressed in previous work (e.g., see Wilcox et al. 2009; Vitell and Muncy 1992, 2005). To address the research question of whether human values influence consumer complicity we tested whether the constructs of

Table 5.3 Categories where counterfeit potential is the highest overall

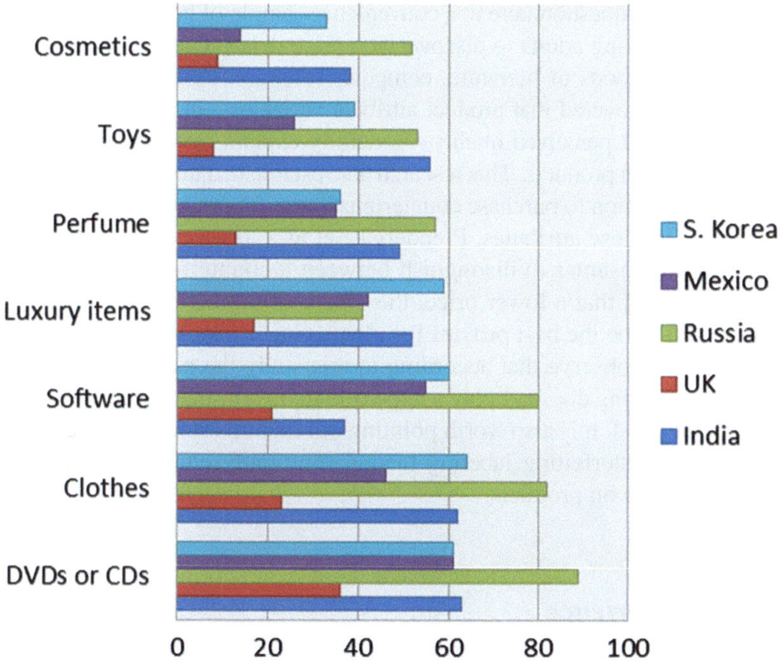

Source: Adapted from *Research Report on Consumer Attitudes and Perceptions on Counterfeiting and Piracy* 2009, p. 57.

"idealism" vs. "relativism" were antecedents of "ethical concerns" that ultimately effect a consumer's willingness to obtain fake products (Chaudhry and Stumpf 2011). Overall, we found that a US consumer with a high idealism ideology would not find the shopping experience in counterfeit markets a hedonic (enjoyable) shopping experience nor would they be willing to use fake goods. However, we found no statistical correlation between a consumer's relativism and their ethical behavior in the context of obtaining counterfeit products (Chaudhry and Stumpf 2011, p. 146).

Product Attributes

A wide variety of products are now counterfeited and the BASCAP research survey of consumers in distinct country markets reveals the counterfeit products most frequently purchased. The results in Table 5.3 are not surprising with DVDs, CDs, clothing, and computer software being the most frequently purchased fake goods across the five country markets.

As indicated in Table 5.1, the major product attributes that affect the purchase of counterfeit goods are image or perceived fashion content, price, quality, performance, investment-at-risk, and purpose of purchase. For example, Wee et al. (1995) conducted a self-administered questionnaire to a convenience sample of both Singaporean undergraduates and working adults to discover non-price determinants of intention to purchase counterfeit goods of literature, computer software, leather wallets/purses, and watches. They discovered that product attribute variables—in particular, appearance, image, purpose and perceived quality—generally explain intention of consumers to purchase counterfeit products. This research also established that the product attributes that affect the intention to purchase counterfeits varies by product category.

In addition to these attributes, Prendergast et al. (2002) examined the traits that might enable a consumer to distinguish between a counterfeit vs. real good. This research confirmed that a lower price, the nature of the buying location, and poor packaging tend to be the best proxies for identifying a fake Video CD (Video CD). It is interesting to observe that according to this study the presence of the original logo on the packaging does not play a large role in discriminating between the original and pirated good. It is also worth pointing out that this study does not even mention other anticounterfeiting labeling tactics commonly employed today, such as placing a hologram on products.

Shopping Experience

Overall, it is clear that the supply of counterfeits is prevalent in many countries. Thus, in order to understand consumer complicity, the shopping environment is a major factor that must be considered. For example, consumers seem more tolerant of buying fake goods in certain shopping environments, such as in a flea market or a known counterfeit shopping district, such as the Patpong market stalls in Bangkok. A virtual counterfeit shopping environment is readily available on the Internet. For example, the Replica Watch Center blatantly sells a variety of exclusive "replica" watches that include iconic brands such as Rolex, Cartier, Tag Heuer, and Patek Philippe. The website boasts that, "the time is NOW to get YOUR replica watches that are famous around the world. These affordable imitations make you look rich at a fraction of the cost" (www.replicawatchcenter.com).

The research by Schuchert-Güler and Martin (2003) referred to earlier also examined the impact of shopping environment on German consumers' purchase of counterfeit goods. This study defined the "shopping environment" into the following categories: German residents abroad and/or on holiday that purchase counterfeits as gifts and/or souvenirs. The researchers supported previous studies concerning the relevance of non-price determinants in influencing consumer complicity. They found that, for consumers who do not live near flourishing counterfeit markets in their home markets, such as German consumers, the people of these countries actively engage in counterfeit purchases in a hedonic type of shopping behavior. Overall, the researchers discovered that it is simply an adventure to be a player in the fake trade at any of the many possible counterfeit markets as they travel the globe.

Fig. 5.4 Mission to stop piracy Ad campaign. *Source*: http://www.ipd.gov.hk/eng/home.htm

In our study of the emerging markets, Brazil, Russia, India, and China, we found that three of the variables listed in Table 5.2 were the best predictors of consumer complicity: perceived quality, price, and hedonic shopping experience (Chaudhry et al. 2011a, 2011b, p. 223).

Demarketing Communications

Some of the major demarketing anticounterfeiting campaigns currently used by various industry associations, such as the Motion Picture Association, the Business Software Alliance, and the Recording Industry Association of America are targeted at reducing consumer complicity. A variety of messages include using role models to persuade the consumer not to purchase counterfeits, instilling a fear of prosecution, implying a negative association with fake goods by way of linkages to organized crime, and using peer pressure to decrease demand for counterfeit goods. We discuss the concept of "demarketing" in greater depth in Chap. 6, but, highlight just a few campaigns below.

The famous actors Jackie Chan and Arnold Schwarzenegger, launched a "Fakes Cost More" global ad campaign to effectively use role models to deter consumer complicity. The International Trademark Association organized a skit that shows Chan breaking up an organized counterfeit sales operation. He can also be seen smashing designer watches and using a chainsaw to destroy a street vendor's display of counterfeit bags and clothes. Figure 5.4 depicts an ad campaign in Hong Kong that shows Jackie Chan and Arnold Schwarzenegger riding their motorcycles through a dangerous highway scene on a "Mission to Stop Piracy" and each actor warns the consumer to stop supporting criminals through the purchase of fake products. The Intellectual Property Department of the Government of Hong Kong Special

Fig. 5.5 Disney magical journey anticounterfeiting promotional campaign. *Source*: Fowler, G., "Disney Fires a Broadside at Pirates," *The Wall Street Journal*, May 31, 2006, p. B3

Administrative Region actually provided web casts of their anticounterfeiting skits designed for television advertising at its website. Whether this type of anticounterfeiting technique, that is, using famous movie stars to denounce fake goods effectively deterred consumer complicity in the Asian markets remains to be seen.

The "Disney Magical Journey" consumer-loyalty campaign in China was designed to help the company educate the Chinese consumer about real vs. fake product. In order to enter a contest for free DVDs, televisions, and trips to Hong Kong Disneyland, the Chinese consumer had to attach an authentic red hologram from a Disney product to his or her entry form. The company's television show in China, the Dragon Club, educates young Chinese viewers about how to locate the red hologram of Mickey Mouse and reinforces the firm's promotion with statements like, "As long as you buy the original products, you will get ··· a chance to win big prizes" (Fowler 2006, p. B3). This innovative anticounterfeiting tactic has been successful in educating the Chinese and has resulted in some consumers calling the firm to report stores selling Disney merchandise without the hologram.

Conclusions

In this chapter, we have presented a conceptual framework that includes both intrinsic and extrinsic determinants of consumer complicity. Each dimension, such as demographic variables and shopping environment was described to provide a better understanding of the main concepts influencing a consumer's behavior to engage in illicit trade. Applicable findings from previous research studies were given to reinforce the model given in Fig. 5.2. However, there is still more work required to validate the relevance of both the "intrinsic" and "extrinsic" determinants of consumer complicity outlined in Fig. 5.2. Several studies are narrowly focused on one of these determinants, such as "attitude towards counterfeit" or "ethical perspective" and draw conclusions based on a limited view of the factors that cultivate complicity.

In Chap. 6, we investigate the novel anti-piracy demarketing techniques that have been developed to educate the consumer about counterfeit trade. In Chap. 10, we discuss consumer complicity in context of Internet piracy that has created a lucrative virtual marketplace for counterfeit trade.

Chapter 6
The Use of Antipiracy Marketing Techniques to Educate the Consumer

Introduction

Overall, the key advertisements that are being developed for antipiracy campaigns fall under the domain of social marketing concepts. In *Social Marketing: Improving the Quality of Life*, Kotler et al. (2002) provide this definition:

> Social marketing is the use of marketing principles and techniques to influence a target audience to voluntarily accept, reject, modify, or abandon a behavior for the benefit of individuals, groups, or society as a whole (p. 5).

Currently, the ideas of social marketing are exemplified by ad campaigns that attempt to decrease the public consumption of alcohol while driving or underage drinking. For example, Fig. 6.1 shows a strong visual association of a social situation and imminent death. Saatchi & Saatchi developed this campaign for Mothers Against Drunk Driving (MADD). However, social marketing techniques can also be used to reinforce positive behavior, such as recycling plastic goods. The main goals of a social marketing campaign are to act as a change agent to make the target audience alter his/her behavior. Thus, to protect the firm's IPR, a firm must develop a reasonable advertisement that will appeal to the target market and change its behavior.

The Microsoft Corporation has established worldwide piracy sites for several countries to counter consumer complicity by educating the consumer in his/her local language about the types of counterfeits and how to anonymously report them at its website (see the link to consumers in the Middle East at "How Piracy Affects You" at http://www.microsoft.com/middleeast/piracy/how.mspx).

As mentioned previously, a major problem centers on decreasing the consumer demand for counterfeit goods. For example, the BASCAP (2009) research on consumer attitudes towards counterfeiting and piracy concluded that the top deterrents for consumers to start ceasing their complicity were the following (BASCAP 2009, p. 8):

- Health and safety consequences top the list.
- Threat of legal action or prosecution delivers a wake-up call.

P. Chaudhry and A. Zimmerman, *Protecting Your Intellectual Property Rights*, Management for Professionals, DOI 10.1007/978-1-4614-5568-4_6,

Fig. 6.1 MADD anti-alcohol Ad campaign. *Source*: http://www.coloribus.com/adsarchive/prints/anti-drink-driving-swimming-pool-12045105/

- Links to organized crime have more traction than might be thought.
- People don't want to harm "someone like me."

In this chapter, we will give a brief overview of social marketing (demarketing) concepts, suggest an agenda to change the public perception of piracy, and illustrate several anti-counterfeiting advertisements that use messages employing role models, peer pressure, education, fear, quality of the product, negative association with suppliers of fake goods (e.g., terrorists), and reward/whistle blowing to alter target audience behavior. We also discuss the rebuttals to these advertisements that are found in various "bottom-up" media outlets, such as blogs on the Internet and YouTube.com.

Overview of Social Marketing Concepts

Alan Andreasen (2005) in *Social Marketing in the Twenty-First Century* outlines the three distinct plans that shape how a society accepts (or rejects) social issues in terms of a *public agenda*, *media agenda*, and *policy agenda*. A brief discussion of each type of agenda as it relates to influencing the general public's perception of safeguarding IPR follows.

Public Agenda

The public agenda is a metric that centers on the public's perceptions of the issues that are important and are reflected through polls. A review of two distinct polls centered on piracy reveals that firms may have a difficult task convincing consumers that

Fig. 6.2 Piracy doesn't work campaign. *Source*: http://www.youtube.com/watch?v=6YScoXn31Mg

there should be zero tolerance of this type of theft. The first, conducted by the IPSOS News Center, questioned 1,500 professionals in accounting, architecture, engineering, financial services, and graphic design. One of their main results was that almost one in four of the participants had violated some form of IPR in their workplace (Gross 2004). Other key findings of the study involved a sense of personal risk (45% of respondents felt they could be fired or reprimanded for using counterfeit software) and justified ownership of illegal copies due to cost savings, and the sentiment that larger firms could afford to pay the software firms the innovation reward (e.g., the David vs. Goliath logic that bigger firms should pay and smaller companies can use pirated products at a lower cost). So, even in the work environment, opinion polls have found a mixed review of the reasons to support (or reject) IPR.

Another important segment of the public agenda is cyberspace, especially the plethora of blogs that both support and refute the protection of IPR. Baker and Green (2008) stress the importance of this Internet information channel to shape public opinion. For example, the explosion of information at YouTube, Twitter, Wikipedia, Spam Blogs, Facebook/MySpace, and iTunes are just a few illustrations of potential "bottom-up media" that can become a global source of information. Just go to Google and type "antipiracy advertisements" and 23,400 hits will appear in less than 1 s. For example, Fig. 6.2 reveals the antipiracy public service announcement developed by the US IPR Center (www.iprcenter.gov) and uploaded by the U.S. Immigration and Customs Enforcement (ICE) agency into YouTube on June 9, 2011 to make consumers think about employees in the film industry losing their jobs because of fake movies sold on the street. The closing caption of this public service announcement is, "Whether you get it off the street or off the Internet, digital piracy and product counterfeiting are not victimless crimes. The financial repercussions are very real and cost real jobs" (http://www.youtube.com/watch?v=6YScoXn31Mg).

In our opinion, what is a primary concern is the time that some consumers take to provide their own rebuttals to antipiracy advertisements, such as the response to

Fig. 6.3 Rebuttal to antipiracy campaign in YouTube. *Source*: http://www.youtube.com/watch?v=oSQQ1NqOaA4

the Motion Picture Association of America in Fig. 6.3, that actually runs an overlay message over the original advertisement with facts, such as total revenue for the industry.

There are also many postings that comment on antipiracy advertisements (e.g., CommercialIHate.com) and blogs that support the legitimate sellers of genuine product (e.g., "Piracy? It just doesn't add up" at Microsoft Small Business at http://blogs.technet.com/b/smallbusiness/archive/2012/05/24/piracy-it-just-doesn-t-add-up.aspx) to blogs that openly confront the IP rights holders (e.g., the "Thank You RIAA" blog posting by the Pirate Bay on June 6, 2012 in response the RIAA efforts to curb the use of search engines, such as Google, to index their site at http://thepiratebay.se/blog).

Media Agenda

In January 2012, the media acutely raised consumer awareness of the pending Stop Online Piracy Act (SOPA) and its proposed enforcement of copyright on the Internet by websites. As a protest "English Wikipedia" went "dark" for the day. Thus, we know it is possible to garner the attention of the populous on the subject of intellectual property (even if this resulted in a controversial outcome for IP rights holders). However, looking at the past few decades, the media has given limited coverage to the problem of counterfeit trade in newspapers, television, and talk shows. Naim (2005) did receive a fair amount of media attention, including an interview on National Public Radio, especially since he describes linkages of counterfeit trade to organized crime and terrorism. The first edition of our book appeared in 2009 with initial success in both European and US markets and our work in counterfeit trade was noted in a U.S. Government Accountability Office (GAO) publication, with personal interviews appearing in *The Wall Street Journal, Advertising Age,* and NotoFakes.com.

The recent reports of counterfeit pharmaceuticals, such as the Avastin case, revealed questionable distribution channels to the US market via wholesalers in the UK and Turkey and was widely reported in early 2012 (Faucon and Whalen 2012; Weaver et al. 2012). In May 2012, the G8 summit primarily focused on the Eurozone crisis, but the member countries found time to (the US, UK, Germany, France, Japan, Italy, Canada, and Russia) offer to "exchange information on rogue Internet pharmacy sites in accordance with national law and share best practices on combating counterfeit medical products" (Taylor 2012, p. 2). Overall, there are sporadic articles found in various outlets, but, in our opinion, the coverage does not put the issue of counterfeit trade at the forefront. In the academic literature, the situation is even bleaker and both theoretical and empirical studies on the subject of managerial tactics designed to curb the counterfeit trade are very few in number.

Policy Agenda

It is hard to estimate the policy agenda on counterfeit trade in the United States and its trading partners that is supported by legislation, administration, and trade policy and the like. As reported in various chapters of this book, there has been increased legislation (e.g., the Digital Millennium Copyright Act and the EU IPR Directive), administration (e.g., the StopFakes program in the U.S.), and trade measures (e.g., the priority watch list of the USTR) established by various policy makers to curb the trade in fakes. Other pending legislation, such as the US bill, S. 978, would punish illegal video streaming for commercial purposes to a felony offense (Chaudhry 2012; Engleman 2011). The movement of counterfeit trade into more nontraditional products, such as pharmaceuticals, auto and airlines parts, and foodstuffs, will only strengthen the policy agenda on counterfeit trade. Specific policy measures are explained in further detail in Chaps. 7 and 10.

Setting an Agenda to Change the Public Judgment of Counterfeit Trade

Yankelovich (1992) created a seven-stage process that can guide managers moving an item of concern, such as the protection of their IPR, from the public's initial awareness of the problem to making an ethical and emotional judgment on the illegitimacy of counterfeit trade. In Table 6.1, we use Yankelovich's framework in the context of establishing an agenda to change consumer behavior relative to purchasing fake goods.

Table 6.1 Stages in the agenda-setting procedure

Stage 1: Dawning awareness. Alerting the public about the problem. For example, the Business Software Alliance consistently posts its annual studies on the Internet. In another example, Jackie Chan and Arnold Schwarzenegger used an advertising campaign, "Mission to Stop Piracy" to educate a Chinese audience about the dark side of piracy, such as its linkage to organized crime. Jackie Chan continued to target the Chinese consumer with a more recent campaign, "Protect the movies, say NO to piracy!"
Stage 2: Greater urgency. Raising apprehension about the lack of IPR protection, such as the Motion Picture Association's advertisement "You can click but you can't hide" to garner more personal implications, such as the fear of prosecution from illegal downloads
Stage 3: Discovering the choices. At this point, policymakers and/or managers can use "trial balloons" to educate the consumer
Stage 4: Wishful thinking. A stage where the public thinks it can have it all—both great innovation and fake goods at lower prices
Stage 5: Weighing the choices. After being exposed to the different information in Stages 1–4, the public is engaged and a consumer can now evaluate the personal implications of the issue. For example, a college student can debate whether downloading illegal music is worth losing his/her Internet access at the university
Stage 6: Taking a stand intellectually. A point where the "public" will accept a course of action, such as a strong desire to protect IPR. However, emotionally, some members of the population will still be able to rationalize that a few songs obtained through the Internet is acceptable because this fits their beliefs that the music industry is price-gouging consumers
Stage 7: Making a responsible judgment morally and emotionally. The ultimate goals of any agenda are to sway public judgment on an issue to circumvent the "fuzzy thinking" that surrounds their moral and emotional feelings about upholding IPR

Source: Adapted from Yankelovich, D. How Public Opinion Really Works. *Fortune*, October 5, 1992, p. 102–106

Based on our 20-year experience of studying and reporting on the protection of IPR, we would argue that in terms of Yankelovich's framework, the current public judgment of a university age population (18–22) in the United States would usually not surpass Stage 5. This opinion is based on many lectures to university students where the topic of IPR protection is addressed and the overall sentiment of the students in the class is either (1) starting to be aware of the ad messages designed to persuade them to purchase legal versions of the goods (i.e., Stage 1); (2) exhibiting *wishful thinking* in terms of not seeing the seriousness of the problem—if they can still download novel, creative music for their smartphones on the Internet, why should they pay for them? (i.e., Stage 4), and/or (3) realizing the *choices* they face since the university will punish them for illegally downloading digital media. For example, the punishment can be a black-out of the university's email system for a couple of weeks—an acute punishment given the student's heavy reliance on his/her jane.doe@college.edu personal account for course materials that are delivered via class email distribution lists only (i.e., Stage 5). However, we realize that future empirical studies will give practitioners and policymakers a better understanding of the level of public judgment on the protection IPR in terms of influencing the public opinion discussed in Table 6.1.

Table 6.2 Target audience of consumer campaigns

Target audience	Number of campaigns reviewed
General public/consumers	95
Kid/teenagers	52
Teachers	35
SMEs	29
Students	25
Retailers	24
Law enforcement	18
Parents	13
Policy makers	8
Right holders	6
Journalists	4
Tourists	4
Farmers	1

Source: Adapted from the *Research Report on Consumer Attitudes and Perceptions on Counterfeiting and Piracy*, BASCAP, 2009, p. 25

Table 6.3 Industry focus of consumer campaigns

Industry focus	% of campaigns reviewed
General counterfeiting or piracy	36
Film piracy	26
Music piracy	19
Software piracy	14
Counterfeit medicines	2
Counterfeit apparel	2
Plant piracy	<1
Trademarks	<1

Source: Adapted from the Research Report on Consumer Attitudes and Perceptions on Counterfeiting and Piracy, BASCAP, 2009, p. 26

Anti-counterfeiting Advertisements

The Business Action to Stop Counterfeiting and Piracy (BASCAP) performed an audit of 202 various anti-counterfeiting campaigns launched in the past decade (2000s) by accessing materials from its own resources and the WIPO database. The geographical distribution of these campaigns primarily focused on the developed markets, such as the United States ($n=36$) and the United Kingdom ($n=20$). The results of this comprehensive study are illustrated in Tables 6.2 and 6.3. The BASCAP findings in these tables clearly reveal the use of a broad demographic for the target audience and the dominance of the campaigns focusing on the film, software, and music industries.

BASCAP (2009) summarized their key findings of these 202 media campaigns as follows (p. 8):

- Audience—the research revealed a lack of audience and message targeting prior to the formation and dissemination of campaigns.

- Demographics and geography—additionally, the majority of research and campaigns focused more on affluent markets and less on the developing world.
- Measurement—very few campaigns attempted to measure the effectiveness of messages to deter consumer purchases of counterfeit and pirated products.

Overall, the BASCAP (2009) study of media campaigns concluded that the best messengers for anti-counterfeiting messages were a "person harmed by counterfeit product; mothers whose children have been harmed; [or] a medical expert" (p. 7).

Kotler et al. (2002) offer a comprehensive overview of the role of designing persuasive communications to change the public's behavior in context of social marketing techniques in their book, *Social Marketing: Improving the Quality of Life*. The authors give a compelling example of how to create a media campaign that centers on the prevention of youth consumption of tobacco. Using similar concepts, Table 6.4 illustrates a plausible framework for setting a message execution strategy for an antipiracy campaign.

Previous Advertisements

The owners of IPR have been providing various "trial balloons" of advertisements that center on role models, peer pressure, education, fear, negative association to terrorism, communism and/or organized crime, and whistle-blowing/reward schemes. In this section, we explore various advertisements that provide this type of appeal to the consumer. First, a quick look at a previous anti-counterfeit ad copy from an earlier time frame (circa 1980s) is given to show how messages have evolved during the past three decades.

Figure 6.4 below uses many deterrents to get a person to change his/her behavior towards fake games. The basic ad concepts are peer pressure, fear of prosecution, negative association with pirates, whistle-blowing, and a reward all in the short story being told through the cartoon published in the United Kingdom.

Role Models

Some firms have used the concept of a role model to persuade consumers to stop pirating and/or purchasing fake goods. In Chap. 5, we highlighted the example of the "Mission to Stop Piracy" campaign initiated in 2005 in the Asian market featuring Jackie Chan and Arnold Schwarzenegger in various media spots to denounce piracy. In Fig. 6.5, the Hong Kong Economic and Trade office shows the two Hollywood film stars in their "no piracy" t-shirts. The media blitz even included a webcast of Jackie and Arnold acting out their mission to stop piracy on motorcycles in a scene that links the piracy trade to organized crime. The Intellectual Property Department of the Hong Kong Special Administrative Region provided the webcast in English and three Chinese dialects.

As seen in Fig. 6.6, the campaign continued in China in 2008 with Jackie Chan and this anti-counterfeiting advertisement was erected for 2 weeks as a billboard at the site of the infamous counterfeit district in Beijing, the Silk Market.

Table 6.4 Creative summary for a youth antipiracy campaign

Key message: Don't download digital media without payment

Target audience: Lower school students who are just starting to own a smartphone with an Internet connection

Communication objectives:

To know: Downloading without payment is illegal

To believe:

(1) Firms will prosecute violators—it is a crime

(2) Firms are losing money that will prevent new movies/music/etc. to be created—the innovation penalty is *real*

(3) The links to organized crime/terrorism are true

To do: Refuse to illegally download

Benefits to promise:

You will support innovative firms, such as Apple, by purchasing music at iTunes

Supports to promise:

(1) Testimonials from target audience (e.g., a young adult convicted of illegal downloads)

(2) Testimonials from role models (e.g., Hollywood actors and/or animated characters with a high affinity to the targeted age group)

(3) Testimonials from an average person (e.g., animation artists that worked on the film *Shrek the Third*)

(4) Graphic visuals that show negative association to counterfeit trade (e.g., possible links to terrorism and/or organized crime)

(5) Real data about the trade in fakes (e.g., statistics that really illustrate the effect of counterfeit trade on innovation—such as the reduced number of blockbuster movies due to lost revenues)

(6) Reinforce the negative stigma of consumer complicity to purchase fakes by drawing parallels to other types of crime, such as shoplifting

Openings:

(1) Listening to the radio

(2) Watching television, previews in DVD/cinema

(3) Surfing the Internet

(4) Talking with friends

(5) Listening to a class discussion

Positioning:

People who illegally download are stealing and hurting more than big business and highly paid actors—reinforce that the average person loses his/her innovation reward. Draw analogies to other crime—can you justify shoplifting? If not, why is stealing through the Internet a victimless crime? It's not worth the risk of prosecution, support of organized crime, the loss of jobs by "real people" (the animation artist for *Shrek the Third*) and the like

Source: Adapted from Kotler, Philip, Roberto, Ned and Lee, Nancy R. (2002) *Social Marketing: Improving the Quality of Life*, Sage Publications, Thousand Oaks, California

Peer Pressure

New York City has its own public awareness initiative, the Campaign Against Content Theft & Piracy with the current "Piracy Doesn't Work in NYC" slogan. The website uses peer pressure to develop empathy through the message "Why Should I

Fig. 6.4 Antipiracy Ad, circa 1980s. *Source*: http://www.globalpov.com/archives/2006/05/old_pirates_live_on.php

Care?" by stating that "If you live and work in New York City, there's a good chance you know someone who could be affected by job loss in creative industries" (http://stoppiracyinnyc.com/TheIssue.aspx). The current campaign shows two young male adults losing their jobs in the book publishing industry resulting from piracy with a rap-like beat to the short video clip. A screen shot of the current campaign is illustrated in Fig. 6.7 below.

Fig. 6.5 Arnold Schwarzenegger and Jackie Chan's "Mission to Stop Piracy." *Source*: www.hketo.ca/news/press-releases-2005/November-18-2005_jacky.jpg

Fig. 6.6 Say no to piracy campaign. *Source*: http://jackiechanforum.com/forum/viewtopic.php?f=75&t=5373

Fig. 6.7 Peer pressure in antipiracy message. *Source*: http://stoppiracyinnyc.com/CurrentCampaign.aspx

Fig. 6.8 The "Respect Copyrights" Boy Scouts of America Patch. *Source*: http://arstechnica.com/gadgets/2006/10/8044/

Education

The Boy Scouts of America trains youth in various areas, ranging from Camping to Citizenship in the Nation. A scout will earn a merit badge, such as Citizenship in the World, once he has completed the learning requirements associated with this particular topic. In 2006, the Motion Picture Association of America partnered with this youth organization in Los Angeles to offer the Respect Copyrights patch (not a merit badge) to members of its organization to educate themselves on peer-to-peer websites and possible illegal downloading behavior. The patch is shown in Fig. 6.8.

Fig. 6.9 Authentication technology designed for pharmaceutical products. *Source*: https://its-true.de/en_new/startseite.html

We illustrate several more education antipiracy initiatives targeted at youth groups by the BSA, IFPI, MPA, and RIAA in Chap. 8.

Pharmaceutical manufacturers, such as Pfizer, are currently working on ways in which consumers can use packaging to authenticate products. A short video from Pfizer that focuses on educating the public to the dangers of counterfeit Viagra and the various visual authentication cues for detecting counterfeits is on YouTube at www.youtube.com/user/viagra?feature=results_main#p/p. The fact that Pfizer is posting its antipiracy campaign, "Counterfeiters are smart. You can be smarter." on YouTube demonstrates a novel way to address the dilemma of authentication.

As revealed in Fig. 6.9, telling the difference between the real vs. fake is not obvious and there have been new developments in authentication technology targeted at consumers. Pharmaceutical firms can use a labeling technique, such as IT'S TRUE® (www.its-true.com) for consumers to determine whether they have obtained the legitimate pharmaceutical product in a pharmacy or by way of the Internet. The manufacturer simple affixes a label on the packaging that contains a concealed code that the consumer can validate by way of a smartphone or typed in via Internet or text message (Counterfeit drugs—New technology to combat counterfeit 2012). Figure 6.9 illustrates this new type of authentication technology.

Provalidate® is another example of authentication technology that can be used in conjunction with a variety of consumer products, such as watches and handbags. The technology draws ideas from computer security to deter the counterfeiters' skills of copying by using inexpensive electronic validators and printed codes where the text and numbers that make up these codes are single-use and unpredictable. Consumers can visit the brand owner's website to validate products items, such as using a serial number on the watch and a code from the "electronic warranty card." The technology behind this type of authentication is beyond the reach of the counterfeiters that have easily copied other labeling methods, such as fake holograms.

Fig. 6.10 Electronic warranty card for authentication. *Source*: http://provalidate.net/howItWorks.htm

Figure 6.10 illustrates an electronic warranty card for a luxury watch that would authenticate the product and get the consumer to the company's website where the firm can present other offers at this time.

Fear

The concept of fear can be employed to various types of messages to convince a consumer to stop using fake goods. In 2007, the U.S. Chamber of Commerce and Gallup Consulting study, *Counterfeiting in the United States: Consumer Behaviors and Attitudes,* reported on the results of consumers' responses to, "Do you believe counterfeiting and piracy laws should be stricter, left as they are, or made less strict?" The US respondents felt that the laws should be stricter (72%), left as they are (24%), or less strict (4%). In addition, these respondents felt that it should be illegal (88%) to obtain counterfeit goods and strongly favored (70%) criminal penalties for knowingly engaging in counterfeit purchases (U.S. Chamber of Commerce/Gallup Consulting 2007, pp. 30–32). Reinforcing fear through potential legal prosecution was a viable strategy. Figure 6.11 shows a previous campaign developed by the Motion Picture Association.

Using approaches like the MADD campaign against alcohol consumption and driving shown in Fig. 6.1, managers can persuade consumers to stop purchasing nontraditional goods, such as counterfeit pharmaceuticals through fear of their health and/or possible death. According to the World Health Organization (WHO),

Fig. 6.11 Fear of legal prosecution. *Source*: http://screencomment.com/site/wp-content/uploads/2011/05/you_can_click_but_you_cant_hide.jpg

"there is strong evidence to suggest that the circulation of counterfeit and substandard medicines is increasing globally… the result of the weak and ineffective medicine regulatory systems and poorly managed medicine supply chains that prevail in many countries" (Kohler and Baghdadi-Sabeti 2011). An image developed by IMPACT, the International Medical Products Anti-Counterfeiting Taskforce of the WHO, is shown in Fig. 6.12 to deliver a different type of fear message—untimely death due to counterfeit drugs.

Quality of the Product

A negative association of inferior or cheaper quality has been used by some companies to persuade the consumer to denounce counterfeit goods. Figure 6.13 gives an example from one of the latest MPAA public awareness campaigns that provide an

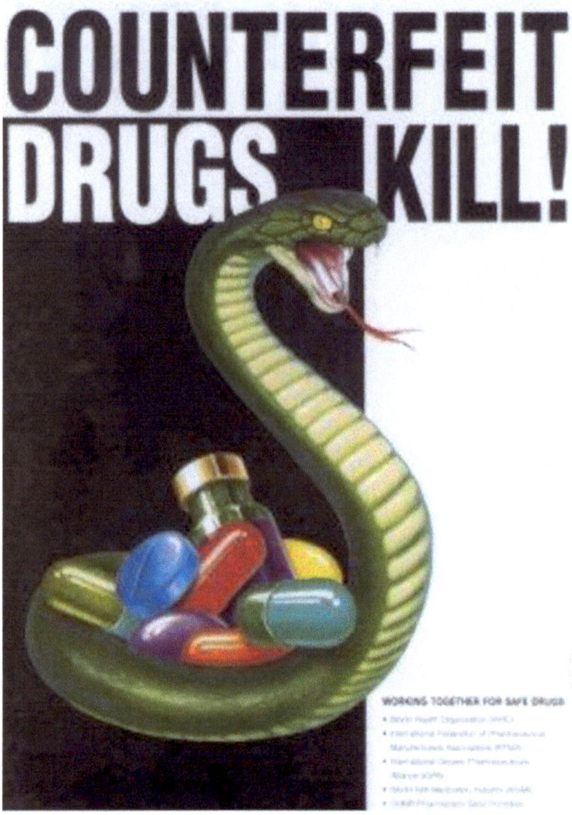

Fig. 6.12 Fear of death—World Health Organization. *Source*: http://www.who.int/impact/activities/en/

overall message emphasizing the risk of purchasing the counterfeit item as ripped-off, poor sound, stupid purchase, obstructive view, and fake.

Negative Association with Suppliers

The 2005 Gallup Poll News Service survey asked respondents, "In your opinion, which of the following groups are involved with producing or distributing imitation or counterfeit products?" The respondents associated these suppliers with importers (84%), organized crime (83%), exporters (72%), terrorist organizations (48%), and government officials (20%) (Stewart 2005). Thus, using ad copy like the message in Fig. 6.14 can reinforce this negative association. The Federation Against Copyright Theft (FACT) developed interesting messages for the United Kingdom that exploited the plausible linkage of terrorism to counterfeit trade. In the article, "British Filmmakers Seeking Crackdown on Piracy," the author highlights a study, "Film

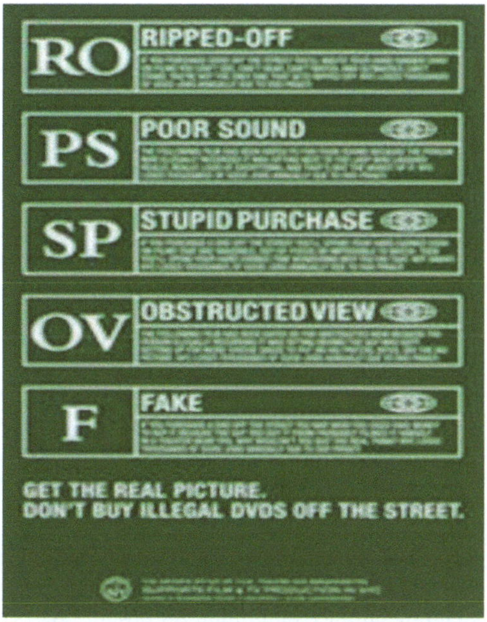

Fig. 6.13 Inferior quality/risk of purchase Ad copy. *Source*: http://www.mpaa.org/contentprotection/public-service-announcements

Fig. 6.14 Negative association to terrorism in Ad copy. *Source*: http://newsimg.bbc.co.uk/media/images/40369000/jpg/_40369411_dvds3_203.jpg

Theft in the UK," reporting many anti-counterfeiting tactics suggested by the UK Film Council. One of these targets public organizations in the UK to create campaigns that emphasize the risk of piracy by stressing the association between piracy and organized crime; the illegal aspects of piracy and file-sharing; the risk to the

Table 6.5 Business software alliance reward guidelines

Reward payment guidelines	
Settlement/damages paid by company	Potential reward payment
$15,000–$100,000	Up to $5,000
$100,001–$200,000	Up to $10,000
$200,001–$400,000	Up to $20,000
$400,001–$600,000	Up to $30,000
$600,001–$800,000	Up to $40,000
$800,001–$1,000,000	Up to $50,000
$1,000,001–$2,000,000	Up to $100,000
$2,000,001–$3,000,000	Up to $150,000
$3,000,001–$5,000,000	Up to $250,000
$5,000,001–$10,000,000	Up to $500,000
$10,000,001–$15,000,000	Up to $750,000
Over $15,000,000	Up to $1,000,000

Source: https://reporting.bsa.org/r/report/usa/rewardsconditions.aspx

growth of inventiveness and culture in the UK; and the menace of unsuitable items becoming available to children and teenagers younger than 18 ("British Filmmakers Seeking Major Crackdown on Piracy," p. 25).

Chris Stewart, a global brand manager, strongly asserts that the best anti-counterfeiting message targeted at the public will provide a negative association with the counterfeit industry. He suggests that the ad copy should develop awareness among potential buyers that these sellers can be involved in either funding terrorist plots and/or organized crime (Stewart 2005).

Rewards Through Whistle Blowing

The Business Software Alliance actually provides a website for reporting piracy at https://reporting.bsa.org/r/report/add.aspx?src=us and a toll free number at 1.888. No.Piracy. The amount of reward depends on the legal settlement. Table 6.5 shows the payout guidelines that the BSA allegedly will give a "piracy snitch" up to $1,000,000 in compensation.

Fisher (2007) claims that almost $22 million has been paid by the BSA in business settlements that were accused of owning pirated software. Thus, Fisher wonders whether the BSA has ever paid close to $1 million to a whistle-blower but the trade association will not comment on the actual amount given to people reporting piracy.

Blog Rebuttals to Advertisements

We cannot conclude the section on antipiracy advertisements without highlighting the fact that the Internet is replete with rebuttals to some of the ad messages

Fig. 6.15 Blog rebuttal to "Fear of Prosecution" message. *Source*: http://www.boingboing.net/2005/02/14/angry-remix-of-you-c.html

described in the previous sections. As previously discussed, there are many sites in the "bottom-up media" that have their own advertisements supporting piracy. Figure 6.15 is an open challenge from one blogger (see Fig. 6.11) for companies to try to prosecute *everyone* in the general public who illegally downloads digital media. This blogger states:

> This website has been erected out of consumer outcry over the passing of sites that facilitate the downloading of perpetually copyrighted motion pictures. The unauthorized downloading of motion pictures denies thousands of dishonest, lazy executives of their crack smoking livelihood, and is the only way to bring an artistically bankrupt monopoly under control. Downloading movies without authorization violates laws distorted beyond their original intent, is not tangible theft, and is impossible to stop. You can't catch everyone. The only way to win is to stop waging war on your customers and accept the fact that we are in control, not you. You brought this on yourself (http://www.boingboing.net/2005/02/14/angry-remix-of-you-c.html, p. 1).

YouTube is also used to post several "anti-anti piracy" parodies that usually take a theme from a legitimate anti-counterfeiting campaign, such as "You Wouldn't Steal a Car," to create a short video clip satire of the original message. As seen in Fig. 6.16, one video clip rebuts the original campaign message with various "You Wouldn't Steal a Liver … a Horse …a Ghost …." Several of these types of video lampoons of original anti-counterfeiting campaigns can be viewed at http://www.youtube.com/watch?v=4gLDekmntEc&feature=bf_prev&list=PL3EAE9FAD263A2150.

Fig. 6.16 Rebuttal to "You Wouldn't Steal a Car" campaign. *Source*: http://www.youtube.com/watch?v=AbIuLHbC5uc&feature=BFa&list=PL3EAE9FAD263A2150

Clearly, these are just two extreme cases of pro-piracy sentiment found on the Internet but firms must use these types of consumer-driven media messages to gauge whether their social marketing techniques have changed the public judgment on the future protection of IPR.

Conclusions

There has been growth of antipiracy advertisement in the media. The ad copy used in this chapter was found in the "images" feature of the Google search engine and also an "antipiracy" search at YouTube to highlight the main messages used by various stakeholders attempting to change a consumer's willingness to purchase counterfeits. The major themes currently employed are role models, peer pressure, education, fear, quality of the product, negative association to organized crime and/or terrorism, and rewards given for whistle blowing. To our knowledge, there have been very few studies that have addressed the effectiveness of these messages in deterring the growth of counterfeit trade (Chaudhry et al. 2011a, b; BASCAP 2009). In fact, we found several "support for piracy" hits in Google and video clips in YouTube that offer numerous rebuttals to antipiracy ad campaigns. This makes us speculate about the efficacy of educating the consumer through these types of messages. Many studies have been conducted evaluating the effectiveness of social marketing campaigns in deterring either cigarette smoking or alcohol consumption. Furthermore, we know that it can take several years, if not decades, to change the cultural acceptance of (or rejection of) a phenomenon like piracy. The key is for companies to actually test the salience of their advertisements to determine whether the message appeal actually *influences* the behavior of the targeted audience.

Chapter 7
Changing Trade Policy: The EU and US Bolster Protection of Intellectual Property Rights

Introduction

Current events on each side of the Atlantic center on movements to revise patent protection. In 2011, President Obama signed the American Invents Act that will reshape the US patent law and the European Commission proposed a single European patent for 25 Member States (excluding Spain and Italy). In 2010, the Prioritizing Resources and Organization Property Act of 2008 (PRO IP Act) created a position within the Executive Office of the US President, the Intellectual Property Enforcement Coordinator (IPEC). The protection of intellectual property rights (IPR) through trade initiatives such as the STOP! Program in the United States and the EU Enforcement Directive are examined in this chapter. This chapter is designed to provide a synopsis of the latest government policymakers' tactics designed to battle counterfeiters. The question of whether the STOP! Program in the United States, the novel directive in the EU on enforcement, and recent patent protection legislation will reduce fakes is a matter for future assessment. However, previous studies have already established that *enforcement* of any type of government and/or multilateral agency-sponsored anti-counterfeiting strategy remains a leading concern in the continuing battle to reduce the proliferation of fake goods (Chaudhry and Stumpf 2010).

U.S. IPR Enforcement Initiatives

The advent of the Department of Homeland Security has changed the hierarchy of governance of IPR in the United States. This department now governs and/or is strategically aligned to several different agencies, such as the U.S. Secret Service (USSS) and Customs and Border Protection (CBP) (i.e., the U.S. Customs). The USSS was actually established in 1865 for the sole objective of suppressing one of the oldest forms of piracy: counterfeit currency. The British counterfeited the US currency during the American Revolution to make the local currency worthless and

P. Chaudhry and A. Zimmerman, *Protecting Your Intellectual Property Rights*, Management for Professionals, DOI 10.1007/978-1-4614-5568-4_7,

Fig. 7.1 Major players in the U.S. IPR Enforcement

"not worth a Continental" was a common expression at the time (www.dhs.gov). Figure 7.1 is a schematic showing the various agencies governing the IPR environment in the United States.

This diagram of the US agencies is just the beginning of understanding the various layers of government sectors involved in the protection of IPR. The key player is the U.S. Department of Homeland Security that governs two principal agencies: CBP and Immigration and Customs Enforcement (ICE). A good example of the labyrinth of strategic alliances is the *Global Intellectual Property Education Training Program Database* sponsored by the US government to provide IP enforcement training materials that was designed to "promote greater consistency and to avoid duplication and waste or resources" (www.usipr.gov). The members of this program are: Executive Office of the President of the United States; the U.S. Department of State; the U.S. Department of Commerce [includes the International Trade Administration and Commercial Law Development]; the U.S. Department of Justice [Office of Overseas Prosecutorial Development Assistance & Training, Criminal Division and Computer Crime and Intellectual Property Section, Criminal Division]; the U.S. Department of Homeland Security [CBP and ICE]; and the U.S. Agency for International Development (Fig. 7.2).

Fig. 7.2 Global intellectual property education. *Source*: http://www.usipr.gov/

To this list of government agencies are added the following private sector organizations who also provide IPR-related information programs, training and technical assistance to foreign officials and policy makers: Coalition of Intellectual Property Rights (CIPR); Interactive Digital Software Association (ISDA); International Anti-Counterfeiting Coalition (IACC); International Intellectual Property Alliance (IIPA); International Intellectual Property Right Institute (IIPI); and Pharmaceutical Research & Manufacturers of America (PhRMA).

The question becomes how many of the already established agencies will effectively interface with the different layers of governance, such as the newly established IPEC. For example, the National Intellectual Property Rights Coordination Center is supervised by the ICE and is supposed to "coordinate a unified response regarding IPR enforcement issues through core staffing from ICE and the FBI…particular emphasis is given to investigating major criminal organizations and those using the Internet to facilitate IPR crime" (www.ice.gov).

Intellectual Property Enforcement Coordinator

The Intellectual Property Act of 2008 created a new position, the U.S. IPEC. Victoria Espinel is currently serving in that role and this agency provides reports on IP, such as the *2011 U.S. Intellectual Property Enforcement Coordinator Joint Strategic Plan*, the *Intellectual Property Spotlight* and the *Counterfeit Pharmaceutical Inter-agency Working Group Report to the Vice President of the United States and to Congress*.

Espinel highlighted the six over-arching goals of this new agency in its *2010 Joint Strategic Plan on Intellectual Property Enforcement* as follows (p. 3):

> Through this process [consultation with many other government agencies, such as DOC, DHS, DOJ, USTR], we identified a number of actions the Federal government will take to enhance the protection of American intellectual property rights (pp. 2–3):

1. We will lead by example and will work to ensure that the Federal government does not purchase or use infringing products.
2. We will support transparency in the development of enforcement policy, information sharing and reporting of law enforcement activities at home and abroad.
3. We will improve coordination and thereby increase the efficiency and effectiveness of law enforcement efforts at the Federal, state and local level, of personnel stationed overseas and of the US government's international training efforts.
4. We will work with our trading partners and with international organizations to better enforce American intellectual property rights in the global economy.
5. We will secure supply chains to stem the flow of infringing products at our borders and through enhanced cooperation with the private sector.
6. We will improve data and information collection from intellectual property-related activity and continuously assess domestic and foreign laws and enforcement activities to maintain an open, fair and balanced environment for American intellectual property rightholders.

America Invents Act

In 2011, President Obama signed into law the America Invents Act (AIA) that reshaped the US patent law. Singer (2011) summarizes the changes to patents that the AIA will change as of September 16, 2012 as (pp. 2–3):

- *Post Grant Review*: The USPTO will implement a post-grant review (PGR) process in which it may reconsider a patent grant if a petition is filed within 9 months of the date of the grant. Much like the opposition process that is available in Europe, the USPTO's PGR process will allow patents to be challenged on any invalidity ground—including prior art, lack of enablement, or inadequate written description. The petitioner and the patent holder may respond to each other's filings during PGR, engage in limited discovery, and stop the proceeding through a settlement. PGR is not available to any petitioner who is also challenging the patent in a court proceeding.
- *Employer Corporation as Applicant*: An entity to whom an inventor has assigned (or is under an obligation to assign) the patent will be permitted to file the application instead of (or on behalf of) the inventor. In addition, if an inventor refuses to assign an oath, an employer or assignee can make the oath upon showing that the entity was entitled to assignment from the inventor.

Singer (2011) also provides a synopsis of other changes that will be effective after March 16, 2003, such as first to file, an expanded definition of "prior art," and derivation proceedings. The "first to file" is considered to be a landmark change since it governs the problem of two inventors independently creating the same invention—overall the first inventor to file gets the patent (with a few exceptions). A detailed overview of the AIA is beyond the scope of this book; however, the U.S. Patent and Trademark Office (USPTO) provides a blueprint of guidance on the AIA

Fig. 7.3 America Invent Act. *Source*: http://www.uspto.gov/aia_implementation/index.jsp

that includes: implementation information (e.g., patent examination), AIA resources, AIA informational videos, AIA frequently asked question, and even a Blog on the new legislation (see Fig. 7.3).

Strategy Targeting Organized Piracy

On October 4, 2004, several US government officials from the Department of Homeland Security, the U.S. Trade Representative (USTR), the Department of Commerce, and the Department of Justice provided information on the Strategy Targeting Organized Piracy (STOPfakes) in an effort to build anti-counterfeiting coalitions with governments and the private sectors in foreign markets. In a press release, former Commerce Secretary Donald L. Evans described the evolution of STOPfakes as "[W]e've been pushing the door closed on fakes for 3 years and today [2004]; we're working towards slamming it shut. Today's STOP! initiative allows us to leverage our experience and integrate government resources to better protect America's intellectual property in a systematic way … Why now? We recognized, for some time, that we need to take intellectual property protection to the next level and STOP! is the weapon that will get us there. We're elevating our cooperation between the federal government, the private sector, and many of our trading partners in an aggressive, unified effort against piracy and intellectual property rights theft" (Evans 2004).

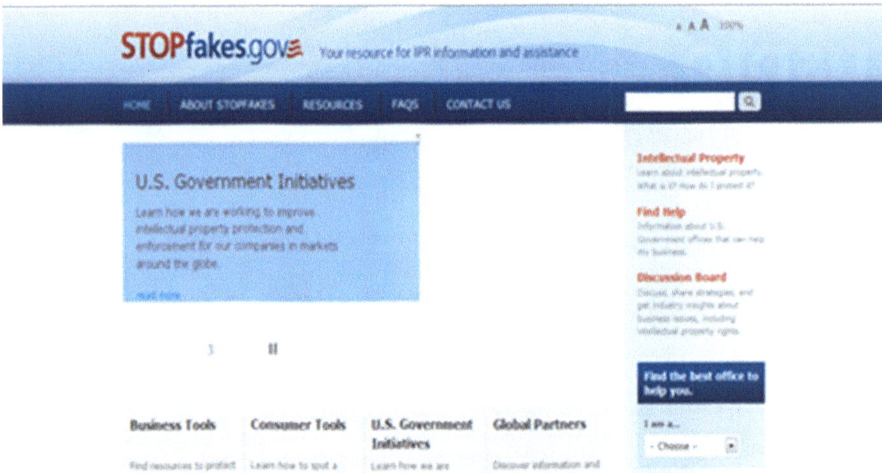

Fig. 7.4 STOPfakes program. *Source*: http://www.stopfakes.gov/

The STOPfakes program provides resources for four key areas of IP: business tools (e.g., how to protect your innovations); consumer tools (e.g., to education on how to spot fakes); the US government initiatives (e.g., enforcement in global markets); and global partners (e.g., information about partner governments, private sector groups, and international organizations). For example, the global partners' page at this site immediately links to INTERPOL, the World Customs Organization, the World Intellectual Property Organization (WIPO), the World Trade Organization, Asia Pacific Economic Council, Trans-Pacific Partnership and Anti-Counterfeiting Trade Agreement (Fig. 7.4).

The U.S. State Department allocated funds in Phase 1 and 2 of the STOP! program ($1.31 million and $1.19 million, respectively) to assist projects to deter intellectual property theft in Brazil, Pakistan, Republic of Korea, Malaysia, Panama, and the like (Ereli 2004). The main focus of each program was to train the indigenous police, prosecutors, and customs officials in each country/region in order to effectively investigate and prosecute infringements of IPR. However, a review of the monetary grants for each country/region questions whether this "level of funding" was adequate funding to reduce the trade in counterfeits. For example, the region of China/East-Asia Pacific received the largest amount of funding of $210,000 while the Republic of Korea, Malaysia, and Panama were awarded $75,000 each. This is a paltry amount of funding when compared to the magnitude of losses of IPR in these countries and/or regions and in comparison to company-level funding of anti-counterfeiting tactics. Today, in its *2011 U.S. Intellectual Property Enforcement Coordinator Joint Strategic Plan* the US government reports that the funding of IP initiatives is now transparent through its training database described in Sect. 7.2, the Global Intellectual Property Education at www.usipr.gov.

The key elements of the STOPfakes program were the following:

- Helping and empowering American businesses, investors and innovators, particularly small businesses, secure and enforce their rights in overseas markets.
- Ensuring consumer safety by securing America's borders and marketplaces from fakes.
- Raising the stakes and making life more onerous for intellectual property thieves through new customs methods that increase costs to violators far beyond seizing shipments and by naming and shaming global pirates and counterfeiting who are producing and trafficking in fakes.
- Developing a "No Trade in Fakes" program in cooperation with the private sector to ensure that global supply chains are free of infringing goods.
- Working to dismantle criminal enterprises that steal intellectual property using all appropriate criminal laws, and overhauling, updating, and modernizing the US intellectual property statutes.
- Joining forces with like-minded trading partners concerned about the growing global IPR piracy problem, such as the European Commission, Japan, the United Kingdom, and France who have all launched initiatives (United States Trade Representative 2004, p. 4).

The U.S. Department of Commerce established a hotline that provides a one-stop-shop for businesses to protect their intellectual property at home and abroad—1-866-999-HALT; build a bridge between companies and the U.S. Customs to block bogus goods at the border; develop a comprehensive web-based guide for American innovators and businesses on how to safeguard their ideas and innovations; and challenge industry leaders to develop voluntary guidelines/corporate compliance programs to ensure that their supply chains are free of trade in fakes (Strategy Targeting Organized Piracy Cracks 2004).

European Commission Taxation and Customs Union (TAXUD)

The parallel agency to the U.S. CBP is the European Commission's Taxation and Customs Union. The best place to keep up-to-date in government initiatives is at http://ec.europa.eu/taxation_customs/customs/customs_controls/counterfeit_piracy/index_en.htm. Various data are presented at this website in terms of both the EU and specific Member States information regarding seizure data. As a point of clarification, the EU TAXUD reports its counterfeit seizure statistics as the "number of cases," where the U.S. CBP, uses the "domestic value" of seized goods in annual time frames.

In 2010, the TAXUD opened a consultation regarding customs legislation and enforcement of IPR to seek input from various stakeholders, such as IP right holders, shippers and holders of customs procedures (for a copy of the initial enquiry and results of this consultation, see http://ec.europa.eu/taxation_customs/

common/consultations/customs/ipr_2010_03_en.htm). The consultation resulted in 89 responses from a number of individuals and non-registered organizations (number=42), public authorities (n=4), and registered organizations (n=43). Walter Deffaa, the Director General, Taxation and Customs Union, European Commission, raised many issues related to customs enforcement in the EU and stated (New measures to bolster customs enforcement of intellectual property rights 2011, p. 4):

> Today, [2011] the only type of trademark infringement upon which customs can act under EU legislation is the classic 'counterfeit' product, but there are several other variations, for example where the fraudster produces something similar to an original logo, such as a "*hike*"T-shirt, or where a well-known brand is used for a completely different category of product. These would all be covered by the new rules. In addition to covering certain situations currently excluded, such as "lookalikes" and illegal parallel trade, it is now proposed that customs should enforce all types of rights recognized at the EU level. New rights include topographies of semi-conductors and utility models. Even if counterfeit products remain the core business for customs, these new rules will enable customs to take action where suspect shipments are identified.

As discussed in Chaps. 2 and 3, the source country for most of the confiscated goods in the EU is clearly China, which accounts for the majority of all fake goods seized in this trade bloc. In 2012, in its press release of the 6th meeting of the EU-China Joint Customs Cooperation Committee (JCCC), the current TAXUD Commissioner, Algirdas Šemeta, raised his concerns with the EU–China trade as follows (Taking stock of the EU–China cooperation in customs 2012, p. 2):

> However, it must be clear: More trade should mean more legitimate trade. IPR enforcement, supply chain security and fraud prevention are part and parcel of our efforts to create a fair trading environment. Customs must stop the violators who distort competition and threaten public safety and security.

An in-depth analysis from TAXUD is found at *Report on EU Customs Enforcement of Intellectual Property Rights: Results at the EU Border—2010*. In 2012, the TAXUD website illustrates that the growth of counterfeit trade is exponential and claims that "[C]ustoms in 2010 registered about 80,000 cases, a figure that has *almost doubled* since 2009 … on-line sales caused a spectacular increase of detentions in postal traffic where 60% of the goods detained were medicines" (Statistics of customs detentions recorded at the external borders of the EU 2011).

In April 2004, in an effort to curb the problem of counterfeit cigarettes and the subsequent loss of significant government tax revenue in the EU (estimated at hundreds of millions of dollars per year in lost tax revenue), Philip Morris International, Inc. agreed to pay $1.25 billion over a 12-year time frame to assist the EU government develop procedures to curb the counterfeiting and smuggling of cigarettes in this region—the first of the so-called EU Cooperation Agreements (Philip Morris to Back EU Counterfeit Fight 2004). Since that time, three other major cigarette manufacturers have been involved in the EU Cooperation Agreements to secure the legitimate supply chain of genuine cigarettes and have scheduled payments to the EU: Japan Tobacco International (JTI), British American Tobacco

(BAT); and Imperial Tobacco Limited (ITL). For a comprehensive report on the illicit trade in counterfeit cigarettes, see our report, *The Impact of Plain Packaging on the Illicit Trade in Tobacco* (June 2012). For a detailed overview of the US and EU seizure data, refer back to Chaps. 2 and 3.

EU Patent Reform

The EU government has been negotiating for unitary patent protection in the regional trade bloc for decades. Barker (2012) in *The Financial Times* describes the fragmented patent system in this trade block as (EU reform: Wrangle over patent court site near ends, June 14 2012, pp. 6–7):

> Businesses have long lamented Europe's baffling patchwork of patent laws. They have to defend their inventions separately in each EU member-state – a costly process that critics say has hurt competitiveness. According to EU estimates, it costs about €30,000 to get a bundle of national patents for all 27 member states, about 15 times the cost of a typical US patent. For decades, EU countries have squabbled over the language rules for a single patent regime – an issue that was potentially resolved last year by 25 EU countries agreeing to move ahead with a treaty without Spain and Italy, which were implacably opposed.

Ironically, Barker (2012) comments that after decades of forums on unitary patent protection, the final decision is where to locate the new patent court—the UK, France, and Germany are all viable contenders for this new governing body and the final decision is supposed to be made on June 29, 2012 between whether to locate the court in London, Paris, or Munich. The result was a compromise and the Unified Patent Court will have a presence in all three cities as described below (Thom 2012, p. 2):

> As previously suggested it appears that the seat, along with the office of the President of the Court of First Instance, will be located in Paris and that two sections of the Central Division will be created, one in London (chemistry, including pharmaceuticals, classification C, human necessities, classification A), the other in Munich (mechanical engineering, classification F).

In 2011, the European Commission claimed that language translation and other costs associated with patent protection would be greatly reduced in the 25 Member States [excluding Spain and Italy]. The European Commission made the following points about the patent reform (Commission proposes unitary patent protection to boost research and innovation 2011, pp. 5–6):

- The translation costs for a European patent with unitary effect in 25 Member States would be €680 in the long run, and less than €2,500 during a transitional period.
- Holders of European patents can apply for unitary patent protection for the territory of 25 Member States at the EPO. The patent will ensure the same level of protection for their inventions in all 25 countries.

- Patent applications can be submitted in any language, however, building on its existing working procedures, the EPO will continue to examine and grant applications in English, French, or German (the official languages of the EPO). For applicants residing in the EU who file their patent application in a language other than the three EPO languages, the cost of translation to one of the official languages of the EPO will be compensated. Finally, the patent claims, defining the scope of the protection, are to be translated to the other two official languages of the EPO.
- For a transitional period of a maximum of 12 years, European patents with unitary effect that were granted in French or German will need to be translated to English. The ones granted in English will need to be translated to another official language of the EU. These translations will be required until high-quality machine translation becomes available to ensure the accessibility of patent information. The additional translations during the transitional period will directly help the development of high-quality machine translations.

A detailed discussion of the EU patent reform is beyond the focus of this book. However, it is clear that both the U.S. AIA discussed in Sect. 7.2.2 and the changes to the EU patent system are both designed to improve the competitive and innovative landscape of the creators and/or businesses that operate in these countries.

IPR Enforcement Initiatives in the European Union

The EU currently has distinct directives that govern some aspects of IPR. As illustrated in Table 7.1, three of these directives specifically have power over the sectors of satellite and cable, computer programs, and semiconductors.

For a more detailed synopsis of each of these directives, consult the European Commission website (http://ec.europa.eu) and review more specific information on the European Commission publication on EC Directives on Copyright and Related Rights at http://ec.europa.eu/internal_market/copyright/copyright-infso/index_en.htm. For the purposes of this book, we would like to focus on the directive related to set minimum enforcement standards in the EU that was adopted on April 29, 2004.

Retaliation: Understanding the Enforcement Directive in the EU to Pursue Counterfeiters

Of the nine directives mentioned in Table 7.1, the first directive governs the rental and lending rights related to copyright protection and was adopted into the EU legislation in November 1992. Thus, in relative terms, this supranational government agency

Table 7.1 List of EU directives on IPR

Name of directive	Brief description	Adoption date
Enforcement	Harmonizes enforcement procedures for Member States	29.04.2004
Resale right	Resale rights for the benefit of the author of an original work of art	27.09.2001
Copyright in the information society	Harmonizes certain aspects of copyright and related rights in the information society	22.05.2001
Protection of databases	Legal protection of data bases	11.03.1996
Term of protection	Harmonizes the term of protection of copyright and certain related rights	29.10.1993
Satellite and cable	Coordination of certain rules concerning copyrights in this industry	27.09.1993
Rental right	Governance of rental right and lending rights related to copyright	19.11.1992
Protection of computer programs	Legal protection of computer programs	14.05.1991
Semiconductors	Legal protection of topographies of semiconductors products	16.12.1999

Source: http://ec.europa.eu

began to develop and adopt the EU-wide measures to protect a company's IPR in this time frame. The more recent policy changes center on the Enforcement Directive that was adopted on April 29, 2004 to establish minimum enforcement of IPR standards in the EU. In 2012, the European Commission describes the problem of enforcement of IPR as (Enforcement of intellectual property rights 2012, pp. 1–2):

> Over the last decade, the counterfeiting and piracy phenomenon has risen to very dangerous dimensions and has become one of the most devastating problems facing world business. With direct links to organized crime, counterfeiters have become extremely skilled entrepreneurs operating on a global scale. Counterfeiters make expert use of current technology and trade and succeed in producing every imaginable type of fake.

The ten Member States which joined the EU on May 1, 2004 were Cyprus, the Czech Republic, Estonia, Hungary, Latvia, Lithuania, Malta, Poland, Slovakia, and Slovenia. Thus, one of the major reasons to adopt a directive on the enforcement of IPR in the EU was to strengthen the ability to fight the counterfeit traffickers in Member States with weak enforcement regimes. However, there was debate as to whether the directive provided enough incentive for these ten Member States to protect IPR. Phillips (2004) describes the legal quagmire for protection of IPR in the EU as "[E]nlargement means that, with respect to pan-European IP rights such as the Community trade mark and the Community design, the same right may be the subject of dispute in up to 25 jurisdictions. If the IP right dispute involves a substantial number of jurisdictions, almost anything is preferable to litigating the same dispute simultaneously in a large number of different countries (sic)" (p. 1).

Table 7.3 Synopsis of EU directive of IPR

Scope of directive	Sets minimum standards for enforcement by reference to best practice in the Member States
	Applies to infringements of any IP rights arising from Community or national law regardless of the degree of harmonization of the underlying rights
	Three measures—relating to orders for the disclosure of certain types of evidence, orders for the disclosure of information, and freezing orders—apply only where the act of infringement is carried out on a commercial sale
	Criminal sanctions are left up to the Member States that must apply penalties that are "effective, dissuasive and proportionate"
Impact on member states	All member states will have to adapt their legislation to a greater or lesser degree to meet the requirements in terms of:
	Disclosure of evidence
	Search and seizure orders
	Seizure of infringing goods
	Injunction against an intermediary
	Freezing orders
	Damages
	Corrective measure
	Cash alternative for innocent infringers

Source: Knapper 2004 and the *Economist Intelligence Unit*, 2004

The major provisions of the EU directive in terms of its "scope" and "impact on Member States" is summarized in Table 7.3. The directive *does not harmonize* but sets minimum standards for enforcement in current Member States. For a more detailed legal evaluation of the directive, review Knapper 2004 and the *Directive 2004/48/EC of the European Parliament and of the Council of 29 April 2004 on the Enforcement of Intellectual Property Rights* that is published in the *Official Journal of the European Union.*

At a 2005 press conference in Brussels, Belgium, László Kovács, European Commissioner of Taxation and Customs Union outlined the leading tactics of the Enforcement Directive for key players, such as business, the EU Customs, and the international and national government policymakers. Basically, this directive will increase cooperation and information exchange in the business community to promote a better dialogue with shipping lines, express carriers, and airlines; to work with business to produce practical guides for customs and promote targeted actions in high risk areas; to establish regular meetings with business to focus on joint efforts; and to provide training for business on customs requirements. In addition, international actions would include using the customs cooperation agreements to create feedback systems to cut off counterfeiting at the source; and increased partnership with other international organizations such as the World Customs Organization and Interpol (Kovács 2005).

In terms of the *scope* of this Enforcement Directive, the legislation sets minimum standards for enforcement by reference to best practice in the Member States; applies to infringements of any IPR arising from Community or national law regardless of the

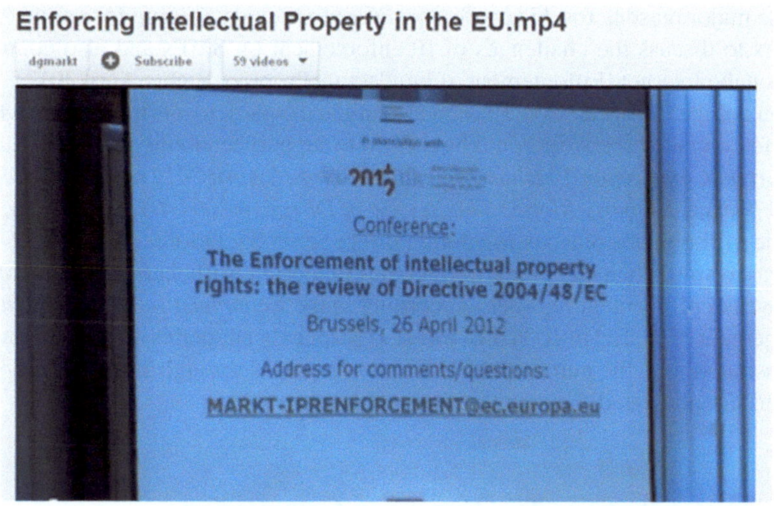

Fig. 7.5 Highlights of meeting on the enforcement directive. *Source*: http://www.youtube.com/watch?v=R9rtWZzBt6U

degree of harmonization of the underlying rights; establishes three measures—relating to orders for the disclosure of certain types of evidence, orders for the disclosure of information, and freezing orders—that apply only where the act of infringement is carried out on a commercial sale; and appeals to the 25 Member States to develop criminal sanctions that must apply penalties that are "effective, dissuasive and proportionate" (European Commission 2004). In terms of the impact of this directive on the protection of IPR in each Member State, the national governments must adapt the legislation to a greater or lesser degree to meet the requirements of the Enforcement Directive.

Knapper (2004) described the controversy that embroiled the adoption of this directive, noting that the scope of the directive was too broad in terms of its application to consumer piracy, such as file-swapping; and for introducing criminal measures outside the jurisdiction of the European Commission. Again, this directive places the burden on each Member State to change its legislation in terms of enforcement mechanisms ranging from disclosure of evidence to damages. The Business Software Alliance (BSA), the International Federation of Phonographic Industry (IFPI), the Motion Picture Association, and the like, expressed a discouraged outlook regarding the level of protection given to IPR under this Directive and stated that the Directive does not give adequate protection since the measures proposed do not reach the level of protection offered in laws of certain Member States (International Federation of the Phonographic Industry 2005).

The implementation of this directive is a continual focus of the governing bodies in the EU, and highlights of the most recent meeting on April 26, 2012 in Brussels, Belgium are available as a webcast, a report (http://ec.europa.eu/internal_market/iprenforcement/docs/conference20120426/summary_en.pdf) or a 5.44 min summary of the meeting available via YouTube (see Fig. 7.5).

The major reasons for this conference were to provide a forum for various stakeholders to discuss the challenges of IP enforcement by SMEs and also counterfeit trade on the Internet (Enforcement of Intellectual Property Rights April 2012). Pierre Delsaux of the European Commission also urged the participants to "explore whether it [Enforcement Directive] should be revised to support economic growth in Europe" (*Report on Commission/Presidency Conference of 26 April 2012 on the Enforcement of Intellectual Property Rights: The Review of Directive 2004/48/EC, 2012*, p. 5).

One of the major reasons to adopt a directive on the enforcement of IPR in the EU was to strengthen the ability to fight the counterfeit traffickers in Member States with weak enforcement regimes. According to the *Economist Intelligence Unit*, the enlargement of the EU in 2004 drove the EU to quickly adopt this directive. However, as illustrated with the number of EU IP cases reported through TAXUD, this directive has not alleviated the counterfeit trade problem.

Seeking Retribution: The European Commission Develops Action Plans to Bolster IP

In October 2005, the European Commission announced an *Action Plan* to further strengthen the level of IPR protection in the trade bloc. At this time, the policymakers were disturbed by recently released seizure data that revealed a significant growth in counterfeit trade, an estimated increase of 1,000% from 1998 in terms of reported cases of pirated goods (European Commission 2005). In addition, government decision-makers were concerned with the health and safety of consumers as a result of the consumption of fake foodstuffs and medicines, or use of fake household items and car parts. Thus, the Commission's 2005 *Action Plan* included the following proposed measures:

- A new business-customs working group to consider whether there is a need to refine the EU anti-counterfeit legislation in order to increase protection for legitimate business while keeping down costs.
- A new Task Force of Member States' Customs experts with the task of improving anti-counterfeiting controls.
- The completion of an anti-counterfeiting risk management guide to be distributed to Member States as well as to our international partners.
- A new electronic system of secure, real-time transmission of information.
- Memoranda of understanding with major trade representatives such as airlines, shipping companies, and express carriers with a view to improving information exchange and creating a better awareness of the risks posed by the traffic in fakes.
- With regard to reinforcing international cooperation, the Commission will, together with Member States, consider possible amendments to the World Trade Organisation Intellectual Property Rights ("TRIPS") Agreement so that countries apply anti-counterfeiting controls not only on imports but also on exports, transit and transshipment movements (European Commission 2005, p. 3).

Immediately after this 2005 press release, Francis Moore, Regional Director of Europe for the IFPI, the organization representing the recording industry worldwide enthusiastically supported this *Action Plan* by stating that "it is a multi-pronged approach which for the first time is commensurate with the size of the problem. For the music industry, the pirate market is estimated to be worth $4.6 billion at pirate prices worldwide" (International Federation of the Phonographic Industry 2005, p. 1). An example of a multiagency cooperation is the successful EU joint customs operation codenamed "FAKE." This sting operation was conducted during a 2-week period in May 2005 where counterfeit products of Chinese origin were monitored through 250 customs officers in the EU throughout the 25 Member States. The FAKE project was coordinated by both the European Anti-Fraud Office (OLAF) and the EU Taxation and Customs Union. This first joint operation was extremely successful in seizing counterfeit goods through the timely exchange of information between Customs Officials in order to detect fake products in commercial transactions entering the majority of the EU's borders (International Customs Operation "FAKE" 2005).

In 2009, the EU Council adopted the "EU Customs Action Plan" to further support the IPR environment with a multitude of goals that centered on (Commission initiatives for fighting counterfeit and other IPR infringements 2012, p. 2):

- Improving and where necessary modifying, existing IPR legislation.
- Strengthening operational cooperation between customs in the EU and with third countries.
- Improving cooperation with right holders.
- Developing further international cooperation on IPR enforcement.
- Improving publicity and awareness.
- Responding to the problem of Internet sales and delivering ad hoc training to customs officers.

In October 2010, the European Commissioner, Algirdas Šemeta applauded the joint collaboration of several countries and agencies known as Operation Sirocco that included "27 EU Member States, 11 non-EU partner countries from the Union of the Mediterranean (Albania, Croatia, Egypt, Jordan, Lebanon, Palestinian Authority, Montenegro, Morocco, Syria, Tunisia and Turkey), with the support of the European Commission, the World Customs Organization, Europol and Interpol" (European Commission 2010b, p. 4). This collaborative effort resulted in the seizure of counterfeit cigarettes, hand-rolled tobacco, alcohol, clothing, shoes, toys, and electronics.

EU-US Action Strategy for the Enforcement of Intellectual Property Rights

On June 21, 2006, at the US–EU Summit in Vienna, government officials endorsed the, "EU-US Action Strategy for the Enforcement of Intellectual Property Rights." The main objectives of this joint effort were to curb the growth of counterfeit trade by way of promoting strict enforcement, strengthening bilateral cooperation; and fostering public–private partnerships to protect intellectual property. The United States Mission to the European Union summarizes the main points of this bilateral agreement in the key areas of *enforcement* and *public–private partnerships* as follows (U.S., EU Adopt Action Strategy for the Enforcement of Intellectual Property Rights 2006):

1. *Enforcement*
   (a) *Customs and Border Control*
   Increase cooperation to strengthen border enforcement of IP rights, taking fully into account the five-point plan agreed in the framework of the JCCC by exchanging IPR border enforcement practices and experiences; operational staff to jointly target and examine shipments; enforcement information on IPR seizures and trends enhancing targeting and controls for counterfeit goods posing health and safety or security risks is a priority for cooperation in this area.
   (b) *Bilateral Measures*
   Step up our actions to encourage third countries to enforce IPR and to combat counterfeiting and piracy. This should be done inter alia through coordinated efforts that draw upon information from industry; coordinated messages on key enforcement issues and active complementing of each others' bilateral efforts working with third countries; and exchange of information about significant IP-related meetings and other events that provide opportunities to advance these objectives.
   (c) *Multilateral Measures*
   Facilitate the ongoing OECD IP study by providing data and any other necessary and available resources, recognizing that current, independent, and reliable information on the scope and effects of IP theft will shape a more compelling pro-IP enforcement message for consumers and governments worldwide. Support implementation of the 2005 G8 Leaders Statement on Reducing IPR Piracy and Counterfeiting through More Effective Enforcement, in particular in the area of the fight against criminal infringements of IP rights to reduce substantially global trade in pirated and counterfeit goods.

2. *Promoting public–private partnership*
   Involve industry by providing information on IPR-related meetings and activities in third countries, to launch joint public–private roundtable discussions in third countries, to assist small- and medium-sized enterprises with IPR protection and enforcement challenges in third countries; and to increase public awareness of the need to address IPR infringements at trade fairs and share ideas on ways to improve enforcement against such infringements, in cooperation with the interested parties.

   The agreement also invites industry to enhance a public–private relationship by sharing information with government authorities; sharing IP strategies in terms of an industry model to curb counterfeit trade; divulging enforcement problems in third countries; and giving government officials an idea of what type of public awareness programs have been designed to educate the consumer on the illicit trade. For a more detailed report of each measure, consult the United States Mission to the EU website at http://useu.usmission.gov.

In 2010, the U.S. State Department summarized progress of this initiative in its Framework for Promoting Transatlantic Economic Integration, Annex III: Intellectual Property Rights (March 2010, p. 4):

- The United States and the European Union (together with others) continue to negotiate an Anti-Counterfeiting Trade Agreement to enhance international leadership on IPR enforcement and cooperation.
- The EU–US cooperation on IP enforcement has been a success story. The IPR Working Group meets formally each year, seeking industry input and collaboration for further joint initiatives.
- The US and EU IPR enforcement experts are deepening their information-sharing about key countries, such as China and Russia, by means of regular meetings and joint IP networks of diplomats.
- Activities have focused in particular on joint enforcement efforts at the WTO and in third countries, in particular in China and Russia; and joint organization of seminars in Russia (digital piracy), in Latin America (tri-border region) and in ASEAN countries.
- Closer customs cooperation, including joint border enforcement actions, has been an area of particular attention. The first joint customs cooperation project (Operation INFRASTRUCTURE) was a success; the U S and EU customs authorities seized 360,000 counterfeit semiconductors and computer network hardware components.
- On global patent law harmonization, the United States and the EU continue to meet within the "Group B+" to advance discussions on patent law harmonization in the WIPO.

Operation Infrastructure

In February 2008, both the EU and US authorities released the information that Operation Infrastructure was the first successful outcome of the EU-US Action Strategy (U.S. CBP and European Commission Announce First Joint Operation Combating Counterfeit Goods 2008). The CBP and the TAXUD selected semiconductors and computer networking equipment for their first joint IPR border enforcement action. These categories were selected, since in addition to IPR infringement, the counterfeit goods in this area also represent safety and security risks. Dan Baldwin, the U.S. CBP assistant commissioner commented that "[C]ounterfeit hardware lacks the quality assurance and manufacturing standards of genuine hardware. As a result, there is a much higher failure rate for counterfeit hardware. Many counterfeit products fail on installation and more fail weeks or months after installation. Failures impose significant labor, equipment and lost productivity costs on individuals and organizations that depend on these networks" (US, EU seize counterfeit computer goods 2008).

Operation Infrastructure was a 2-month joint operation conducted in November and December 2007 that led to the seizure of over 360,000 illicit computer central processing chips and circuit boards that had been shipped from primarily China, Taiwan, and Hong Kong. The fake merchandise contained the brand names of over 40 leading manufacturers in this sector, including Intel, Cisco, Philips Electronics, Siemens and the like. The EU and US authorities in Operation Infrastructure worked closely with key airports in the United States and the EU and air freight operators, such as Federal Express, United Parcel Service, and DHL to detect the counterfeit merchandise.

In February 2008, R.Verrue, Director General for Taxation and Customs at the European Commission, stated: "We will continue to build upon this operation and a growing cooperation with our U.S. colleagues to combat the global trade in fake goods. The EU and US are fully committed to combating counterfeiting and piracy at home and abroad. In addition, this also shows that Customs administrations are prepared to tackle difficult enforcement challenges and issues, especially when the health and safety of our citizens is at stake" (U.S. Customs and Border Protection and European Commission Announce First Joint Operation Combating Counterfeit Goods 2008, p. 2). CBP Assistant Commissioner Baldwin mirrored his counterparts comments stating, "The success of Operation Infrastructure clearly demonstrates our commitment to jointly working with our European counterparts to stop the international flow of illicit goods, and protect our consumers and businesses from these harmful products" (U.S. Customs and Border Protection and European Commission Announce First Joint Operation Combating Counterfeit Goods 2008, p. 4).

EU Third-Country IPR Enforcement Strategy

In November 2004, the European Commission released its new tactics for enforcing IPR beyond its borders in "third countries." Pascal Lamy, the (former) EU Trade Commissioner states, "[P]iracy and counterfeiting continue to grow every year and have become industries, increasingly run by criminal organizations. This is a serious problem for us but also for third countries whose companies are also suffering the consequences of violation of their intellectual property rights. Some of these fakes, like pharmaceuticals and foodstuffs constitute an outright danger to the public, while others undermine the survival of EU's most innovative sectors, confronted with the misappropriation of their creations. Adopting new legislation on intellectual property is one thing. But devising the right tools to enforce it is another. This is now our priority...." (EU Strengthens Fight Against Piracy and Counterfeiting Beyond its Borders 2004).

In July 2003, the European Commission conducted a detailed survey assessing enforcement issues related to IPR in third countries. The study concluded that the most difficult countries were China, Thailand, Ukraine, Russia, Indonesia, Brazil, Turkey, and South Korea in terms of both the export and domestic consumption of counterfeit goods. The major tactics of this trade strategy towards third-country IPR infringement is to (EU Strengthens Fight against Piracy and Counterfeiting Beyond its Borders 2004):

- *Identify priority countries*: The EU action will focus on the most problematic countries in terms of IPR violations. These countries will be identified according to a regular survey to be conducted by the Commission among all stakeholders.
- *Awareness raising:* Promote initiatives to raise public awareness about the impact of counterfeiting [e.g., loss of foreign investment and risks to health].
- *Political dialogue, incentives, and technical cooperation*: Ensuring that technical assistance provided to third countries focuses on IPR enforcement, especially in priority countries. Exchanging ideas and information with other agencies, such as the WIPO, the United States or Japan, with the aim of avoiding duplication of efforts and sharing best-practices.
- *IPR mechanisms in multilateral (including TRIPs), bi-regional, and bilateral agreements*: Raising enforcement concerns in the framework, consulting trading partners in terms of an initiative with the WTO TRIPs Council, and the like.
- *Dispute settlement—sanctions:* Recall the possibility that right-holders have to make use of the Trade Barriers Regulation or of bilateral agreements, in cases of evidence of violations of TRIPs.
- *Creation of public–private partnerships*: supporting/participating in local IP networks established in relevant third countries, and the like.

Future research will have to examine whether these strategies designed to strengthen the EU IPR in countries such as China and the Ukraine, are going to assist businesses fight the fakes in the global marketplace.

Conclusions

The primary purpose of this chapter was to provide a synopsis of the IPR initiatives designed by the US and EU government officials. There have been several changes to IP protection in the past few years: IPEC, the AIA, and the conclusion of negotiations for unitary patent protection in the EU are just a few leading examples. It is clear that a business manager simply does not have the time to sift through the labyrinth of information on this topic. For example, news on the FAKE sting operation in the EU was found imbedded at the Europa website for the European Commission and was distributed by the EIU Newswire—the story was not published in more common business sources, such as *The Wall Street Journal* or the *Financial Times*. Therefore, both international and government policymakers, trade consortiums, such as BSA, and companies must work to find a better way to disseminate information related to the protection of IPR to the global business community. One suggestion might be a global anti-counterfeiting blog. The main issue will be to find an agency that is willing to take ownership for this central blog. Suggestions would include the U.S. Department of Commerce, the OLAF, or the World Customs Organization.

Most of the current literature on counterfeits centers on the description of various anti-counterfeiting measures that are developed through international and national government agencies, industry associations, and businesses to deter counterfeit traders. There are a myriad of reports stemming from the US and EU agencies that are available from a plethora of agencies, Fig. 7.1 is just a brief synopsis of some of the major players in the United States that provide IP information and assistance. However, there have been few, if any, studies to determine whether adding new layers of IP governance, such as IPEC, or legislation, such as the EU Enforcement Directive, have effectively deterred the growth of illicit trade.

Chapter 8
Government and Industry Led Operations to Curb Counterfeit Trade

Introduction

The purpose of this chapter is to give a succinct overview of the leading multilateral organizations and industry associations that safeguard intellectual property rights. First, a quick overview of the Trade-Related Aspects of Intellectual Property Rights (TRIPS) in the World Trade Organization (WTO), the World Intellectual Property Organization, the IP-related governance in the Organization for Economic Cooperation and Development (OECD), and the enforcement of IP through the International Criminal Police Organization (Interpol). These four international agencies were selected for illustration purposes and many more global organizations could have been selected for this chapter. Second, a description of some of the principal industry associations that have IP at the forefront of their mandates—the International AntiCounterfeiting Coalition (IACC), the Business Software Alliance (BSA), the Software Information Industry Association (SIIA), the Motion Picture Association of American (MPAA), the Recording Industry Association of America (RIAA), and the International Federation of Phonographic Industry (IFPI) are highlighted in this chapter. Again, these six associations were selected due to their high profile for collecting data on piracy in their respective market segments. There are many more trade associations that exist with strong linkages to IP protection.

The goal of this Chapter is to provide as many resource links as possible to academics, managers, and public policy decision makers in order to guide their future IP agendas. This chapter is replete with websites that yield current information.

Multilateral Organizations that Govern IPR

The main multilateral decision-making bodies that have a significant impact on dealing with global IP concerns are the WTO, the World Intellectual Property Organization, and the Organization for Economic Cooperation and Development.

P. Chaudhry and A. Zimmerman, *Protecting Your Intellectual Property Rights*, Management for Professionals, DOI 10.1007/978-1-4614-5568-4_8,

A brief synopsis of each agency is given in the next section to provide a general overview. Several websites are listed to provide the means to educate the reader on the specific intricacies of each agency.

World Trade Organization: TRIPS

Without question, one of the leading multilateral organizations for the protection of intellectual property rights is the TRIPS in the WTO. The TRIPS was negotiated in the Uruguay Round (1986–1994) and became the first agreement governing IP in a multilateral trade organization. The WTO commenced in 1995, as an outgrowth of its predecessor, the General Agreement on Tariffs and Trade (GATT) that was established in 1948. It is the main multilateral trade forum for member countries to negotiate trade liberalization and disputes. As of May 10, 2012, there are 155 members of the WTO ranging from Albania to Zimbabwe. Other countries, such as Azerbaijan, are categorized as "observer governments" and must start accession to the WTO within 5 years of reaching this status. With such a large membership, it is clear that the WTO is the largest forum for IP trade issues.

The specific details of the WTO are found at http://www.wto.org. A quick pursue of this website gives updated information on a variety of global trade issues, such as the June 2012 dispute settlement report on the countervailing and anti-dumping duties on US imports into China (World Trade Organization (WTO) 2012) and WTO Director-General Pascal Lamy's address to a global commodities conference in Geneva, Switzerland ("Global Commodities Trade: Perspective of the WTO," 2012). On the IP front, the most current news centers on the WTO and WIPO training course held in March 2012 for 24 government leaders of both developing and transition economies to provide IP education.

Overall, the TRIPS agreement recognizes these categories of intellectual property: copyright and related rights; trademarks, including service marks, geographical indications, industrial designs, patents, layout designs (topographies) of integrated circuits; and undisclosed information, including trade secrets. A good example of a geographical indication is wine produced in "Napa Valley" or the well-known "Champagne"—this is why similar products produced in other regions are called "sparkling wine" since the product does not originate in the Champagne region of France. Astra Zeneca's submission of data for FDA approval is an illustration of trade secrets that must be protected.

The TRIPS governs five main areas (Intellectual Property: Protection and Enforcement, n.d.):

- How basic principles of the trading system and other international intellectual property agreements should be applied
- How to give adequate protection to intellectual property rights
- How countries should enforce those rights adequately in their own territories

- How to settle disputes on intellectual property between members of the WTO
- Special transitional arrangements during the period when the new system is being introduced

There have been 31 cases filed related to IP under TRIPs in the WTO (for a detailed list, see "Disputes by Agreement," at http://www.wto.org). The most recent case, "Certain Measures Concerning Trademarks and Other Plain Packaging Requirements Applicable to Tobacco Products and Packaging," (DS435) was filed by Honduras against Australia on April 4, 2012. A number of countries have since joined Honduras in this consultation: Brazil, Canada, El Salvador, the EU, Guatemala, Indonesia, Nicaragua, New Zealand, Norway, the Philippines, Ukraine, Uruguay, and Zimbabwe. The dispute involves a consultation with Australia regarding its recent Tobacco Plain Packaging Act 2011, which results in trademark restrictions and plain packaging requirements on tobacco products and packaging ("Australia—Certain Measures Concerning Trademarks," 2012, p. 2).

A former dispute within the TRIPS was filed by the United States against China for consultations on the level of thresholds for criminal actions to be taken against acts of trademark counterfeiting and copyright piracy; the disposal of goods confiscated by the Chinese government; the range of criminal procedures and penalties for producing and distributing pirate goods; and the problem of the lack of observance of copyright and other IP for sound recordings that have no authorization to be distributed in China. Other third parties that joined the consultations with the United States were Argentina, Australia, Brazil, Canada, EU, India, Japan, Korea, Mexico, Taiwan, Thailand, and Turkey. Known as "DS362," a WTO panel made its decision in March 2009 with China fulfilling its obligations for the settlement the following year by making amendments to its copyright law (World Trade Organization 2010).

The Doha round of trade negotiations is still in progress 10 years after its initial meeting in Qatar in 2001. Several key issues, such as revising intellectual property and anti-dumping rules, are currently on the agenda. For example, in 2001, the Doha Declaration adopted an agenda related to the dissemination of medicine to developing countries—the key focus is how patents are used to exclude developing countries from principal pharmaceuticals that safeguard public health (for detailed discussions see http://www.ielrc.org/content/f0201.htm and http://www.who.int). Seven years later, Williams (2008) reported that this round was facing its "moment of truth" since many policymakers questioned whether the talks could move forward with key political elections in the United States and India and changes in the executive of the European Commission. He reports that the familiar stumbling blocks, such as farm trade, are an issue, but, other goals such as market access to developing countries by way of reduced tariffs are still a contentious concern. In terms of intellectual property, a few of the key issues being negotiated are "the possible establishment of a multilateral register for Geographical Indications [GIs] on wine and spirits and possible strengthening of the TRIPS rules on GIs for products other than wines and spirits; and the question of patentability or non-patentability of plant and animal inventions and protection of plant breeders rights" (Intellectual property and the development aspects of the WTO's Doha round negotiations 2011).

In 2011, *The Economist* claimed that a decade of trade negotiations had "sharpened divisions, not smoothed them" and reports on the shift of trade goals by member countries, such as Brazil and India concerned about opening their markets to cheap imports from China ("The Doha Round: Dead Man Talking," April 28, 2011, p. 1).

World Intellectual Property Organization (WIPO)

The World Intellectual Property Organization (WIPO) was established in 1967 and is the current agency in the United Nations that governs IP. There are currently 185 Member States ranging from Afghanistan to Zambia. The WIPO includes more member countries than the TRIPS accord within the WTO. An alliance between the WIPO and the WTO was forged in 1996 with an agreement between the two multilateral regimes especially in the area of assisting developing countries achieve their TRIPS requirements by 2013. In addition to the WTO, the WIPO also works closely with other agencies, such as the World Health Organization (WHO), the International Labor Organization (ILO), and intergovernmental (IGOs), and nongovernmental organizations (NGOs). The WIPO offers several distinct types of interdisciplinary courses for (WIPO Academy, n.d., p. 2):

- Students from a range of disciplines (e.g., law, engineering, business) can grasp the fundamentals of the IP system
- Policymakers and diplomats can examine and discuss the pivotal importance of IP for development and economic growth
- Administrators can explore best practices to improve the delivery of IP services back home
- Academics can widen their understanding of emerging trends in IP
- Legal professionals can hone their practical IP skills and knowledge

In its 2011 annual report, the WIPO outlined its nine strategic goals as (WIPO Overview, 2011, p. 7):

- A balanced evolution of the international normative framework for IP
- Provision of premier global IP services
- Facilitating the use of IP for development
- Coordination and development of global IP infrastructure
- World reference source for IP information and analysis
- International cooperation on building respect for IP
- Addressing IP in relation to global policy issues
- A responsive communications interface between WIPO, its member states and all stakeholders
- An efficient administrative and financial support structure to enable WIPO to deliver its programs

Fig. 8.1 First prize poster in WIPO IP day in Brunei. *Source*: http://www.brunei-patents.com.bn/index.php/component/k2/item/35-26-April-prize-presentation-ceremony-of-iposter-competition

In the WIPO's 2011 Annual Report, the Geneva-based agency gives detailed information regarding its current endeavors to support IP through public outreach and communication, promoting the strategic use of IP for development, copyright in the digital environment, and the like. As discussed in Chaps. 5 and 6, there is a need for policymakers to communicate to consumers a more holistic perspective of the damages to the IP industry. The WIPO has begun this effort through its public outreach campaign via the web, film and television, publicity events, seminars, and publications. One example of this type of social marketing is its "World Intellectual Property Day" on April 26, 2012 that sponsored events around the globe to raise public awareness of the benefits of IP, such as IP Poster Competition for Youth in Brunei illustrated in Fig. 8.1.

The WIPO also raises public awareness at its own YouTube Channel by profiling several professions affected by IP protection, such as an entrepreneur and fashion designer in Sri Lanka. Figure 8.2 is a screen shot of one video clip that highlights musicians in Kenya and how piracy has negatively affected their ability to earn a living.

Fig. 8.2 WIPO YouTube channel. *Source*: http://www.youtube.com/user/wipo

A detailed overview of the WIPO's recent initiatives is beyond the scope of this chapter, however, their annual report, *World Intellectual Property Organization: An Overview 2011* can be obtained at http://www.wipo.int/export/sites/www/freepublications/en/general/1007/wipo_pub_1007_2011.pdf.

Organization for Economic Cooperation and Development

The OECD is well-known as a multilateral forum that includes countries committed to a free market economy. The OECD was established in 1961 and has a current membership of 34 countries with its secretariat in Paris. After 50 years of existence, the OECD lists its four main overarching goals at its website as (OECD at 50 and beyond, n.d.):

- First and foremost, governments need to restore confidence in markets and the institutions and companies that make them function. That will require improved regulation and more effective governance at all levels of political and business life
- Secondly, governments must reestablish healthy public finances as a basis for future sustainable economic growth
- In parallel, we are looking for ways to foster and support new sources of growth through innovation, environmentally friendly "green growth" strategies and the development of emerging economies
- Finally, to underpin innovation and growth, we need to ensure that people of all ages can develop the skills to work productively and satisfyingly in the jobs of tomorrow

The OECD is another forum where governments can voice their public policy concerns and debate future domestic and international policy on an array of topics that includes the protection of intellectual property rights. The organization addresses issues related to IP under its Directorate for Science, Technology, and Industry. A good way to keep updated on the various IP publications stemming from this part of the OECD is to bookmark their site at http://www.oecd.org/sti/ipr. The OECD is one of the largest sources of publications that cover subjects ranging from statistics and economic data to social changes—that can shape global policymaking decisions. The OECD report, *The Economic Impact of Counterfeiting and Piracy 2007*, is still widely quoted due to the comprehensive nature of this study. As discussed in Chap. 2, this report gives estimates of the size of the counterfeit market, the current IP environment (such as linkages to organized crime), the economic effects of piracy, suggestions for disseminating information on counterfeits, and an overview of government and industry initiatives. The report also gives specific attention to the audio and visual, automotive, electronic components, food and drink, pharmaceuticals and tobacco sectors affected by IP infringement. An Executive Summary of this 2008 publication can be obtained at http://www.oecd.org/dataoecd/21/20/40896133.pdf. Another report,

Piracy of Digital Content is available through their website.

The role of the OECD is both similar, in terms of fostering global policymaking on IP issues, and dissimilar to the WTO and WIPO since it does not provide a dispute settlement mechanism for IP trade disputes. However, given the prestige of this multi-country forum and its undeniable role in publishing leading works in IP, the OECD website should be consulted regularly by academics, policymakers, practitioners, and lawyers working in intellectual property concerns.

The International Criminal Police Organization (Interpol)

There may appear to be a disjunction between discussing multilateral trade policymaking agencies such as the WTO in the same category as an international police organization, Interpol. However, the various enforcement issues related to intellectual property are as important as the forums used to discuss and negotiate IP. In October 2000, this global police organization added IP crime to its mandate and strongly recommend that various stakeholders keep current with the issues reported via Interpol at http://www.interpol.int. Under the section "Financial and high-tech crimes," Interpol identifies currency counterfeiting, cybercrime, intellectual property crime, and health and safety consequences of IP crime. As illustrated in Fig. 8.3, Interpol is educating law enforcement, regulatory authorities and private sector IP investigators through its International IP Crime Investigator's College (IIPCIC). The College uses video content to train, such as its "Introduction to Organized Crime Funding and Intellectual Property Crime Module" linked to its website.

The Interpol IP Crime Program faces the formidable challenge of combating multinational organized crime and the program goals are to (Interpol's IP Crime Program, n.d., p. 11):

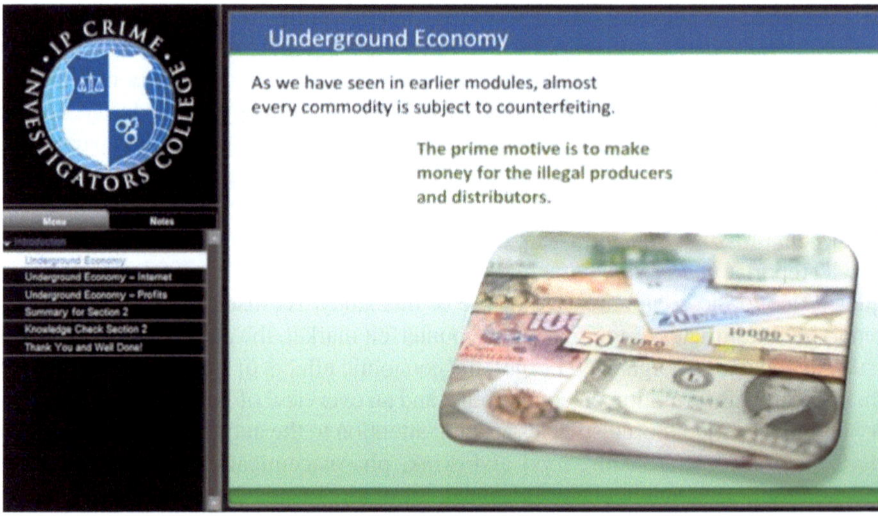

Fig. 8.3 Web training on IP linked through IIPCIC. *Source*: http://content.learnshare.com/courses/73/320870/player.html

- Develop strategies and programs to combat transnational organized criminal activity linked to IP infringement
- Develop the Database on International Intellectual Property (DIIP) Crime to improve the exchange of information and intelligence on transnational organized IP crime
- Raise awareness among policymakers, stakeholders, and the public about the central role of organized criminals in transnational IP crime
- Increase national and regional law enforcement efforts to combat transnational organized IP crime
- Develop a systematic worldwide operational capability to facilitate and coordinate regional enforcement action against transnational IP crime
- Provide police with support and training on IP crime

As discussed in Chap. 6, this organization supports raising public awareness of the role of organized crime in IP theft and maintains that the high profit/low risk incentives of product counterfeiting provide lucrative funding opportunities for terrorist organizations and organized criminal groups.

Industry Associations that Govern IPR

An overview of principal industry associations that are at the leading edge of global IP issues is given in this section. The IACC, BSA, SIIA, MPAA, RIAA, and IFPI were selected due to the industry sectors that they represent and the in-depth level of resources available at their websites. A concise review of each association follows.

Fig. 8.4 Quiz on real vs. fake at the IACC. *Source*: http://www.iacc.org/gallery/index.php

International AntiCounterfeiting Coalition

The IACC was established in 1979 and is based in Washington, D.C. This nonprofit agency represents a cross-section of industry sectors including pharmaceuticals, software, food, autos, and the like. In one of our managerial studies (refer back to Chap. 4), the respondents favored using this organization in their efforts to combat pirates. The IACC has a good website (http://www.iacc.org) and presents information on its public awareness campaigns (e.g., "When you buy counterfeit goods, you cost your city $1 Billion,"), IACC conferences, college outreach program (e.g., educating students on the real vs. fake product), and its infamous "counterfeit gallery." As shown in Fig. 8.4, the current counterfeit gallery offers an interactive quiz on the "real vs. fake" to educate the consumer. Once you have selected your "answer" another screen provides a detailed explanation for detecting counterfeits in a product category.

The IACC site will also give access to other studies and links to other agencies involved in IP protection, such as the WIPO. The separate "News & Media Resources" section includes a multitude of current events. In addition to representing a cross-section of brand owners (e.g., Apple and Motorola), the IACC also includes members from product security firms (e.g., Authentix), government agencies (e.g., Canada Border Services Agency), law firms (e.g., Arnold & Porter LLP), investigative agencies

Fig. 8.5 BSA country page for China. *Source*: http://www.bsa.org/country.aspx?sc_lang=zh-CN

(e.g., Pinkerton Consulting), and industry associations (e.g., Automotive Aftermarket Industry Association). This inclusive membership truly makes the IACC a coalition that represents the viewpoints of many decision makers in the IP arena.

Business Software Alliance

The BSA proclaims itself as the "voice of the world's commercial software industry" and represents several of the leading names in the industry, such as Adobe, Apple, Cisco Systems, Dell, HP, IBM, Intel, McAfee, Microsoft, and SAP. The BSA offers a wealth of information related to IP issues in this sector at http://www.bsa.org. On the BSA homepage, a link to an "anti-piracy portal" will send the reader to a variety of current events and a general description of software piracy and statistics (piracy rates by region). The annual "Global Piracy Study" has been cited several times in various chapters and the BSA provides this information as a pdf file at its site (http://portal.bsa.org/globalpiracy2011/).

The BSA provides a link to its "Public Policy" portal providing information on topics such as intellectual property, cyber security, innovation, and global trade and commerce. A country menu is also furnished to give a direct link to the BSA homepage that presents policy issues in the native language of the country selected. Figure 8.5 shows the BSA homepage for China.

The BSA supports an interactive website (http://www.cybertreehouse.com) for youth to access with links to "smart and uncool" (i.e., it is uncool to download software, movies, or games without paying for them) and other activities, such as

Fig. 8.6 SIIA ad campaign targets corporate America. *Source*: http://www.siia.net

games. This site is another excellent example of social marketing concepts being used to foster good cyber behavior in children.

Overall, the BSA offers many valuable links and resources that will keep academic, managers, and policymakers up-to-date on trends in this high growth sector. The coalition even offers quick fact sheets on software piracy, education, Internet piracy, online shopping, cyber security, and public policy for a succinct synopsis of the current issues.

Software Information Industry Association

The SIIA is a major trade group that represents the software and digital content industry. As part of their objectives, the agency oversees issues related to IP and offers valuable information at its anti-piracy link at http://www.siia.net/piracy/. The SIIA provides a link to whistleblowers, gives education on software management, proclaims its "Certifies Content Rights Manager" program will educate managers that oversee copyright issues in their firms, and suggests education materials. The *SIIA Anti-Piracy 2011 Year in Review* report gives a succinct accounting of software piracy for professionals working in the field. The reports include statistical evidence of share of pirated software by category (e.g., security and utility software), an overview of notice and takedown on the web (e.g., eBay and iOffer), and enforcement of Internet piracy and education programs.

The SIIA is an excellent resource for any firm that is trying to educate or supervise its workforce on IP-related issues. Figure 8.6 depicts a previous SIIA "big elephant" ad that portrays illegal software sharing in an office environment.

Motion Picture Association of America

The Motion Picture Association of America (MPAA) and its international branch, the Motion Picture Association (MPA) are obvious advocates of IP issues related to film, video, and television markets. This association also represents producers, distributors of media content, and any future delivery system created (such as the iPhone). The trade association was established in 1922, but has evolved to embrace other current issues, such as IP protection of creative works. The MPA oversees the global aspect of the industry—films can now be launched in over 150 countries—the Disney launch of *Ratatouille* occurred simultaneously in multiple languages. At the MPAA homepage (http://www.mpaa.org) the association immediately provides information on counterfeit problem with a link to "content protection," with a drop-down menu to salient IP topics, such as copyright information, camcorder laws, types of content theft, public awareness campaigns, report piracy, and rogue websites.

The MPAA is definitely targeting youth in the United States at these links and practitioners could use their examples to develop some of their own anti-piracy campaigns. As discussed in Chap. 6, social marketing techniques to educate the consumer are being used by various stakeholders. In the past, the MPAA has used novel education materials, such as "Lucky and Flo" in the Weekly Reader that was given to fifth to seventh grade children in 20,000 US schools to educate them about the validity of copyright protection. The campaign issued a curriculum that provides a teacher's manual, a workbook for the students, and posters of the two dogs (Lucky and Flo) that were used to "sniff out" fake DVDs by US Customs.

Recording Industry Association of America

The RIAA is the trade representative of the music industry. The agency is located in Washington, D.C. and boasts a long list of members ranging from 111 Records and Daddy Yankee to Walt Disney Records. The Board of Directors consists of some of the largest names in the business—EMI Recorded Music, Sony Music Entertainment, Universal Music Group, and the Atlantic Group.

The RIAA website (http://www.riaa.org) has a piracy link on the top banner of its homepage. To highlight the scope of the problem, the RIAA provides these statistics at its site ("Scope of the Problem," p. 2):

- Since peer-to-peer (p2p) file-sharing site Napster emerged in 1999, music sales in the United States have dropped 53%, from $14.6 billion to $7.0 billion in 2011
- From 2004 to 2009 alone, approximately 30 billion songs were illegally downloaded on file-sharing networks
- NPD reports that only 37% of music acquired by US consumers in 2009 was paid for

Fig. 8.7 Education of youth via music rules! *Source*: http://www.music-rules.com

- According to the Information Technology & Innovation Foundation, the digital theft of music, movies, and copyrighted content takes up huge amounts of Internet bandwidth—24% globally, and 17.5% in the United States
- Digital storage locker downloads constitute 7% of all Internet traffic, while 91% of the links found on them were for copyrighted material, and 10% of those links were to music specifically, according to a 2011 Envisional study

The RIAA provides specific programs for educators of children, such as Music Rules! that targets students in grades 3–8. Figure 8.7 illustrates the homepage for Music Rules! The Higher Education Opportunity Act of 2010 mandates that universities in the United States are required to provide some type of program to tackle illegal file-sharing using a campus network (Sandoval 2010). Thus, the RIAA in conjunction with American Council on Education and EDUCAUSE have developed video content to be used to educate young adults in a campus environment (see Fig. 8.8).

Overall, the RIAA gives a variety of information for parents, educators, and students at its website. The site also hosts a reporting mechanism for consumers to report both online and physical piracy via email or by calling 1-800-BAD-BEAT.

Fig. 8.8 Education video for university students. *Source*: http://www.campusdownloading.com

International Federation of Phonographic Industry

The international counterpart to the RIAA is the IFPI with at least 1,400 members in 66 countries that represent the music industry. The website at http://www.ifpi.org immediately links to a "Pro-Music" page (http://www.pro-music.org/), where educational materials, such as the Childnet International guide for parents and teachers, "Music and the Internet," can be viewed online or downloaded (see Fig. 8.9). This website also provides advice on "free music myths" and the "legal do's and don'ts" to raise awareness on the issue of content theft.

The association provides its own "Record Industry in Numbers," 2012 report for a fee which summarized the efforts made to combat piracy as part of this report. The IFPI Piracy issued reports during the 2000–2006 time frame that covered a range of topics from physical and Internet piracy, pre-release piracy, enforcement issues, and priority (e.g., Brazil and Canada) and special focus (e.g., Bulgaria and Pakistan) countries. An archived list of these reports can be accessed at http://www.ifpi.org/content/section_resources/piracy-archive.html. The last report was replete with relevant information about counterfeit trade in this sector and IFPI cautions about the growth of fakes through other means, such as "digital stream ripping" and mobile phones. Basically, stream ripping allows someone to convert a radio or Internet webcast into a copy—that is, he or she can create a collection of songs in a MP3 format through these "free" channels. Bluetooth enables a consumer to transfer content to another phone and swap memory cards. The increased technology that

Fig. 8.9 Pro-music. *Source*: http://www.pro-music.org/

gives the consumer distribution choices will also augment the growth of piracy. The concluding section of their report offers a "call to governments" to ensure adequate criminal penalties for copyright crime, highlight the fact that music piracy is not a victimless crime, enforce the regulation of optical disc factories, educate the public about copyrights, and achieve cooperation from Internet service providers.

Both the RIAA and IFPI give similar types of information related to the global protection of the music industry. Each website provides clear information targeted at youth to protect the copyrights of the innovative industry that the national and international agencies represent.

Conclusions

The information available on the Internet is endless and several multilateral organizations, industry associations, and national decision-making bodies exist to support the protection of intellectual property rights. As discussed in Chap. 7, even trying to develop a roadmap of these agencies for the US market is a cumbersome task. In a previous chapter, we suggested a central blog to be developed where all current information related to IP could be posted—a sort of Wikipedia for IP—to allow many of us involved in the area to keep abreast of current IP initiatives. In this chapter, several examples of anti-piracy programs targeted at consumers were highlighted to complement our work in Chaps. 5 and 6.

We have found social networking with others IP colleagues in the field, such as IP lawyers, to be a productive but not a comprehensive way to stay current. In general, the main issue is the explosion of information available at various websites that can be channeled into moving IP into the forefront of public policy agendas and ultimately effective enforcement of IP infringement.

In this chapter, a few resources were briefly described designed to help managers develop a better understanding of IP issues. Several sources of information are available for the legal community and have merit also but were not included in this chapter. In addition, we did not offer a critique of the effectiveness of each IP-related agency nor possible bias of its data collection/resources posted at its website. These related issues are discussed in separate chapters of the book.

Chapter 9
The Special Case of China

Introduction

The problem of piracy in China remains challenging. Just about every product is being pirated, sold in country and exported. At the end of 2011 USTR identified more than 30 "notorious markets." Eight of these are located in China. An amusing example of trademark infringement is seen below—the invention of "W&Ws" copying M&Ms packaging in every detail (Fig. 9.1).

A full review of current IPR conditions requires a look at the Chinese economy as well as Chinese history. For hundreds of years the Chinese economy experienced minimal growth and in fact from 1300 to 1950 per capita GDP decreased. Under the Communist regime economic conditions did not improve much and it was not until Deng Xiaoping took over that the so-called Chinese miracle began. Since 1978 annual GDP growth has been about 10%. Foreign direct investment (FDI) has been a major reason for this rapid growth and as a result exports have increased exponentially. With the growth of exports has come the growth of exported counterfeit product. China is the main source for pirated goods coming into the United States and the EU. While it is virtually impossible to estimate the value of counterfeit product originating in China, it is evident that the total is significant and growing.

Looking at the history of IP in China, it is clear that Chinese political culture did not lend itself to the concept of ownership of intellectual property. Confucianism required control of information and a traditional Chinese belief is that inventions draw on past knowledge which belongs to all citizens. The basic beliefs of Communism dovetailed with these traditional attitudes. Censorship was more important than copyrights and inventions belonged to the state.

Over the last hundred years under pressure from foreign powers, China has enacted a series of copyright, trademark, and patent laws and at this point the laws appear to be adequate. The most recent problems come from weak enforcement. Mertha (2005) describes the "opaque" bureaucratic apparatus attempting to enforce these laws and shows how a combination of pressure at the national and local level results in both better laws and enforcement. Nevertheless both firms doing business

P. Chaudhry and A. Zimmerman, *Protecting Your Intellectual Property Rights*,
Management for Professionals, DOI 10.1007/978-1-4614-5568-4_9,

Fig. 9.1 Trademark infringing W&Ws packaging. *Source*: Mertha, pg 21

in China and foreign governments are dissatisfied with the level of IPR protection. The US government asked for a WTO Dispute Settlement Panel to review China's legal regime related to copyrights and trademarks. The WTO findings only partially supported the US claims and are explained later in Sect. 9.6.

The Growth of the Chinese Economy

For centuries the Chinese economy was stagnant. According to Maddison (2001) total Chinese GDP in 1500 was about $62 billion in constant 1990 US dollars. This grew to about $230 billion by 1820 and only to $240 billion by 1950. Over the same period total GDP in Western Europe advanced from about $44 billion in the year 1500 to nearly $1.4 trillion in 1950. In China, per capita GDP actually fell from about $600 in 1300 to only $439 in 1950.

Overall total GDP did not improve much under Chairman Mao. In fact as Mao's biographer Philip Short understated, "economics was not Mao's strong point." Mao himself recognized his weakness in this area saying to businessmen in 1956, "I am an outsider in the field of economics" (Short 2000, p. 439).

The advent of Deng Xiaoping as leader of the Communist Party drastically changed the economic fortunes of the People's Republic of China. His famous saying "whether a cat is black or white makes no difference, as long as it catches mice it is a good cat" (CNN 1997) made possible the changes allowing the transition to what he called a "socialist market economy." From 1978 when Deng took power, the Chinese economy has grown rapidly. Much has been written about the Chinese "economic miracle." Looking at important indicators graphically gives a clear picture of this unprecedented growth.

As can be seen in the graph below (Fig. 9.2), China has maintained an astounding annual average GDP growth rate of about 10% for the last 30 years. For 2011 China's total GDP is the second-largest in the world at $11.3 trillion (CIA World Factbook 2012).

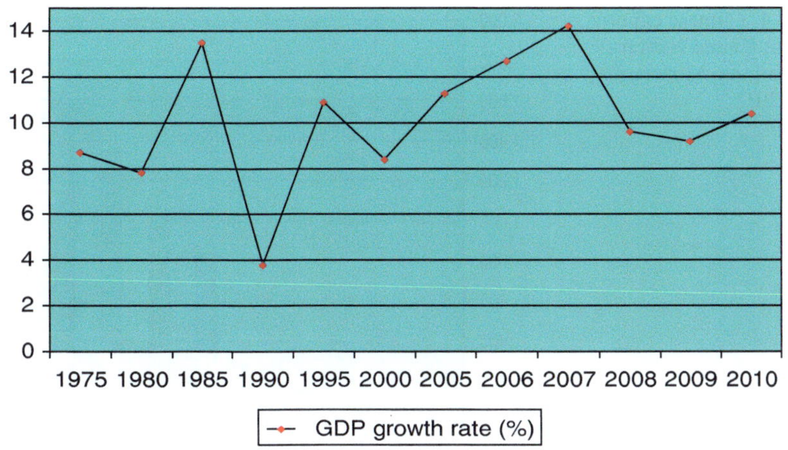

Fig. 9.2 China GDP growth rate. *Source*: The World Bank, National Bureau of Statistics

Fig. 9.3 China FDI. *Sources*: United Nations Conference on Trade and Development, Ministry of Commerce of the People's Republic of China 2012

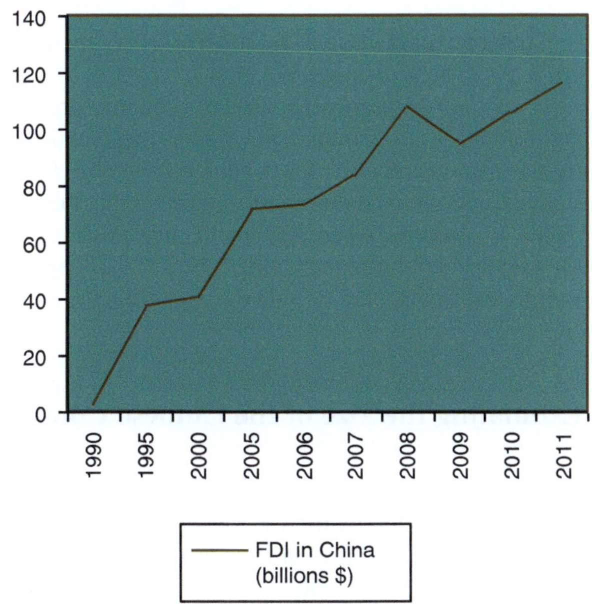

Wu (2000) reports Maddison's estimates of China's GDP growth at a little over 4% per year in the period 1952–1978 and 7.5% annually from 1978 to 1995. He states that even at this rate China's GDP had probably been underestimated by at least 10% of the official figures.

One driving force for this rapid GDP growth has been inward FDI. FDI into China has continued to increase rapidly, rising to a record $116 billion by 2011. The growth of FDI over the last 20 years is shown in Fig. 9.3.

Fig. 9.4 Chinese exports. *Source*: United Nations, International Monetary Fund 2012

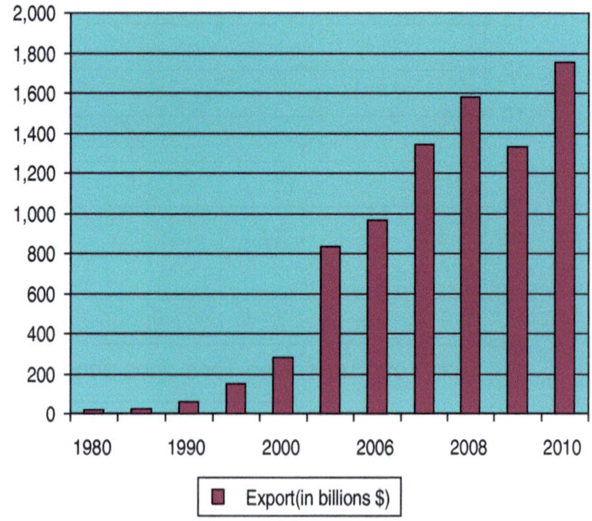

Chinese exports have also grown at a very rapid rate, approaching $2 trillion for 2010 as can be seen in the Fig. 9.4.

It may not be surprising that an economy growing in one generation from an eighteenth century level to a powerhouse with exports to virtually every other country has also become the chief source of counterfeit products. Despite this, in our study of international managers, we found that these managers plan to make investments in countries where the intellectual property environment is less than ideal. This is especially true for China where the strategic importance of the market outweighs any managerial trepidation regarding the lack of IPR protection.

Estimating the Size of the Chinese Counterfeit Market

As we have seen in Chap. 3, China is the most important source for counterfeit products intercepted by the US Customs (US Customs-Border Protection 2012) and reported by the EU Taxation and Customs Union (2010). In recent years, about two thirds of counterfeit products seized in the United States came from China and more than 80% of counterfeit goods seized at EU borders in 2010 were from China. In addition the OECD (2007c, d) identifies China as a country where IPR problems persist. Naim (2005) and Hopkins et al. (2003) cite China as the most important source for counterfeit product. As mentioned in Chap. 3, China remains on the USTR's Priority Watch List. After an in-depth study of the problem, the U.S. International Trade Commission (May 2011) estimated that US businesses suffered a total of $48 billion in lost sales, royalties, and license fees in 2009 as a result of IPR infringement in China.

It is impossible to accurately estimate the value of counterfeit product originating in China but it is evident that counterfeit production has grown right along with the economy and exports. In 1998 a confidential report by the Chinese State Council stated that the country was "drowning in counterfeits" and placed the value of counterfeit production at $16 billion for 1998 (Hopkins et al. 2003). In 2002 a reporter for the *Christian Science Monitor* stated that the piracy industry produced something between $40 and $80 billion and directly or indirectly employed three to five million people (Marquand 2002). He reports a common joke in China, "everything is fake but your mother." The production of counterfeit goods often occurs primarily in countries which lack the capacity or political will to regulate the industrial sector as noted by Global Financial Integrity (2011):

> Some might argue that, in places like China, counterfeiting employs people, produces goods, and benefits the economy. This report, however, holds the position that any short term benefits come at the substantial cost of human rights and the development of strong, internationally reputable Chinese brands. In fact, counterfeiting benefits mainly those criminal elements which put personal wealth ahead of state stability and social well-being. In short, for any developing country, counterfeiting is an unsustainable and potentially dangerous enterprise.

According to testimony by Chow (2005), a later study by the same government agency placed the value at $19–24 billion by 2001. He estimated in 2005 counterfeit product accounted for approximately 8% of China's GDP and that percentage has been cited frequently ever since. In 2011 this would imply that the total of counterfeit products produced in China exceeded $900 billion, an estimate far greater than most estimates for the entire worldwide counterfeit goods market.

Some estimates claim 60–70% of worldwide counterfeit goods are produced in China (Economist Intelligence Unit 2006; Schwarz and Wong 2006). Using the $250 billion estimate from the OECD (2009) this would place the value of counterfeit products from China between $150 and $175 billion annually, radically different from the total based on Chow's estimate. Calculations completed by Havocscope (2012) conclude that the Chinese counterfeit goods and piracy market amount to $60 billion. Pirated products include Chateau Lafite Rothschild Bordeaux, Budweiser beer, Gillette razor blades, Marlboro cigarettes, Yamaha motorcycles, and Skippy peanut butter (Dunlop 2012; Hopkins et al. 2003). In fact any product with a well-known brand is probably a victim of product counterfeiting in China.

The *Economist Intelligence Unit* (2012) ratings of the "degree of property rights protection" in China show an erosion from 1995 to 2002. There is some improvement in 2003–2012 but the expectation is IP protection will remain at a modest level for the foreseeable future (Fig. 9.5). (The rating scale is 1–5 with five meaning the highest degree of protection.)

A survey of its members by the Quality Brands Protection Committee (QBPC, an organization of more than 190 IP holders in China) revealed that nearly 42% felt that economic losses caused by C/P (counterfeit and pirated) goods were serious or extremely serious (Quality Brands Protection Committee 2012). According to the USTR (2007b) in 2006, 85–93% of all copyrighted materials sold in China were pirated with very little improvement since 2005.

According to the US Embassy in Beijing (2012), "auto parts, watches, sporting goods, shampoo, footwear, designer apparel, medicine and medical devices, leather

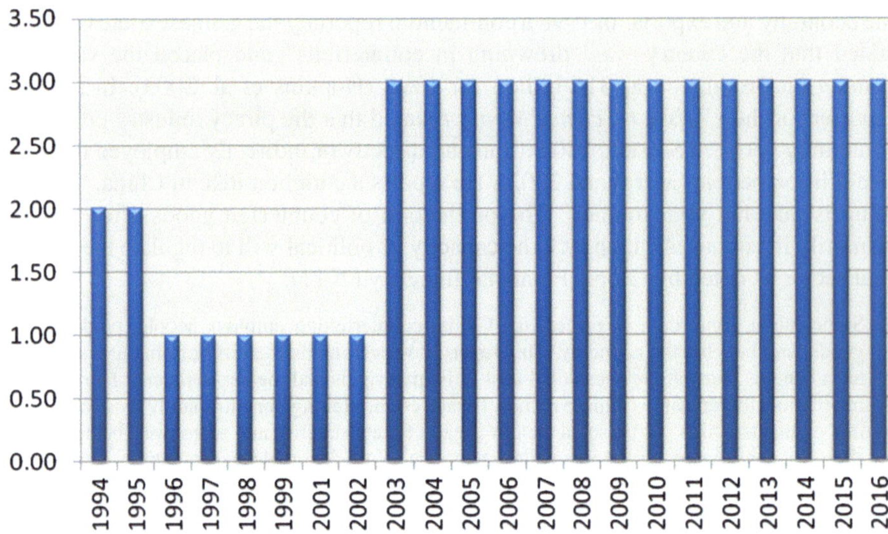

Fig. 9.5 Degree of IPR Protection in China. *Source*: The Economist Intelligence Unit, (2012)

goods, toys, batteries, and other non-consumer products—the seemingly endless array of counterfeit products that are manufactured and distributed within China, or exported to other countries, continues to grow." An inspection by the China Healthcare Association revealed that "more than 25% of healthcare products in China were fakes" and between 200,000 and 300,000 Chinese die every year because of counterfeit or substandard medicine (Schwarz and Wong 2006). According to the Business Software Alliance (2012) the value of China's illegal software market is nearly $9 billion while the legal market is only about $3 billion. The BSA claims the piracy rate in China has only declined marginally from 2010 to 2011, from 78 to 77%. According to the National Electrical Manufacturers Association (NEMA) three quarters of a million counterfeit ground connectors were imported from China and India in 2007. Jim Pauley of Schneider Electric says that most counterfeit products are manufactured in China (Griffin 2012). The list of fake electrical products made in China and exported includes batteries, smoke detectors, circuit breakers, wire/cable, and relays. The association also reports counterfeit certification marks including those of Underwriters Laboratories and the Canadian Standards Association. False certification labels and substandard versions of these products are a threat to health and safety (NEMA 2005). Figure 9.6 shows the results of substandard wiring.

China has also been a major source of counterfeit cigarettes, producing 190 million annually. About 15–20% of these are exported, mostly for European and North American destinations (Allen 2011). In China, the national government's previous efforts to fight the illicit trade in cigarettes have faced difficulty because of the increasingly covert and entrenched nature of the businesses. In some cases, the

Fig 9.6 Faulty cable can cause a fire. *Source*: Griffin (2012)

illegal production of cigarettes was so deeply rooted in local communities that whole villages were engaged in it under "the protection of local governments" (Von Lampe et al. 2012).

The International Anti-Counterfeiting Coalition (Quam 2002) said "the trademark community confronts a market filled with counterfeit goods… affecting every conceivable product." They claim a wide range of products are subject to counterfeiting, from auto parts to industrial lubricants to chewing gum and razor blades. Naim (2005) reports that a Chinese expert on intellectual property had his IP books pirated and placed on the Internet.

An embarrassing moment occurred back in 1998 when even the US Trade Representative, Charlene Barshefsky, brought back counterfeit products from China. Hers were "Beanie Babies," a popular variety of stuffed animals (e.g., the Garcia bear) that collectors' highly coveted in this time frame (NY Times 1998). It is clear that there is widespread counterfeiting in the PRC of nearly every type of product. In addition, although the Chinese government has been taking more action against counterfeiters in recent years, the scope and size of the problem is extremely large and appears to be growing.

History of Intellectual Property in China

To understand the difficulties of protecting intellectual property, one must look back through history, not only to the Communist regimes of the People's Republic but even to the early dynasties. Alford (1995) contends:

> The most important factor in explaining the late appearance and relative insignificance of the idea of intellectual property in the Chinese world lies in … its political culture, and especially in the central importance to the state, for purposes of legitimation and power, of controlling the flow of ideas. A system of state determination of which ideas may or

> may not be disseminated is fundamentally incompatible with one of strong intellectual property rights in which individuals have the authority to determine how expressions of their ideas may be used and ready access to private legal remedies to vindicate such rights (Alford, p. 119).

He explains that a pillar of traditional Chinese belief is that individual inventions draw on past knowledge which belongs to all citizens. In addition Confucianism requires the control of information. Contrary to conventional wisdom, copyright did not evolve in China with the invention of printing. Alford finds there was neither a "formal or informal counterpart to copyright or other major forms of intellectual property law in Imperial China (221 BCE to 1911 CE)." Alford dates the earliest efforts to regulate publication of particular works to 835 CE. These regulations were not designed to protect the property rights of authors but to ensure pre-publication review so that the state could prevent nonconforming ideas from being distributed. This emphasis was clearly in line with ancient Chinese precepts regarding the role of the state vs. individuals. As Alford (1995) puts it, rulers were seen to be in a parent-like position and therefore it was their responsibility to "nurture the populace [and]… determine which knowledge warranted dissemination and which ought to be circumscribed in the best interests of the Commonwealth." On the other hand there was no sanction against the pirating of many more ordinary works.

Until the twentieth century, there was far more interest in the control of publications than in trademarks or patents. The main interest was to prevent ordinary people from reproducing official symbols. While some guilds and clans used brand names and symbols, there was widespread counterfeiting and copying of secret manufacturing processes. There was little intellectual property owners could do to put a stop to it. In the late nineteenth century Western interest in intellectual property revived. The formation of the Paris convention in 1883 dealing with patents and trademarks and the Berne convention which addressed copyright in 1886 focused more attention on intellectual property within the country, even though China was not a party to either convention. Although negotiations with Chinese officials began, it took about 20 years for laws to be passed related to copyright, trademarks, and patents. Even these were unsatisfactory to the treaty powers working in China and in 1924 the US Consul in Shanghai said there was "widespread unauthorized reproduction of foreign patented articles." (Alford, p. 43) In fact although the Chinese believed that economically successful countries had patent and trademark law, they did not easily understand the Western concept of intellectual property. In one case, the Jiangnan Bureau of Commerce issued patents to Chinese for *imitation* rather than innovation.

Although new, well-designed laws were passed to protect intellectual property during the reign of the Nationalist Guomindang government in the 1920s and 1930s, there was little improvement in IPR protection since there were a few trained government people or judges who understood intellectual property. In addition the government continued to see the control of ideas as paramount.

When the Chinese Communists took over in 1949, they found a commonality with the Soviet approach toward intellectual property because it reflected traditional Chinese attitudes toward both inventions and the control of information. Mertha (2005) points out that inventors' rights touch on "the set of core assumptions that separate socialist from capitalist systems." Although laws were passed giving recognition and some monetary rewards to inventors and authors, apparently few took advantage of them. Instead, there was unauthorized copying and trademark use in the 1950s. A major problem was that there was neither basic contract law nor any effective legal redress. During the 1960s the minimal patent protection of the earlier years was removed from the law and trademark guarantees were weakened. The intellectual property environment reached its low point during the Cultural Revolution where even the meager payments for inventions were eliminated. After the Cultural Revolution, starting in the mid-1970s, the Chinese moved to create new laws for patents and trademarks. This was difficult for China since these laws established new private ownership rights in an ostensibly Socialist country. Copyright law took an even more torturous path before being finally issued in 1990. Alford (1995) explains that this law allowed only limited payments and excluded "works prohibited by law to be published and disseminated," and that the copyright holder could not violate the Constitution and the law or infringe upon the "public interest," an obviously vague term.

Mertha (2005) describes in great detail the role of the United States in pushing China to enact IPR protections. From the time of normalizing relations with China in 1979, the United States began negotiations aimed at convincing the Chinese to improve their patent, copyright, and trademark laws. China agreed to protect foreign patents, copyrights, and trademarks in the US–China bilateral trade agreement of 1979. As a result China issued new patent and trademark laws, and joined the Paris Convention. By 1984 the US Trade and Tariff Act included inadequate protection of intellectual property as one of the "unreasonable" practices of foreign governments and in 1988 a new US Trade Act provided for trade sanctions against countries who were abusing the US firms' intellectual property. This law also established the annual report from the USTR on unfair trade practices and the "priority foreign country" designation for countries whose actions had an adverse impact on the US products including failure to provide intellectual property protection. The United States continued negotiations with China, pressing them to fulfill all the commitments in the 1979 agreement. The repression of Tiananmen Square put these negotiations on hold for more than a year. By late 1991 IPR issues became central to the negotiations between the United States and China. Although agreements were reached in 1992, IPR violations continued at a high level in China. The United States pressured China using the provisions of the 1988 Trade Act and issuing deadlines for changes in IPR protection. An important agreement was reached in 1995 but the United States again found the Chinese enforcement of the 1995 agreement less than ideal and the United States threatened another set of trade sanctions in 1996. Negotiations have continued to this day although the tone since the late 1990s has been less confrontational.

According to a USTR (2011a, b) report prepared at the end of 2011 China has enacted a relatively good set of IP laws since its accession to the WTO when the country had to adopt the IP principles of the TRIPS accord. However, the USTR report states that, although the Chinese government has initiated many antipiracy campaigns, counterfeiting remains a serious problem which causes significant harm to US businesses. Despite the fact that China is a member of the WIPO, the Paris Convention, the Berne Convention, and the Madrid Protocol, the USTR report goes on to say that "effective enforcement of China's IPR laws and regulations remains a significant challenge."

Some contend that the tight control of information dissemination exacerbates the counterfeiting problem. Pang (2004) states that the Chinese government's insistence on "ideological purity" and resulting tight restrictions on film production and distribution only encourages cinema piracy. While the laws described above were improvements over those in the past there was a lack of provision for resolving disputes. The lack of enforcement and corrective mechanisms will be examined next.

(Much of the above section is based on Alford (1995), who provides a detailed and well-reasoned discussion of intellectual property law and Chinese culture, and Mertha (2005) who provides a fascinating look at the workings of the Chinese bureaucracy as it relates to IPR).

IPR Enforcement

As can be seen in Fig. 9.7 below, the *Economist Intelligence Unit* sees a significant risk in the legal and regulatory environment in the People's Republic of China. This facet of the Chinese economy is perceived as significantly more important than nearly all of the other risk factors measured (Fig. 9.7). (On this scale, 100 equals the highest level of risk.)

A study conducted by one of the authors with (Chaudhry and Stumpf 2007) found that managers who had recently visited China identified weak enforcement of IPR and limited criminal/civil penalties as two of three important reasons that suppliers offer counterfeit goods. The most important reason was obvious—profitability.

Understanding the IPR environment in China requires a careful review of the enforcement of existing laws. Chow (2005) identified two main barriers to effective enforcement—local protectionism and inadequate punishment. The protectionism comes about despite the best intentions of the central authorities because particular localities may benefit from counterfeiting. This activity provides jobs and generates revenue and may be vital to the local economy. He states "some local areas in China are entirely supported by the trade in counterfeit goods and local residents are ready to use any means necessary to protect their illegal trade." Regarding inadequate punishment, he points out that there is enforcement activity but the fines and prosecutions are so minimal that they do not create a level of deterrence. As he puts it, "enforcement in China does not create fear in counterfeiters."

One author's conversation with a Chinese Customs official reveals the attitude which has been prevalent in China. The official restated the opposition of the Chinese government toward fraudulent product, while acknowledging that many industries discourage "government interference." (It should be noted that Mertha (2005) identifies the word interference as a euphemism for effective enforcement). The official also noted that "it is unrealistic to expect the average citizen to think about the illegality of products" (Name Withheld, personal communication).

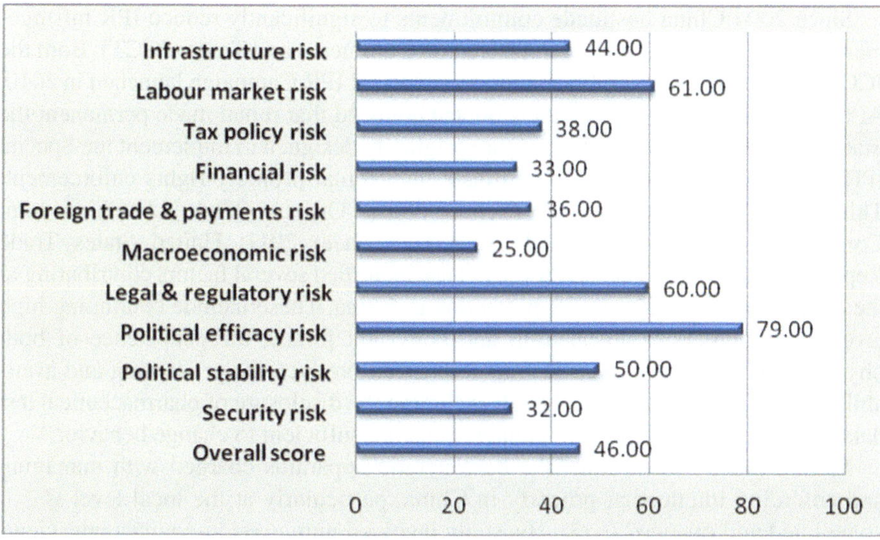

Fig. 9.7 Business operations risk in China. *Source*: *The Economist Intelligence Unit*, (2012)

The national government seems to launch one program after another to put a stop to piracy. In November 2011 the Ministry of Public Security announced the results of a "national crackdown on counterfeit goods" (Di 2011). They claimed they had uncovered nearly 29,000 cases of IPR infringement, that they had raided 22,000 production centers and taken down nearly 7,000 criminal gangs with a total value of nearly $3 million. In May 2012, The General Office of the State Council announced a new "IPR Protection, Anti-Counterfeiting Agenda" (PRC Central Government 2012). This agenda includes campaigns focused on trademark rights, copyrights, patents and online websites with a special emphasis on counterfeit foods, cosmetics, medicines, chemicals, and auto parts. Over the past years at least seven campaigns such as Mountain Eagle, Sunshine, and Blue Sky were launched. As long ago as the mid-1990s a campaign called "Strike Down Fakes" was started. Local offices were established using personnel from the Administration for Industry and Commerce (AIC) and the Quality Technical Supervision Bureau (QTSB). Because of inter-agency conflict the system was ordered to be dismantled in 1998 but Mertha (2005) found that offices related to this effort still existed at the national and local level as of 2003. Operation Blue Sky was designed to help companies at trade fairs. The government has designated a week in April of each year to stress the importance of enforcing patents and copyrights (US Chamber of Commerce 2007). In the past pirate factories were related to the Ministry of Electronics Industry and the People's Liberation Army (PLA) although interviews conducted by Mertha (2005) indicate that the press had overstated the role of the military. *The Economist* (2007) reported that by the late 1990s, the central government had changed its view about the PLA being involved in business. They were asked to give over these enterprises to civilians and the government made up for it by increasing budgets for the PLA.

Since 2004 China has made commitments to significantly reduce IPR infringement at the US–China Joint Commission on Commerce and Trade (JCCT). Both the JCCT and the USTR favorably mention the Special IPR Campaign launched in 2010. At the most recent JCCT meeting China announced that it had made permanent the State Council-level leadership structure originally designed to implement the Special IPR Campaign to continue to coordinate intellectual property rights enforcement. This group is chaired by Vice Premier Wang Qishan (22nd U.S.-China Joint Commission on Commerce and Trade Fact Sheet 2011; United States Trade Representative 2012). The USTR (2012) has identified several factors contributing to the continuing challenge to IPR protection in China. These include continuing high levels of trademark counterfeiting and copyright piracy, the persistence of both physical and Internet markets selling counterfeit product, the production and availability of counterfeit pharmaceuticals including the disclosure of pharmaceutical test data, and the failure to impose "penalties that are sufficient to change behavior."

Mertha (2005) states that "the bureaucratic apparatus charged with managing and enforcing intellectual property in China, particularly at the local level is . . . convoluted and opaque" (p. 3). His study involved numerous in-country interviews with various Chinese sources over a period of 5 years. Mertha makes a clear division between enforcement of copyrights and patents and trademarks. The success realized in each of these areas varies considerably partly because of the independence of the particular bureaucracy charged with enforcement and therefore its reliance on a superior agency for personnel and budgets. In his opinion, success is also related to the level of external pressure from foreign governments and companies and the competition of particular bureaucracies with each other. The Chinese bureaucracies charged with implementing intellectual property policy are an excellent example of "fragmented authoritarianism," meaning that authority below the top of the Chinese political system is disjointed. Mertha identifies two dimensions of fragmentation—functional and geographic differences separating agencies. These differences allow agencies to effectively veto the implementation process.

An example of this fragmentation is described by Mertha (2005) and augmented by Chang (2012): the State Intellectual Property Office (SIPO), a bureaucracy established specifically to manage patent protection was assigned to coordinate all IP protection. Mertha states, "In reality SIPO is an organization largely adrift and often disconnected from the actual institutional and political arena in which . . . IPR protection and enforcement in China take place." Its predecessor was the China Patent Bureau, established in 1980. This agency was moved from one "host" organization to another over 13 years. While its technical abilities developed, it had no real political power. Eventually it was renamed SIPO but its political abilities remained relatively weak. In addition the relationships between the local patent bureaus and the national government agency create another level of confusion, as can be seen clearly in Fig. 9.8.

Although SIPO was to be the agency coordinating all intellectual property, the State Administration for Industry and Commerce (SAIC) is the national bureaucracy which manages the Trademark Office. According to Mertha (2005), the Trademark Office is "a cash cow for the SAIC" and therefore is highly resistant to a merger of that office into SIPO. The National Copyright Administration (NCA)

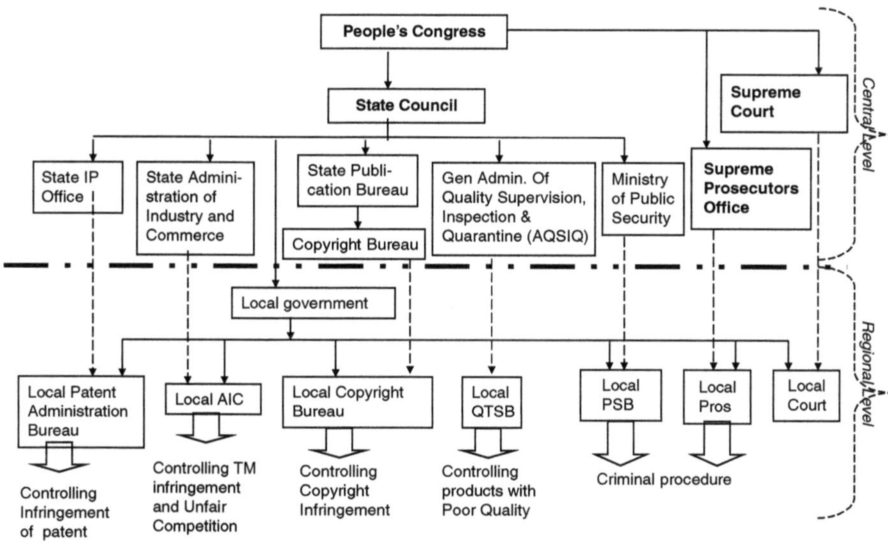

Fig. 9.8 IP Enforcement in China. Adapted from Tabata (2003)

also had not been moved under SIPO because of concerns about culture and propaganda. In the end, one of Mertha's interviews called SIPO "the Patent Bureau with a different name."

While the national SAIC and the local AICs are responsible for registering and enforcing trademarks, at the local level, the AICs are branches of local governments. They invest in creating markets, issue licenses to businesses, and collect management fees from proprietors. This puts the AIC in a compromised position with counterfeiters from whom they are collecting large fees (Kearney and Inc 2005). In a study of the Chinese counterfeit DVD market, Wang (2010) agrees concluding that many local officials, while responsible for both regulation of IP laws and developing entrepreneurship, are under "tremendous pressure to produce significant economic development" results so they resist strong enforcement of IP regulations. Although the AIC is responsible for trademark enforcement, a competing agency, QTSB, saw an opportunity to expand its influence where the AICs were not vigorously protecting trademarks. The QTSB is formally responsible for product quality and consumer protection. But it has expanded its mandate by identifying counterfeit product as potentially harmful to consumers. The QTSB's actions prodded the local AICs to take on more vigorous enforcement against pirates (Mertha 2005). The QTSB is a bureau of the AQSIQ (General Administration of Quality Supervision, Inspection and Quarantine) who have a specific mandate to fight counterfeit goods (Zhao and Graham 2006). The complex arrangements for IP enforcement are shown in Fig. 9.8 above. Note that the local bureaus report directly to provincial and regional governments while receiving direction from the national agencies (dotted-line relationships).

Effective Firm Action in China

Successful foreign companies have established alliances with various enforcement agencies on the local level. They have also used private investigation agencies and law firms who establish good relationships with particular local AIC or QTSB officials. Some of these agencies are foreign and others are Chinese owned. In fact some of them are essentially state owned or closely aligned with governmental agencies. One company includes on its staff former members of the Public Security Bureau, the AIC, and the China Patent Bureau. Trademark agents also play an important role in fighting piracy by filling out a complaint letter which is similar to a search warrant in the United States. Because foreign firms can afford to pay larger fees than Chinese firms, much of the enforcement action is on behalf of these foreign IP holders. Mertha (2005) describes an anticounterfeiting raid in which he was an eyewitness. This involved private investigators as well as AIC agents. After the raid the "sponsor" bought everyone dinner and an evening at a karaoke place. Mertha concludes that although enforcement actions are often quite different, common elements are important for success. First, private investigators lay the groundwork and absorb the costs while the officials provide authority and take credit for the raids. Second, either direct or indirect payments are expected as well as a symbolic giving of "face." This would be accomplished by publicly recognizing the important role of the official(s) in any actions taken. (In the Chinese culture the concept of "face" is quite important. Generally this means looking good, or not being humiliated, in the eyes of others. To give face at the simplest level would be to politely agree with someone publicly even if privately one disagrees. At a higher level it would require more effort. The more difficulties one need overcome to honor another person, the more face is given to that other person.) (Jieming 2004). Discussions with Chang (2011) reinforce this point. The strategy of the QBPC has been to "share the honor" for putting a stop to counterfeit trade by focusing on cooperation with local law enforcement. Chang believes using both honor and shame will be effective in motivating officials to move against counterfeiters.

According to Pfizer's Director of Global Security, the company works on many levels to protect its intellectual property rights. In addition to engaging law enforcement, Pfizer organized roundtable discussions and seminars with Chinese ministries to exchange information and experience related to fighting drug pirates (Schwarz and Wong 2006).

Mertha (2005) concludes that top-down pressure on the national government can help to change policy but this must be combined with what he calls lateral pressure focused on the local level to improve enforcement. Chang (2011) feels that many top officials in China want to stop counterfeiting but must rely on local law enforcement to carry out the work in the field. A number of these individuals are interested in reducing counterfeiting while some have other priorities. In some cases actions taken at the international level by the US government result in counterproductive ramifications at the local level. For instance the recent WTO disputes brought by the US government may have had the effect of raising nationalistic feelings and reducing local cooperation. Alford (1995) advises that one must take into account the political culture in order to understand the difficulties of developing effective intellectual property law in China. He describes the difficulties in "efforts to graft limbs grown in one setting onto trunks that have matured in another."

Some firms are trying new tactics. Chanel filed a lawsuit in Las Vegas against a counterfeiter in China for selling fake goods in the United States via the Internet. Following a judge's ruling that defendants could be served notice by e-mail, the firm filed another lawsuit against nearly 400 websites, many based in China. Similar cases have also been filed in federal court in Las Vegas by Tiffany and Louis Vuitton. The suits request orders to disable or seize website domain names such as chanelOnline.com, replica-coco-lv.com, tiffanyand-co.com, and chanelhandbags-outlet.net which sound similar to the legitimate corporate names (Ritter 2011).

Another novel approach has been taken by Gucci and Tiffany. These firms have petitioned in federal court to freeze assets of counterfeiters in Chinese banks. Each of the Chinese banks has branches in New York. This followed a judgment against counterfeiters which enabled the designers to recover damages from the counterfeiters. The firms face an uphill battle since the Federal Reserve Bank of New York fears this kind of judgment might drive foreign banks out of the country (Reuters 2011).

Recent Events

The Chinese themselves are beginning to put pressure on the government to improve IP enforcement. In 2011 China filed more patents than any other country surpassing both the United States and Japan (Maleske 2012). And according to the *Economist* (Chinese consumers are falling out of love with fakes 2012) a recent study by consulting firm Bain reveals that demand for counterfeit luxury products is decreasing. The *Economist* also reports that McKinsey has found the proportion of consumers willing to buy fake jewelry dropped from 31% in 2008 to 12% in 2011. More indigenous manufacturers have their own intellectual property to protect. Firms like Lenovo and Haier as well as other innovators are putting pressure on the government to enforce anti-pirating laws. Most recently General Electric, Philips, and Panasonic working with Chinese Customs and various provincial police forces successfully put a stop to counterfeit lighting being sold to Africa. The entire counterfeit production network was arrested and the ringleader received a sentence of more than 5 years. Suppliers of packaging and labels were also arrested and prosecuted (Chang 2012). Despite what the USTR calls "welcome progress" including completion of the accession to the WIPO Internet treaties, China remains on the USTR (2012) Priority Watch List.

In February 2012 an ABC television report (Jackson 2012) identified China as a major source of fake antimalaria drugs such as artemisinin. Tablets with low levels of the active drug have increased drug resistance and even caused the deaths of some patients while also reducing confidence in the legitimate drugs. A few years ago, the Chinese government took drastic action against one individual, Zheng Xiaoyu, former head of the State Food and Drug Administration. Xiaoyu was executed for taking bribes to approve untested medicine. Despite this draconian measure, the Chinese face daunting problems in regulating the safety of products, and struggle to enforce intellectual property rights. As we have seen, many different bureaucracies have been given responsibility for intellectual property. In the food and drug area alone, the Ministry of Health, the Ministry of Agriculture, the State Administration of Industry and Commerce, and the AQSIQ all have some role. Since each distinct government agency wishes to collect license fees and fines to supplement their budgets, inspectors are tempted to accept bribes to ignore violations (Kahn 2007a, b; Castle 2007; Barboza 2007).

In September 2007, the US government requested a WTO panel to hear a case related to "specific deficiencies in China's legal regime for protecting and enforcing copyrights and trademarks" (United States Trade Representative 2007b). This followed 3 years of bilateral discussions and formal WTO consultations. In March 2009, after nearly 2 years of deliberation, the Panel failed to support the US claims "that the criminal thresholds [for product counterfeiting] are inconsistent with China's obligations under . . . Article 61 of the TRIPS agreement." The Panel did conclude that China's copyright law is inconsistent with the Berne Convention and the TRIPS agreement and recommended that China bring this law into conformity. The Panel also found that China's practice of removing trademarks and selling pirated goods into markets violated the TRIPS agreement and that changes should be made in Customs measures to prevent this. China has since completed all required legislative changes to implement the WTO's rulings (WTO 2012).

The Economist Intelligence Unit (2006) reemphasized the point that at the state level China's government seems to be aware of the importance of solving the piracy problem since this issue could have a negative effect on trade relations or investment. But "as is the case with so many problems in China, the farther you get from Beijing the more difficult it is to police." On the other hand The QBPC recently asked its members about the current state of IP enforcement. More than 80% said the level of cooperation and administrative and criminal effectiveness of administrative and police agencies as well as intelligence sharing between enforcement agencies had improved somewhat or significantly (Quality Brands Protection Committee (QBPC) 2012). One important change made recently is that the coordination function for intellectual property protection has been given to the Commerce Ministry as opposed to SIPO (Chang 2012).

Alford (1995) takes the broadest view of the problem. He believes the political culture in China is the greatest barrier to the growth of effective intellectual property protection. He explains that political liberalization and a greater commitment to "a rights-based legality" are needed to produce better IP protection. He recognizes that this is a difficult problem because political culture includes values and practices that are central to a nation's identity. Foreigners should not assume they have the capacity to change these values and practices. In short he believes that improve-

Fig. 9.9 State Intellectual Property Office of the PRC. *Source*: http://english.sipo.gov.cn/

ments in the protection of basic civil and political rights are a necessary precursor to improvements in protection of property rights.

Information Sources

The US government, while extolling the outstanding growth of the Chinese economy and the opportunities in China, cites legal issues, especially IP infringement, as "a particularly damaging issue for many American companies" (http://www.export.gov 2011). This country report provides a separate section on "Protecting Your Intellectual Property Rights in China" and links to all the important agencies that have jurisdiction over patents, trademarks, and copyrights.

The SIPO of the PRC has an English version of its website as illustrated in Fig. 9.9. This websites lists current events, such as the 2012 US–China Intellectual Property Adjudication Conference held in Beijing on June 19, 2012 where David Kappos, Director of the U.S. Patent and Trademark Office, and Tian Lipu, SIPO Commission, addressed the opening ceremony. Tian focused on the New Tendency of China Patent System in his recent speech (sipo.gov.cn 2012).

Figure 9.10 is the homepage for the US Embassy information related to IPR for China and can help the manager navigate several of the salient issues related to IP infringement. The site provides an excellent overview of conditions in China and enforcement mechanisms.

Fig. 9.10 Embassy of the US information on IPR in China. *Source*: http://beijing.usembassy-china.org.cn/ipr.html

Conclusions

The problem of counterfeit goods originating in China continues to be a major concern for both managers and government officials. That China is the main global source of counterfeit goods is beyond dispute. The total of this counterfeit production and distribution is not clear but the value may easily be over $150 billion annually. Products counterfeited in China range from motion pictures to pharmaceuticals to cigarettes, including nearly every industrial and consumer product.

Looking at Chinese history explains the reasons for the difficulties both governments and manufacturers have encountered in trying to establish effective IPR protection. Traditional Chinese beliefs about the ownership of inventions and the need for controlling information from the earliest days of the nation through Mao's regime yield valuable insights. After more than 100 years and constant pressure from foreign governments, Chinese laws related to copyright, trademarks, and patents are acceptable but enforcement continues to leave much to be desired. China's arcane bureaucracy makes it difficult even to understand how IPR laws are to be enforced. Despite nearly constant national antipiracy campaigns, functional and geographic fragmentation, protection of revenue sources at the local level and outright corruption allows most of the counterfeit industry to stay in place. It remains to be seen whether the new efforts headed by high-level officials will change the trajectory of IPR enforcement.

To many, intellectual property remains a foreign concept in China. It seems the best course for managers includes establishing alliances with local enforcement agencies, using private investigation agencies or law firms while keeping pressure on at the national and international level. While there are many hopeful signs, it may be that real change in China will not happen until there are major changes in the overall approach to individual rights.

Chapter 10
Internet Piracy: The Virtual Marketplace for Counterfeit Goods

Introduction

Managers need to monitor several trends to protect their firm's intellectual property on the Internet. In this chapter, we report global growth of Internet penetration rates and highlight piracy in both the motion picture and software industries that include ethical perceptions of this illicit behavior. We show that pirates on the virtual sea can be very sophisticated. One formidable opponents, is the warez group. Various stakeholders create the supply and demand for fake goods by way of a pyramid of Internet piracy. We provide a synopsis of the recent US government sting operations conducted with the assistance of other countries to target Internet piracy. Finally, we address the problem of educating the consumer that obtaining music, software, movies, and the like without compensation is *unethical*. This is a key issue in terms of decreasing the demand for counterfeit goods in the virtual marketplace where a consumer can exhibit more rogue behavior with a limited fear of prosecution (Chaudhry et al. 2011a, b). As discussed in Chap. 6, social marketing tactics have been employed by both the Motion Picture Association of America (MPAA) and the Business Software Alliance (BSA) to educate the consumer about fake products.

The Growth of Counterfeits in the Virtual Marketplace

As reported in Chap. 2, the problem of counterfeit trade is growing and the seizure statistics for the infringement of IPR reveals a change in total domestic value of goods from $45.3 million in 2000 to $178.3 in 2011 (U.S. Customs and Border Protection 2011). However, this data collected by the U.S. Customs and Border Protection represents *physical goods* seized at some port of entry into the United States. Thus, the problem of counterfeit trade in a virtual marketplace, such as Internet auctions on eBay, commercial websites, peer-to-peer (P2P) downloading, and video streaming is an activity that cannot be measured accurately, if at all, but

P. Chaudhry and A. Zimmerman, *Protecting Your Intellectual Property Rights*, Management for Professionals, DOI 10.1007/978-1-4614-5568-4_10,

one that many industry associations claim is growing, especially with Internet penetration expanding in many global markets.

In 2011, the Internet World Stats estimates that there are 2,267,233,742 Internet consumers in the world (www.internetworldstats.com). This site categorizes regions by Internet penetration rates as a percent of total population. Figure 10.1 illustrates the divergent penetration rates by region, with a world market Internet penetration rate at 32.7%.

It was telling to observe that increased measures to enforce IP for manufacturers of goods and services on the Internet, through the proposed Stop Online Piracy Act (SOPA) engendered massive protests from consumers and was abandoned by policymakers as a result of this controversy (Pignal 2012). Figure 10.2 is just one example of the "blackout" that occurred across the Internet on January 18, 2012 at Wikipedia (and other sites, such as Google) that inflamed consumer fears about Internet censorship. Schatz (2012) describes the rationale behind adversaries to this new enforcement (Schatz 2012, p. 9):

> Opponents of the legislation worry that the language in the House bill [SOPA] is so broad that it would allow content owners to target U.S. websites that aren't knowingly hosting pirated content. This has been a particular concern of bill opponents Facebook, Wikipedia and Twitter, all of which have sites that depend heavily on content uploaded by users.

The BSA, an initial advocate of SOPA, pulled its support of the pending legislation since the President and CEO, Robert Holleyman, indicated on his blog that "Due process, free speech, and privacy are rights that cannot be compromised. And the security of networks and communications is indispensable to a thriving Internet economy. Some observers have raised reasonable questions about whether certain SOPA provisions might have unintended consequences in these areas" (Baker 2011, p. 4).

Buzzeo, focusing on counterfeit pharmaceuticals reports the success of the U.S. Drug Enforcement Administration sting operation, Operation Cyber Chase, that shut down 200 illegal e-pharmacies associated with a sophisticated black market industry (Buzzeo 2005). A few years ago, 11 persons were indicted on the premise of their involvement in an Atlanta-based generic drug scam on the Internet. This recent case is testimony to the fact that many consumers can "unknowingly" purchase counterfeit via the web. Indeed, in this situation, the customers actually thought they were purchasing prescription drugs such as Ambien, Xanax, and Viagra, by way of a Canadian firm on the Internet. However, according to the indictment, the entire operation began in 2002 by Jared Wheat, principal owner of Hi-Tech Pharmaceuticals, who lured Internet customers through "spam." The drugs were allegedly manufactured in unsafe conditions in a house in Belize (United States Department of Justice 2006b).

In March 2012, *The Wall Street Journal* reported the problem of a counterfeit cancer-treating drug, Avastin, distributed by way of Canadian online pharmacies, which had a trade route that, "illustrated the circuitous path that pharmaceuticals can take before reaching consumers. Wherever the counterfeit Avastin was manufactured—possibly China—investigators are examining a zigzagging route that may have taken the product through Turkey and Egypt before it was sold to Swiss and

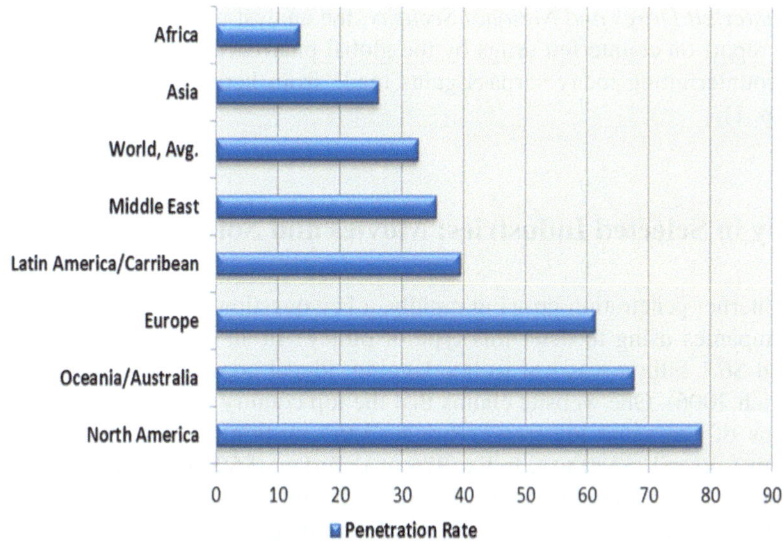

Fig. 10.1 World Internet Penetration Rates by Geographic Region, 2011. *Source*: Adapted from www.internetworldstats.com/stats.htm

Fig. 10.2 Wikipedia blackout protests SOPA. *Source*: http://abcnews.go.com/blogs/technology/2012/01/sopa-blackout-wikipedia-google-wired-join-protest-against-internet-censorship/

Danish wholesalers and then to Mr. Haughton's [a Canadian citizen] UK wholesaler, River East Supplies Ltd…." (Weaver, Whalen and Faucon, p. 9).

Overall, the increase in fake drugs is a result of large profit potential, anonymous distribution channels by way of the Internet, and price sensitive consumer demand.

In *Counterfeit Drugs and National Security*, the analyst reports, "[A]ccording to a recent report on counterfeit drugs by the global pharmaceutical firm Pfizer, profits from counterfeiting today surpass gains made from heroin and cocaine" (Finlay 2011, p. 1).

Piracy in Selected Industries: Movies and Software

With Internet penetration growing rapidly, a key question becomes what strategies are companies using to deter this type of piracy? In an earlier study, the MPAA claimed $6.1 billion was lost to bootlegging, illegal copying, and Internet piracy (Horwich 2006). One website claims that the top country markets for video piracy in terms of estimated losses are Russia ($250 million), China ($168 m.), Italy ($140 m.), Brazil ($120 m.), India ($75 m.), Turkey ($50 m.), Malaysia ($42 m.), Taiwan ($42 m.), Columbia ($40 m.), and Saudi Arabia ($40 m.) (Top Ten Countries with Highest Video Piracy 2012). TorrentFreak boasts the "Top Ten Most Pirated Movies of 2011" (see Table 10.1) by reporting the number of illegal downloads at its website with the byline of "The place where breaking news, Bit Torrent and copyright collide."

The TorrentFreak website even explains its data collection methods to be a list compiled from several thousands of Bit Torrent trackers in a variety of release formats that include "cammed versions" of the movies. Even trends are reported. The top pirated movie of 2010, Avatar, had at least 16 million illegal downloads as compared to Fast Five in 2011 at 9.2 million.

The MPAA's "pyramid of Internet piracy" illustrates a smaller number of suppliers (e.g., camcorder theft of movies in theaters) and other release groups (e.g., pirated movies posted at topsites) at the top of the pyramid that supply facilitators (e.g., search engines) in the middle of the pyramid that ultimately channel into numerous file-sharing/downloading of people at the bottom of the pyramid (MPAA explains pyramid of Internet piracy 2006). The MPAA says that there are a variety of means to perform content theft that include (Types of Content Theft n.d.): camcorders in theaters; P2P; streaming (watching unauthorized copyrighted movies and/or television online); optical disc (hard copy "bootlegs"), theatrical print (stealing a film from a theater, courier service, etc., to make illegal copies); screener (illegal copies are made of advanced previews used for marketing purposes); signal (obtaining content through unauthorized satellite signals); broadcast (unauthorized on-air broadcasting of films/television); and viewing illegal public performances.

The BSA claims that the demand for pirated computer software will go up or down as a function of consumer education, law enforcement, the number of new users coming into the market, the ease of access to pirated software, and external factors such as political conditions (www.bsa.org). The industry alliance says culture, institutional effectiveness, and even geography having an impact on the abilities of countries to reduce piracy (www.bsa.org). Overall, the BSA forecasts that the

Table 10.1 Most downloaded movies on bit torrent, 2011

Rank	Movie	Downloads	Worldwide grosses ($)
1	Fast Five	9,260,000	626,137,675
2	The Hangover II	8,840,000	581,464,305
3	Thor	8,330,000	449,326,618
4	Source Code	7,910,000	123,278,618
5	I Am Number Four	7,670,000	144,500,437
6	Sucker Punch	7,200,000	89,792,502
7	127 Hours	6,910,000	60,738,797
8	Rango	6,480,000	245,155,348
9	The King's Speech	6,250,000	414,211,549
10	Harry Potter and the Deathly Hallows Part 2	6,030,000	1,328,111,219

Source: Adapted from http://torrentfreak.com/top-10-most-pirated-movies-of-2011-111223/

increased use of the Internet, the proliferation of P2P networks, and the growth of broadband access will increase software piracy rates, especially in emerging markets, such as China, India, and Russia.

The problem of software piracy continues and Table 10.2 clearly shows that significant markets are affected by large piracy rates, such as China. The BSA determines the values in Table 10.2 by estimating how much packaged software was used in 2010 and comparing this figure with how much packaged software was paid for in 2010 to formulate piracy rates for each country. The BSA cautions that some of the lower software piracy rates in the United States, Germany, the UK, and Japan are misleading since these are large markets for software vendors and losing a 19% share to pirates in the United States results in an estimated $9.773 billion commercial loss of business in 2011 (Business Software Alliance 2012, p. 1). Thus, a more accurate way of determining the significance of piracy is to estimate the lost revenues per market. In addition, the BSA *2010 Piracy Impact Study: The Economic Benefits of Reducing Software Piracy* assert that in the 42 countries that comprise 93% of the PC software market, that (p. 1):

> [R]educing the piracy rate for PC software by 10 percentage points in four years would create $142 billion in new economic activity – more than 80 percent accruing in local industries – while adding nearly 500,000 new high-tech jobs and generating roughly $32 billion in new tax revenues.

Table 10.2 clearly reveals that no country, whether developed or developing, is immune to consumer demand for pirated software. The country effects of consumer demand for counterfeit software is a result of many factors that include the strength of intellectual property right protection, the supply of counterfeits, and cultural differences that affect demand of the fake goods. This report also indicates that a manager must not generalize a country's piracy rate since the incidence of piracy can vary by city, region, or industry within each national market.

We cannot conclude this section without a note on the difficulties presented in collecting precise statistics on this clandestine activity. There are several blogs on the Internet that claim that these statistics have been over exaggerated by various constituents, such as the MPAA, in order to effectively lobby legislators to protect

Table 10.2 Top 10 economies in commercial value of pirated PC software, 2011

	Pirated value ($M)	Legal sales ($M)	Piracy rate (%)
US	9,773	41,664	19
China	8,902	2,659	77
Russia	3,277	1,895	53
India	2,930	1,721	63
Brazil	2,848	2,526	53
France	2,754	4,689	37
Germany	2,265	6,447	26
Italy	1,945	2,107	48
UK	1,943	5,530	26
Japan	1,875	7,054	21

Source: Adapted from *Shadow Market*, 2011 BSA Global Software Piracy Study, Ninth edition, May 2012, p. 1

their intellectual property. A debate on the accuracy of the various methods used to calculate counterfeit trade is beyond the scope of this chapter. However, an awareness of the inaccuracies involved in guesstimating the size of the problem is necessary.

Ethical Perceptions of Internet Piracy

Figure 10.3 shows that a study of 1,644 youth conducted for the BSA by Harris Interactive found that young people clearly viewed downloading music in cyberspace without payment (60%) less harmful than stealing from a store (92%).

The Vice-President of Public Affairs for the BSA, Diane Smiroldo, states that "[T]he discrepancy among youth in their decision-making between the real world from the online world indicates an unrealistic view of the consequences of cyberspace. It underscores how important it is for parents and teachers to educate the new generation of cybercitizens about good ethical conduct and the proper use of resources in the digital world" (www.bsa.org). Table 10.3 reveals the high level of consumer complicity to download music, games, and the like without paying for the product.

As previously discussed in Chaps. 5 and 6, companies are struggling with an effective way to decrease Internet piracy since the consumer demonstrates more rogue behavior and erroneously misjudges his or her ability to be punished for this type of intellectual property theft (Chaudhry et al. 2011a, b). As outlined in Chap. 8, the RIAA, the MPAA, and the IFPI have developed social marketing communications to target consumers who are at the bottom of the Internet piracy pyramid.

Pirates on the Virtual Sea

It is well known that common distribution channels for items such as fake clothes and accessories are street peddlers, flea market vendors, "fake purse parties," and discount outlets. However, the virtual marketplace offers an even more lucrative distri-

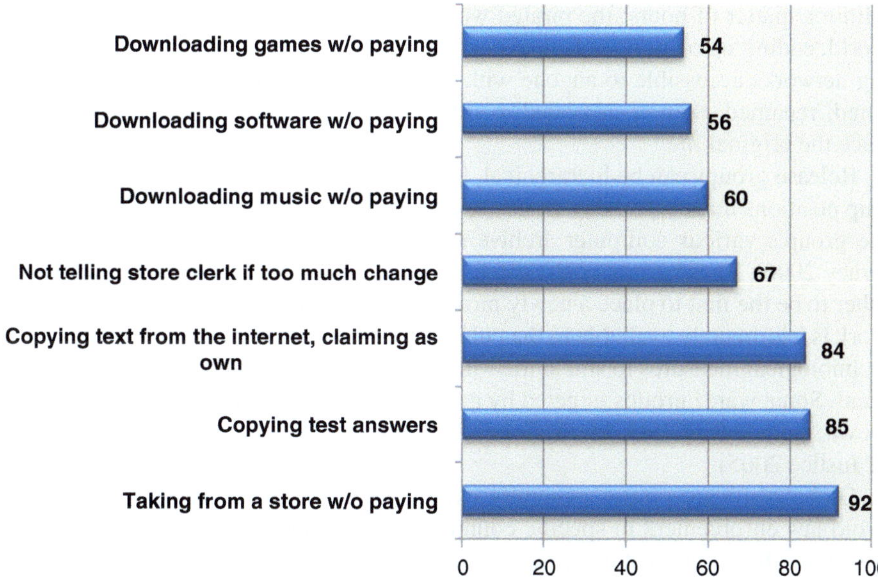

Fig. 10.3 Percentage of youth who report the following activities as "always wrong." *Source*: www.bsa.org

Table 10.3 Propensity to download without paying for the good

"What have you ever downloaded without paying for it?"	% of all youth	% of 8–9 year olds	% of 10–12 year olds	% of 13–15 year olds	% of 16–18 year olds
Music	32	9	21	39	52
Games	25	22	23	27	27
Software	14	3	7	18	24
Movies	10	1	3	11	21
None of these	57	75	68	52	41

Source: Adapted from www.cybertreehouse.com and www.bsa.org

bution channel for fake goods. In this section, we discuss the warez community that has fed illegal content on the web, various Internet sites, and video streaming.

The Warez Scene

Warez is a generic term used to describe software that has been stripped of its copyright protection and placed on the Internet for downloading *without* financial compensation. Members of this illicit group can be the first-providers—the original source for the illegal trading and online distribution of pirated works. Once a release group prepares a stolen work for distribution, the material is distributed in minutes to secure, top-level servers and made available to a select clientele. From there, within a matter of hours, the pirated works are illegally distributed throughout the world, ending up on public channels on IRC (Internet relay chat) and P2P file sharing networks accessible to anyone with Internet access. Since one release is duplicated, renamed, then re-uploaded to different sites, it can become impossible to trace the original file.

Release groups can be hierarchical, highly structured organizations with leadership positions that control day-to-day operations, recruit new members, and manage the group's various computer archive sites (MPAA explains pyramid of Internet piracy 2006). These groups exist solely to engage in piracy and compete with each other to be the first to place a newly pirated work onto the Internet, often before the work is legitimately available to the public. The groups employ highly sophisticated technological measures to shield their illegal activity from victims and law enforcement. Some warez groups targeted by government-led sting operations, such as Site Down, include RiSCISO, Myth, Goodfellaz, and the like (United States Department of Justice 2005).

Global software pirates generally exploit the national nature of copyrights to avoid law enforcement in specific countries. The production and/or distribution of warez are illegal in most countries. Developed countries have loopholes in legislation that allow the warez to continue. Moreover, it is typically overlooked in poorer developing countries with weak or nonexistent IP protection.

Internet Sites

A virtual counterfeit shopping environment is readily available on the Internet. Luxury Replica (http://luxuryreplica.net/), an online seller that claims to be the "largest online retailer of Replica watches with Free Shipping" blatantly offers consumers replica Rolex, Cartier, and other iconic brand name watches. The Luxury Replica website even provides customer satisfaction reviews, such as "If you are looking for a well-made, high quality watch…look no further. This website is amazing. I am very pleased. It is definitely a watch that will attract attention. It is a work of art." (posted by Jonathan A. of Tennessee, USA). Figure 10.4 shows a screen shot of a search for Rolex watches [239 available on June 16, 2012].

The Pirate Bay (PirateBay.org) in Sweden has also drawn media attention as this site provides a "Bit Torrent tracker" directory of music, movies, college textbooks, and the like to augment copyright infringement by giving the information for the buyer/seller exchange.

Figure 10.5 is a screen shot of the infamous website that allows consumers to perform specific searches of audio, video, applications, and games.

In February 2008, the Swedish government sought legal prosecution of the four men associated with Pirate Bay: Frederik Neij, Gottfrid Svartholm Warg, Carl Lundstrom, and Peter Sunde (Pfanner 2008). The initial legal battle was decided in April of 2009 and each of the four defendants were sentenced to 1 year in jail and

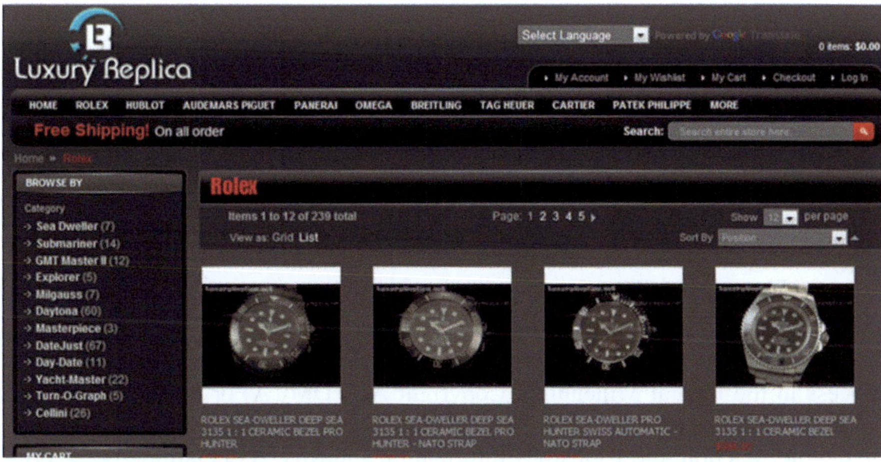

Fig. 10.4 Rolex watches available at Luxury Replica. *Source*: http://luxuryreplica.net/

Fig. 10.5 The Pirate Bay. *Source*: http://thepirateBay.se/

$4.5 million in damages to be paid to such companies as Warner Brothers, Sony Music Entertainment, EMI, and Columbia Pictures. On the day of the verdict, the BBC News quoted Peter Sunde as follows (Court jails Pirate Bay founders 2009, April 17, pp. 7–8):

> It's so bizarre that we were convicted at all and it's even more bizarre that we were [convicted] as a team. The court said we were organized. I can't get Gottfrid out of bed in the morning. If you're going to convict us, convict us of disorganized crime. We can't pay and we wouldn't pay. Even if I had the money I would rather burn everything I owned, and I wouldn't even give them the ashes.

The Guardian in the UK later reported that the Pirate Bay defendants had lost their appeal with an ironic outcome: the prison sentences had been reduced to between 4 and 10 months, but their fines had increased to $6.5 million (Halliday 2010).

Industry watchdogs, such as the Software Information Industry Association (www.siia.net), are constantly "trolling" Internet auction sites, such as eBay and Yahoo! to detect pirates and, for example, can use the "notice-and-takedown" process in the Digital Millennium Copyright Act (DMCA) or the Verified Rights Owner (VeRO) program in eBay to slow the growth of software piracy at this type of Internet auction site (Software Information Industry Association 2005). eBay boasts that over 10,000 firms and individuals in such sectors as software, video games, music, and luxury goods protect their intellectual property through its VeRO program (http://pages.eBay.co.uk/vero/about.html). eBay lists the benefits of joining this program as (About Vero 2012, p. 4):

- Dedicated eBay staff to assist you in getting the most out of the program.
- Rapid response by eBay in ending listings reported by you as allegedly infringing, pursuant to the VeRO program notice of infringement.
- Dedicated priority email queues for reporting alleged infringements.
- The ability to obtain identifying information about eBay users.
- eBay member rights and privileges as described in the eBay User Agreement.
- Automatic updates on new benefits available under the program.

A quick perusal of the apparel sector companies that are participants in this program reveals the following firms—Abercrombie & Fitch, Burberry Limited, Hermès, Kate Spade, and Vera Bradley, to just name a few (http://pages.eBay.co.uk/vero/participants-apparel.html).

The virtual distribution channel is obviously a problem, but it also represents a *legitimate* way to do business. Some articles refer to the metamorphosis of a legal distribution channel in the music industry to the *Steve Jobs Effect.* In other words, a new product, the iPod, created a consumer market to buy authentic music over the Internet. As early as 2006, a *Business Week* article reported on the push of Hollywood to offset declining DVD sales and Internet piracy through Movielink, owned by five movie studios and CinemaNow, that distributes films from Sony, MGM, and Lionsgate only. These two services released movies at the same time as their DVDs were available at Wal-Mart and Blockbuster thus creating a virtual distribution channel. The downloaded movies were kept on PCs, but using digital rights management (DRM) techniques, the consumer was not able to burn and copy to use in another device, such as a DVD player (Grover 2006). The download restriction was to provide a different type of competition to the DVD market available through traditional outlets such as Wal-Mart. Six years ago, this type of service questioned the future validity of pay-for-TV services, like HBO or Showtime that rely on timing of releases to maintain their customer.

Video Streaming

Today, the rise of video streaming through sites such as Netflix shows that the changing technology did shift consumer demand for digital entertainment. In the first edition of this book, we speculated whether copyright holders in the movie/television industries would start to compete with the pirates on price. In the fall of 2011, the media on the web was picking up on this idea with statements, such as, "Netflix is doing its job to reduce piracy in North America" (Wong 2011). The study that stimulated the buzz in the Internet media was the *Global Internet Phenomena Report* since the analysts at Sandvine found that the "four largest Internet services on North America's fixed access networks, by daily downstream volume," are (1) Netflix (27%); (2) HFTP (17.8%); (3) YouTube (10%); and (4) Bit Torrent (9%) (Sandvine 2011, p. 1). Analysts at Sandvine also suggest that the North American market is now in its "post-PC era" with the majority (55%) of "real-time entertainment" traffic channeled through fixed-access networks stemming from game consoles, set-top boxes, smart TVs, tablets, and mobile devices (Sandvine 2011, p. 1).

As expected, the pirates are keeping up with the technology and several websites offer illegal video streaming of digital content. In June 2012, a German court sentenced 39-year-old "Dirk B." to 4.5 years in jail and a $4.7 million fine for an alleged 1.1 million incidents of copyright infringement at his website, www.Kino.to that was alleged to earn $8 million in advertising revenues (Epstein 2012). The US government is also pursuing these illegal websites, and shortly before the February 2012 Super Bowl, the Immigration Customs and Enforcement agency (ICE) seized sites that were allegedly streaming sports events: Firstrowsports.tv, Firstrowsports.com, and Soccertvilive.net (Santo 2012). Visiting one of these sites, one will see the ICE/DOJ/DHS banner as illustrated in Fig. 10.6.

US Government: Led Sting Operations to Curb Internet Piracy

The former U.S. Attorney General, Alberto R. Gonzales, cautioned that the Department of Justice would be combating the top of the Internet piracy pyramid in an effort to dismantle these networks that feed the supply chain of illegal digital content on the web. In his statement, he boldly stated that "we have shown that law enforcement can and will find—and we will prosecute—those who try to use the Internet to create piracy networks beyond the reach of law" (United States Department of Justice 2005, June 30.) In 2011, the current ICE Director, John Morton, raised consumer safety issues by stating (ICE announces results of 'Operation Strike Out' 2011, p. 2):

Fig. 10.6 Takedown notice posted on seized websites. *Source*: http://www.pcworld.com/article/227308/mozilla_refuses_to_help_censor_the_internet.html

> Counterfeits products represent a triple threat by delivering shoddy and sometimes dangerous goods into commerce, by funding organized criminal activities, and by denying Americans good-paying jobs. Homeland Security Investigations and our partners at the IPR Center will continue to work together to keep all types of counterfeit products off our streets.

Several articles mention the paradox of enforcing IPR for tangible goods (e.g., see Chaudhry and Stumpf 2011; Chaudhry and Walsh 1995, 1996; Chaudhry 2006; Zimmerman and Chaudhry 2009), but relatively few studies address the ability of governments, firms, and individuals to enforce their IPR via the Internet (Chaudhry 2012; Chaudhry et al. 2011a, b). Some recent sting operations are briefly discussed below.

Operation Buccaneer

In October 2000, the U.S. Customs Service in cooperation with its allies in Australia, Finland, Norway, Sweden, and the United Kingdom, worked together under the codename Operation Buccaneer to commence a string of undercover operations designed to infiltrate the labyrinth of criminals that distribute software, games, and movies over the Internet through the warez scene by targeting such release groups as DrinkorDie, Razor 1911, RiSCISO, Myth, and POPZ (United States Department of Justice 2006a). As a result of this 14-month undercover operation, approximately 70 search warrants were executed worldwide in the initial phase of Operation

Buccaneer, backspace. It is notably the most significant law enforcement penetration to date of international organizations engaged in the criminal distribution of copyrighted material via the Internet.

Law enforcement officials seized several warez archive sites that are described as highly secured computers used to store massive quantities of pirated software, games, and movies. Access to these sites is used as a reward for active warez group members and as an incentive for them to continue their illegal activity. Many archive sites contain 2,000 gigabytes or more of pirated software, equivalent to approximately 1.4 million, 3.5 inch diskettes of copyrighted material (www.cybercrime.gov). Although there is not an exact measurement, the retail value of the pirated software, movies, games, and music seized during the course of Operation Buccaneer is estimated to be in the hundreds of millions of dollars.

In 2005, three men who were part of a huge network of Internet software pirates, known as DrinkorDie, were arraigned at the Old Bailey, England's most important crown court. Judge Paul Focke was quoted in a BBC News release, "Your motivation was not only the benefit of free access—it was to enhance your personal reputation" (BBC 2005, p. 15). The infamous DrinkOrDie were simply a network of computer buffs that derived pleasure from cracking codes protecting copyrighted software such as Windows 95. One of their main goals was to share the material among themselves, with little profit-oriented motive—as is often the case.

Operation Digital Gridlock

Operation Digital Gridlock was a joint investigation conducted by the FBI, the U.S. Attorney's Office for the District of Columbia, and the Department of Justice's Computer Crime and Intellectual Property Section. These joint prosecution maneuvers targeted illegal file-sharing of copyrighted materials over Direct Connect P2P networks that belonged to an online group of hubs known as The Underground Network. These networks required their users to share large quantities of computer files with other network users, all of whom could download each other's shared files. Four people were convicted. This was the first federal felony convictions for copyright piracy using P2P networks, all within about 9 months of the original searches and seizures.

From August 2003 through August 2004, Tanner, one of the defendants, owned, maintained, operated, and moderated a Direct Connect hub named "Silent Echoes." According to court documents, the defendant's hub offered movies, computer software, computer games, and music in digital format. During the investigation, government agents downloaded from the hub numerous copyrighted works worth approximately $7,371. Agents estimated that on any one day, this hub shared an average of 6.72 terabytes of files, which is roughly equivalent in storage space to well over 6,000 movies in digital format (www.usdoj.org).

Operation Higher Education/Operation FastLink

Higher Education is the largest component of the global law enforcement action known as Operation Fastlink, announced by the Department of Justice on April 22, 2004. Twelve nations participated in Higher Education; it ensued as an 18-month, multinational software piracy investigation. Three men were found guilty of assisting in the cracking, storing, and distributing of copyrighted material throughout the world.

Operation Fastlink is presently the largest global enforcement action ever undertaken against online piracy. It was the culmination of four separate undercover investigations simultaneously being conducted by the FBI, coordinated by the FBI Cyber Division, the U.S. Department of Justice, and the Computer Crimes and Intellectual Property Section (CCIPS) of the Criminal Division. This operation focused on the highest levels of release groups—the warez groups. The investigation has so far yielded searches and seizures of over 70 high-level targets that were conducted in Belgium, Denmark, France, Germany, Hungary, Israel, the Netherlands, Singapore, Spain, Sweden, the United States, as well as Great Britain and Northern Ireland.

The release groups targeted by Fastlink specialize in the distribution of all types of pirated works including utility and application software, movies, music, and games. Among the groups targeted by Fastlink are well-known organizations such as Fairlight, Kalisto, Echelon, Class and Project X, all of which specialized in pirating computer games, and music release groups such as APC. The enforcement of Operation Fastlink seized over 200 computers—30 computer servers that functioned as storage and distribution hubs were included. These servers collectively contain hundreds of thousands of pirated copies (www.linuxelectron.com, www.cybercrime.gov).

Operation Site Down

In June 2005, the Justice Department released a joint statement from the former U.S. Attorney General, Alberto R. Gonzales, the former Acting Assistant General, John C. Richter of the Criminal Division and Assistant Director Louis M. Reigel of the FBI Cyber Division regarding a recent Internet piracy initiative, Operation Site Down, that worked jointly with the assistance of ten countries to further apprehend and prosecute the international pirates. In a 24 h time frame, the agencies conducted over 70 searches in the United States and 20 overseas to yield arrests of four individuals in the United States and other actions in Australia, Belgium, Canada, Denmark, France, Germany, Israel, the Netherlands, Portugal, and the United Kingdom.

One of the main goals of this sting operation was to target the individuals and organizations of the warez scene that release a myriad of software, movies, music, and games from such sites as: RiSCISO, Myth, TDA, LND, and Goodfellaz. These sites are part of the distribution channel for other suppliers to obtain the counterfeit goods via the Internet and resell for a profit. For example, a spam email that advertises cheap software is often downloaded from one of these sites at the top of the Internet piracy pyramid and can actually bear the "signature mark" of the warez group responsible for its release. This is a great example of where the "middleman" in the Internet pyramid has the profit incentive of this illicit trade (United States Department of Justice 2005).

Operation Strike Out

In 2011, in the wake of the end of Major League Baseball's World Series, a joint effort of ICE, Homeland Security Investigations (HIS) and the National Intellectual Property Rights Coordination Center (IPR Center) reported on their operation to combat fake sports paraphernalia sold at 58 commercial websites (ICE announces results of 'Operation Strike Out' 2011). Operation Strike Out has been an ongoing sting operation and this represented the seventh phase of "Operation In Our Sites"—a perpetual enforcement initiative to safeguard consumers by focusing on fake goods and piracy over the Internet. The details of the previous six phases of this enforcement program can be reviewed at the website for ICE, http://www.ice.gov/news/releases/1110/111031washingtondc.htm.

ICE reports that of the 200 domain names that were seized, 86 were forfeited to the US government. The owner of the domain name is given a period of time to file a petition after the initial "Notice of Seizure" with a US federal court. The owner is also given the right to appeal after the "Notice of Forfeiture." Thus, the domain name becomes the property of the US government if neither a petition nor a claim is made by the individuals who have an interest in the site.

In April 2011, ICE went beyond just posting its "takedown" banner (refer back to Fig. 10.6) at the 86 forfeited sites and decided to run its public service announcement (refer back to Chap. 6) as a way to raise awareness and further deter criminals.

Enforcement Issues Related to Electronic Piracy

It can very difficult to convince consumers that Internet piracy negatively affects giants such as motion picture firms. As discussed in Chaps. 5 and 6, consumer willingness to purchase counterfeits can center on an anti-big business sentiment and many times the consumer describes a "Robin Hood" (Warez groups stealing from the rich to give to the poor) and/or "David vs. Goliath" (e.g., Internet piracy is a means to attack the price-gouging music, software, and movies industries) type of analogy to justify their actions in obtaining illegal goods. A quick search in Google using "Internet piracy" as a search query produces more individual blogs that support Internet piracy than those against it. The recent consumer activism surrounding the SOPA controversy is testimony to the public opinion regarding safeguarding their access to the Internet.

The message that Internet piracy is hurting more than a "Goliath," such as Microsoft or highly paid screen stars, such as Tom Cruise, is a message that needs to be given to the populous to change this sentiment. The following excerpt from a joint statement from the Directors Guild of America, the Writers Guild of America West, and the American Federation of Musicians, released after the *Metro-Goldwyn-Mayer Studios Inc. v. Grokster Ltd.* case was filed with the U.S. Supreme Court (Internet Piracy Hurts Individual Creators, Not Just Industries Say the Entertainment Unions 2005, p. 2):

> If the work of creators is not protected, and is used around the world without just payment, it is very likely that, in the end, neither the creator nor the copyright holder will be able to continue to make this work available. The losers will not only be those artists whose talent and hard work is the creative heart on each screen, TV and iPod; but also the very public that enjoys quality movies, music and television.

No Electronic Theft Act

The No Electronic Theft Act (NET) is a critical form of anti-counterfeit enforcement, since it was mentioned that warez scene infringements are often not motivated by profit-oriented incentives. The act posits that it is a federal crime to reproduce, distribute, or share copies of electronic copyrighted works such as songs, movies, games, or software programs, even if the person copying or distributing the material acts without commercial purpose and/or receives *no private financial gain.*

Prior to the passage of this legislation, people who intentionally distributed copied software over the Internet did not face criminal penalties if they did not profit from their actions. As such, warez scene involvement, driven by the mere incentive of cracking the code had flourished. The passing of the NET Act in 1997 established a penalty of up to 5 years in prison and a fine of up to $250,000 for electronic copyright infringement. If the defendant reproduces or distributes ten or more copyrighted works that have a total value of more than $2,500, he or she can be charged with a felony. Raising statutory damages in civil cases by 50%, the act was obviously targeting those involved in the warez scene in order to enforce penalties for pirating, regardless of motive or gain.

Digital Millennium Copyright Act

In October 1998, the DMCA was unanimously supported by the U.S. Senate and signed into law by former President Bill Clinton. The four main provisions of this act were (What are the DMCA's Anti-Circumvention Provisions? 2008, p. 2):

1. A prohibition on circumventing access controls (commonly known as digital rights management [DRM]).
2. An access control circumvention device ban (sometimes called the "trafficking" ban).
3. A copyright protection circumvention device ban.
4. A prohibition on the removal of copyright management information.

Basically, the DMCA made it a crime to disable antipiracy measures in goods, such as software; outlaws code-cracking devices; requires service providers to remove items from their websites if one suspects copyright infringement; and limits liabilities of nonprofit institutions of higher education. DRM allows the copyright holder to thwart access, copying, or conversion alteration by the consumer to other formats. Obviously, the advent of personal computers, the Internet, and file-sharing had made digital piracy more accessible to everyone. In the past, a counterfeiter was a specialist in a certain skill-set, such as an artist creating the engraving to make fake currency. However, in today's environment, one is literally just a click away from some type of digital piracy.

The passage of the DMCA was surrounded by controversy in terms of consumer rights and skepticism related to the role of Internet service providers (ISPs) policing their sites for IPR violations. First, consumer advocates, such as the Electronic Frontier Foundation (ETF) have said that technological locks inappropriately limit how the purchaser can play and view his or her CDs and DVDs. Secondly, there is a key provision of the DMCA called the safe harbor that protects ISPs from being liable for the activities of its users. In general, if a service provider qualifies for the safe harbor exemption, only the individual infringing customer is liable for monetary damages; the service provider's network through which they engaged in the alleged activities is not liable.

The "safe harbor" aspect of the DMCA has caused debate in various forms. Cloak (2007) in his *Vanderbilt Law Review* article, provides an outstanding example of how the emergence of video-sharing Internet sites (VSIs), such as YouTube.com, to millions of savvy bloggers has created a significant challenge for any provider that allows this type of digital content. Cloak asks whether "given the current operational framework of VSIs, are owners of these sites liable for copyright infringement when copyright material is illegally posted by their users?" He concludes that many VSIs will be facing multimillion, if not billion dollar, law suits in the future resulting from copyright infringement. The two key questions are whether the VSIs receive financial benefits from the illegally posted copyright materials and whether the VSIs have the "right" and means to effectively control what their users post on the site. We will discuss this point further in Sect. 10.6.4 with the proposed S.978 Bill proposed in the U.S. Congress.

Another dispute involving the DMCA centers on its ability to have copyright holders shut down websites if they *suspect* IPR violations. For example, in a case brought by InternetMovies.com to the District Court for the District of Hawaii, the firm asked the court to require that copyright holders need to provide some type of investigation and/or evidence before asking websites to be shut down. This request for proof of infringement was rejected by the court and a spokesperson for the firm commented that "[T]his decision rules that the DMCA does not require a copyright holder to conduct an investigation to establish actual infringement prior to sending notice to an ISP requiring them to shut-down an allegedly infringing web site, or stopping service all together to an alleged violator (Court Confirms DMCA 'good faith' web site shut down rights 2003, p. 3)." The former Tiffany and LVMH court decisions are clear examples of the legal quagmire facing firms that decide to litigate their IP rights.

Commercial Felony Streaming Act

Pirates have kept up with the new technology and the owners of digital content are providing access via streaming, not just downloading. The Executive Office of the President of the United States published a 2011 report, *Administration's White Paper of Intellectual Property Enforcement Legislative Recommendations* that suggested three additional measures to support enforcement authorities to combat intellectual property infringement as follows (p. 2):

> 1) Clarify that, in appropriate circumstances, infringement by streaming, or by means of other similar new technology, is a felony; 2) Authorize the Department of Homeland Security (DHS), and its component U.S. Customs and Border Protection (CBP), to share pre-seizure information about, and samples of, products and devices with right holders to help DHS to determine whether the products are infringing or the devices are circumvention devices; and 3) Give law enforcement authority to see a wiretap for criminal copyright and trademark offenses.

The legislation designed to curb video streaming piracy, the Commercial Felony Streaming Act, also known as S. 978 (or the Ten Strikes Bill), was sponsored by Senators' Amy Klobuchar, Chris Coons, and John Cornyn to provide increased criminal penalties to fight the illegal streaming of copyrighted content for financial gain (Chaudhry 2012). Senator Klobuchar reassured the public that the Act was targeted for "criminals streaming thousands of dollars' worth of stolen digital content and profiting from it," and not the general public steaming movies in their homes (Engleman 2011, p. 4). OpenCongress, an organization independent of the U.S. Congress, summarizes the penalty provisions of S. 978 as (OpenCongress n.d., p. 1):

> Makes unauthorized web streaming of copyrighted content a felony with a possible penalty of up to 5 years in prison. Illegal streaming of copyrighted content is defined in the bill as an offense that "consists of 10 or more public performances by electronic means, during any 180-day period, of 1 or more copyrighted works" and has a total economic value, either to the copyright holder or the infringer, of at least $2,500.

This proposed Bill has obvious proponents, such as the Copyright Alliance that represents companies like Comcast Corporation, NBC Universal, Time Warner Inc., and Viacom Inc. (Engleman 2011). Peracchio (2011) succinctly stated that this proposed legislation was needed to keep up with the technology since the

DMCA was developed in a time (1998) where digital content was stored on a hard drive or DVD, not in "the cloud." However, the blogs picked up the buzz immediately and consumers worried about streaming on YouTube and possible criminal penalties (Peracchio 2011).

Conclusions

There have been many trends facilitating and hindering digital piracy in the past decade. Overall, the attempts to measure the size of the Internet piracy market are strictly guesstimates. The common denominators one might use to assess the growth of piracy in the global marketplace are growing Internet penetrations rates, continued consumer willingness to video stream, download, and/or purchase (obtain) fake goods in cyberspace through a variety of devices, and the growth of suppliers to the Internet piracy pyramid. The main responses developed to impede this market are the various unilateral and multilateral enforcement tactics, such as Operation Strike Out, and proposed government legislation, such as the Commercial Felony Streaming Act.

One can question how much enforcement is required to seriously demotivate the main actors in the Warez scene to stop feeding the top of the Internet piracy pyramid. Overall, these groups are releasing the illicit products on the web as a matter of pride in an elaborate art of digital war with the copyright holders. In addition, the financial gain for unscrupulous players to sell everything from fake pharmaceuticals to video streaming blockbuster movies is a large incentive. The former polar opposite positions of the United States and French courts on the liability of eBay for counterfeit merchandise being sold at its Internet auction site was just the beginning of the legal controversy on gauging contributory trademark infringement. The controversy surrounding the demise of SOPA reveals that future governance of the Internet will be challenged by various stakeholders. Ironically, the entire topic of digital piracy places the current technology advances on the cusp of a paradox; on the one hand, the Internet has literally exploded with information to aid in the insatiable appetite to purchase digital entertainment through the web, using iTunes or Netflix, or through a variety of new devices, such as iPads and smartphones. On the other hand, advances in technology and Internet access have created a dark side to cyberspace—the challenges of Internet piracy will continue into the foreseeable future.

Chapter 11
Managerial Counterattack: Traditional and Novel Anticounterfeiting Strategies

Introduction

It is clear that governments alone cannot solve the counterfeit product problem. Owners of intellectual property (IP) must take action to protect their rights. There are a number of anticounterfeiting strategies recommended by numerous researchers that target distribution channels, international organizations, and pirates. There are also internal, company-based initiatives. But, few if any of these studies assess the effectiveness of the recommended anticounterfeiting tactics. We have conducted in-depth interviews with US managers to measure their perceptions of the efficacy of various anticounterfeiting tactics. Our research indicates that corporate managers believe registering trademarks and patents is a must. They also believe encouraging distributors to notify the manufacturer about counterfeits, and educating both employees and channel members about the counterfeit problem to be very effective ways to fight pirates. These managers also report that many other tactics are far less effective, for example an acquisition/joint venture with a counterfeiter, aggressively cutting prices, providing financial incentives for distributors to reject counterfeits, or stressing the harmful effects of fake goods in consumer advertising.

In this chapter, we recommend a specific program firms can employ to protect their IP rights (IPR). The action program includes developing a company-wide IP protection strategy based on a cost–benefit analysis; managing the registration of all copyrights, trademarks, and patents in key markets; establishing a brand integrity team; monitoring the marketing of fakes through a central information repository; developing a multipronged education program; preparing to fight pirates through investigative work in conjunction with local law enforcement and a willingness to take legal action, and setting up a regular evaluation system.

P. Chaudhry and A. Zimmerman, *Protecting Your Intellectual Property Rights*, Management for Professionals, DOI 10.1007/978-1-4614-5568-4_11,

Firms Must Act to Protect their IP Rights

As we have seen, IPR enforcement varies widely from country to country. In China the concept of IPR protection is only slowly taking hold. Some consumers are fairly sophisticated decision makers and can tell whether a product is legitimate or counterfeit by price and where they purchase the product. However, other consumers are non-complicit players and unknowingly obtain counterfeits. As discussed in Chap. 5, consumers can be quite willing to purchase counterfeits for a variety of reasons. Furthermore, we find that managers plan to make investments in countries where the intellectual property environment is problematic.

With these facts as background, we have discovered that inadequate government protection of IPR throughout the world forces firms to act on their own. Overall, the problem is not a lack of existing legislation to protect a firm's intellectual property rights but the lack of enforcement caused by budget constraints and the importance of other priorities. For example, there are 155 member countries of the World Trade Organization (WTO) that govern its TRIPS (Trade-Related Aspects of Intellectual Property Rights). Thus, several government policymakers have acknowledged the concept of intellectual property rights. However, this multilateral agreement does not guarantee enforcement of intellectual property rights. Almost 10 years ago, *The Financial Times* (2005), questioned whether the WTO and its TRIPS are providing adequate protection of IPR. In that same time frame, Naim (2005), dealing with the widest range of illegal trafficking, suggested that governments focus on the most harmful kinds of illicit trade such as traffic in sex slaves, nuclear material, or heroine. This places the illegal copying of products (which do not affect health and safety) at a much lower priority for government agencies. Field (2007) points out that government has done little to address the crisis, US Homeland Security is underfunded and US Customs has fallen short in training agents about counterfeiting. There is also a shortage of prosecutors with specialized knowledge required for these kinds of cases. While some believe that TRIPS has been effective in convincing WTO members to strengthen their IPR protection (Cardwell and Ghazalian 2012), IP holders pushed for more protection from governments. The result was the Anti-Counterfeiting Trade Agreement (ACTA) which had been negotiated over 2 years. Before the measure could be ratified by the countries who had signed on, protests began throughout the world (Economist 2012). Various government ministers started backing away from ACTA following the failure in the United States of the proposed Stop Online Piracy Act (SOPA) (Nurton 2012). The net result is that rights holders must develop their own programs for protecting their intellectual property.

Suggestions from Researchers and Authors

Many authors have recognized the magnitude of the product counterfeiting problem and have proposed a wide range of solutions. A sampling of the most notable recommendations follows. More than 25 years ago Harvey (1987) described the types of configurations used by counterfeiters, the legislation relevant to combating the problem, and the need for multinational corporations themselves to take on the fight against counterfeit products. Harvey described technology that could be used to brand products and recommended a three-step anticounterfeiting program which he identified with three A's: Awareness, Action, and Assertion. His basic formula has been enhanced by later researchers.

Shultz and Saporito (1996) offered ten anticounterfeiting strategies:

1. *Do nothing*—based on a cost–benefit analysis
2. *Co-opt offenders*—buy up the counterfeiting factories and make them legitimate
3. *Educate stakeholders*—convince governments to follow international rules
4. *Advertise*—to differentiate real from phony products
5. *Investigation and surveillance*—hire international investigators to find pirates
6. *High-tech labeling*—develop special high-tech labels
7. *Create a moving target*—improve performance, better the price/value offering, or change the packaging or labeling of the legitimate product
8. *Legislation*—recommend changes in laws to better protect IPR
9. *Coalitions*—involvement with organizations that have similar IPR interests
10. *Cede the industry*—leave the market to the counterfeiters

Deng and Townsend (1996) also recommended a cost–benefit analysis of intellectual property protection actions. They also state that "the most common sources of IP losses are employees, as well as outside advisers such as bankers, lawyers, and consultants." These authors emphasize the need to limit exposure of valuable intellectual property to subcontractors and to identify in all agreements information that is considered secret. They also emphasize that a firm should develop a reputation with employees and competitors for vigorously enforcing its intellectual property rights.

Jacobs et al. (2001) identified four different types of international piracy and seven "protective responses." These were summarized as communication, legal, government, direct contact, labeling, strong proactive marketing, and piracy as promotion. Generally speaking these recommendations are slight variations of those already discussed. Staake and Fleisch's (2008) extensive analysis of counterfeit trade includes a detailed literature review and offers a specific anticounterfeiting program. They recommend determining counterfeit goods' market share, investigating producers, understanding the illicit supply chain, analyzing consumers, conducting a risk analysis, analyzing best practices, setting up a brand protection task force, implementing monitoring and reaction processes, selecting preventive measures, implementing product checks, integrating external stakeholders, signaling top management support, and reviewing brand and product protection efforts on a regular basis.

Using Technology

New and clever packaging and marking of products is generally recommended, including special spouts which discourage refilling of bottles, the use of holograms and covert chemical fingerprints and other hidden markers, and even the use of

DNA to give unique identification to products. In fact there are a very large number of firms which sell product identification technologies of all kinds and the software used to track sales to contractors and through retailers. A firm must identify who will benefit from the technology—consumers, retailers, distributors, manufacturers, or law enforcement—to determine what kinds of technology at what expenditure level is appropriate.

Hopkins et al. (2003) and Staake and Fleisch (2008) provide detailed information describing anticounterfeiting technology solutions. These technologies are designed to verify for consumers, law enforcement, or IP owners that products are genuine, what is generally called authentication. The techniques described can be overt such as special colors or type fonts or holograms, which are readable without any special device. Or they can be covert. Covert technologies do require some kind of optical or electronic reading device such as a decoder or lens or specialized laboratory equipment. These technologies include "invisible" printing, RFID (radio-frequency identification), or various types of "taggants" which may be chemical or biological and are read only by special detectors. A new approach uses nanotechnology—called nanosecurity—to prevent counterfeiting of computer chips (ECN 2012). RFID is an identification method which stores and retrieves data using a device called an RFID tag. This device is applied to, or incorporated into a product, for the purpose of identification. Some tags can be read from several meters away and even beyond the line of sight of the reading device.

An example of covert technology is the addition of minute levels of chemicals into fuels to prevent counterfeiting or dilution of the product. A subset of the covert approach is machine-readable technologies which allow high-speed authentication of a large number of products. At the extreme end of covert technology is what is called forensic technology. These techniques are the most difficult to detect or duplicate but require lab testing for verification. These tests may be destructive or nondestructive (Davison 2011a). Various sources (NEMA 2012; Dupont 2012; Davison 2011a) agree with Hopkins et al. (2003) that a layered approach, a combination of overt and covert technology, is the best way to protect IPR and this concept is used by many firms. Establishing a well-designed system based on the above technologies but adding serial number data and RFID allows a company to track and trace its product. This is useful for reducing counterfeiting as well as for combating gray market diversions. Managers interviewed by Staake and Fleisch (2008) had less faith in protection technologies than they did in anticounterfeiting industry groups and legal actions. This was especially true among firms deemed to have the most successful practice against counterfeit products.

A California regulation, the ePedigree law, passed in 2004, originally required that, as of January 1, 2009, prescription drug manufacturers be able to record the movement of every product from manufacturing to sale through an electronic tag. The law requires a unique serial number on the smallest retail unit. After several delays the new deadline is January 2015 when 50% of a manufacturer's product will have to have a unique serialized number on each container. The remaining half must have serialized numbers by the following year (Varney 2012). Although the law does not specify a method, RFID is considered superior to barcoding. RFID has a few advantages. First, a unique serial number is electronically written into a chip at the pharmaceutical plant. To copy that, a pirate would need to be able to make semiconductors rather than a simple photocopier which is all that is required for reproducing a bar code. Another major advantage is that the RFID reader can penetrate sealed boxes and scan multiple labels in a very short time (Parkinson 2008; Davison 2010). The US Federal Drug Administration's Counterfeit Drug Task Force (2008) identified RFID as a technology with the capability of preventing counterfeiting. The pilot test program has been extended by the FDA (2012) to December 31, 2012. Inexpensive scanners can read nearly invisible bar codes printed with special inks (Hattersley 2006). Very sophisticated cryptographic memories embedded in a labeling device provide a very high level of authentication. This approach allows unique information to be transmitted for each transaction. According to the providers these product labels or computer chips are nearly impossible to clone or copy (Asanghanwa 2008; ECN 2012). Nevertheless it is important to remember that counterfeiters need only provide products which look authentic enough to satisfy the buyer. Therefore covert authentication technologies may be less effective against counterfeiters without widespread checking of product as it moves through the supply chain.

The Role of Packaging

There is an active market for the trade in counterfeit packaging (separate from the product). In one historic example, a Shanghai subsidiary of Johnson & Johnson identified a small quantity of counterfeit Band-Aid adhesive bandages in a few Chinese cities. Johnson & Johnson began an extensive program to track down the sources of the counterfeited product. The investigation revealed a counterfeit training group, which provided technology, production facilities, and, indirectly, counterfeit packaging and raw materials to over 100 counterfeiters operating manufacturing sites across multiple locations in China. In this case, the packaging was sourced from the Middle East, and the training group made connections for the Chinese counterfeiters with the packaging counterfeiters (Chang 2011). Much of this counterfeited packaging originated in the UAE, which has established many free-trade zones where sophisticated equipment can be put to work and materials shipped throughout the world (Mutterperl 2007).

One of the authors of this report has found that management in Australia, New Zealand, South Africa, Tahiti, and the United States all perceive innovative packaging to be one of the three most effective methods for reducing consumer demand for counterfeit goods (Chaudhry and Stumpf 2010). Executives in Brazil and the United States believe special packaging to be the most effective anticounterfeit method and 56% of US managers rate packaging an "important influence on consumer determination of legitimacy of a product" (Stumpf et al. 2011).

According to Perkins (2009), the use of color and "stylized elements" on packaging and innovative pack designs that change over time are factors that make the production of counterfeit product packaging more difficult. Another researcher has stated that "many products targeted by counterfeiters are very easy to copy due to their simple-to-copy packaging. Undifferentiated packaging is one of the first

Fig. 11.1 Innovative cigarette packaging

things to be addressed, to stop making it easy for the counterfeiter to copy" (Counterfeiting: The industry is on the wrong track 2009).

The importance of packaging as an anticounterfeiting tactic has is critical in the pharmaceutical industry. As one expert (Davison 2011b) puts it, companies spend a billion dollars developing a high value product and then use standard packaging that is available to anyone over the Internet to package it. He explains "the selection or design of non-standard, product-specific closures, or unusual packaging shapes can be an effective defense against counterfeiting.... [T]he extra cost of non-standard pack shapes and materials, unusual die-cutting, specialist tooling, and other design features is often minimal when spread across the lifetime of the product, but by denying criminals a simple path to replication, they may be a surprisingly effective deterrent to counterfeiting."

The *frequency of change* in packaging is also important. According to an expert in the packaging of cosmetics, a way to increase security of packaging effectiveness is through frequent design changes to stay ahead of the sophisticated counterfeiter. The latest technology, such as scanners and professional software, is also available to the counterfeiter and therefore "the shelf life of some packaging is limited to six months, after which it is better to change the design or content" (Genuario 2006).

From a counterfeiter's perspective, the ability to produce authentic-looking packaging is a key factor in the success of a counterfeit brand and "keeping up" with the evolving packaging of the legitimate product can be an expensive and time-consuming process. This is very much the case with tobacco products where innovative packaging plays a key role in erecting barriers to counterfeiters. Even a cursory look through the offerings of the "world's largest packaging manufacturer," Amcor, shows many packaging innovations including the expensive-to-duplicate "lighter pack" or "scissor pack" seen in the figure above (Fig. 11.1).

According to Amcor, product manufacturers' anticounterfeiting strategies are primarily based on the following two elements: first, packaging design—shape, art-

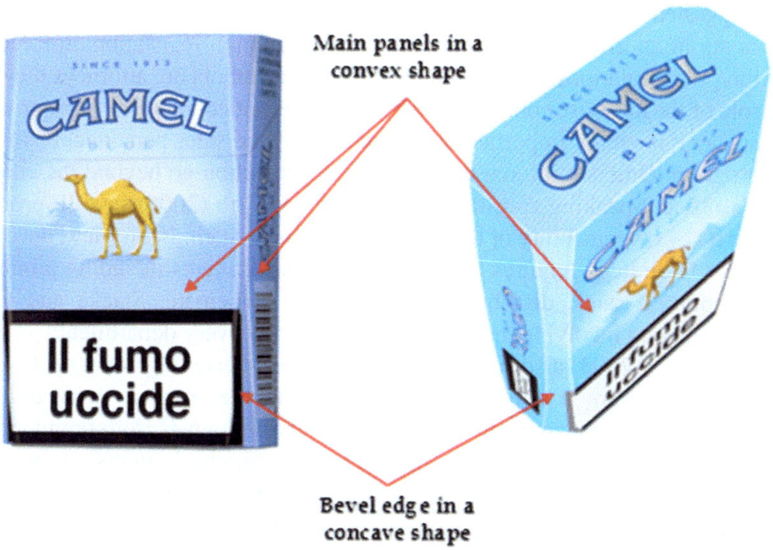

Fig. 11.2 "Camel Curve" pack design. Image provided by JTI, May 2012

work, and complicated manufacturing processes add to the difficulty in counterfeiting; and, second, constant change. Amcor states that "packaging design along with constant changes and updates provide multiple hurdles for counterfeiters, making it more challenging for them to follow the market and replicate products... in our experience, it is only by this constant evolution of the package that product manufacturers are able to increase the reproduction complexity or provide any type of defence to counterfeiting... if either of these two elements become static, a product becomes easier for counterfeiters to duplicate" (Amcor 2011a).

An example can be seen in the figure above (Fig. 11.2). The pack itself is unique to the tobacco industry: its four main panels (front, back, and sides) are in a convex shape and the pack edges are in a beveled and concave shape. An expensive, specialized—and patented—machine is required in order to manufacture the pack. It cannot simply be manufactured using the machinery used to make "traditional" cigarette packs without significant alterations and at a considerable cost.

The print quality of the counterfeit pack and/or individual cigarette can provide a first point of reference in detecting counterfeit tobacco products for consumers, retailers, manufacturers, and enforcement agencies.

Developing a Plan

In *Trademark Counterfeiting,* the extensive work by Abbott and Sporn (2002), Kolsun and Montan offer a 94-page chapter, "Building a Comprehensive Anti-counterfeiting Program." This very thorough section includes sample letters, reporting forms, and even a suggested Freedom of Information Act request. The chapter describes the key components in an effective antipiracy program: planning, legislation, enforcement, education/public relations, and assessment. Since the authors are attorneys they focus on the role of the in-house counsel as the leader of the anticounterfeiting program. But they also say it is vitally important that management and sales personnel be involved in the program. Others reinforce the idea that IP protection go beyond the corporate counsel's office. Speaking specifically about China, Firth (2006) says IP protection should be a key responsibility of the entire management team. In his view, developing an effective IP strategy requires that all company departments including production, human resources, sales, distribution, and finance participate. Staake and Fleisch (2008) recommend involving individuals from virtually every department.

Hopkins et al. (2003) also support the idea that counterfeiting is not exclusively a matter for the lawyers in a firm. They too recommend a company-wide task force supported by senior management and including representatives from brand management, marketing and public relations, manufacturing, purchasing/outsourcing/supply chain management, packaging, sales, research and development, finance, security as well as the law department. In the case of very large organizations, they believe that both regional and national operating companies need to be involved. And they recommend consulting with important outside constituencies including law enforcement, industry associations, various service providers, and lobbyists. They also show the return on investment for establishing a product security system. In their example a firm might realize $4.78 for each dollar spent on its prevention program.

Summarizing the Existing Literature

As is indicated from the discussion above, existing literature provides a variety of suggestions for combating counterfeit goods, starting with the development of a comprehensive plan and including tactics ranging from the development of better relations with the distribution channel to differentiating products based on quality and appearance or emphasizing a prestigious image.

In reviewing all the recommendations, the range of actions can be categorized according to the sector targeted: consumers, distribution channels, international organizations, host/home country governments and pirates, as well as company-based activities. Table 11.1 summarizes all of the frequently suggested tactics resulting from an in-depth review of existing literature.

Effectiveness of Recommended Actions

A decade ago, Green and Smith (2002) recommended more research into "topics related to counterfeiting and its prevention." They also reaffirm that little research has been done which describes companies' perceptions of counterfeiting and their actions

Table 11.1 Frequently used actions to combat counterfeiting

Targeted at consumers	**Targeted at host/home country governments**
Use special packaging and/or labeling; change packaging frequently Stress harmful effects of the counterfeiting in advertising Emphasize benefits of genuine product Create strong brand image, exclusivity and superiority of luxury brands Provide lists of legitimate channel members Emphasize warranties and after-sale service Offer site licenses Offer reduced price, related product lines	Register copyrights, trademarks, and patents Educate and cooperate with local law enforcement Lobby for more stringent laws/enforcement Seek assistance from tax authorities
Targeted at distribution channels	**Targeted at international organizations**
Educate channel members about counterfeits Encourage distributors to notify manufacturer about counterfeit goods Provide warnings to distributors/retailers Give financial incentives to reject counterfeits Solicit channel member suggestions to develop tactics Use authenticating technology, such as RFID tags, holograms, DNA markers, invisible inks and dyes, taggants, i.e., biological or chemical markers Monitor and investigate channel members Maintain surveillance of products in stores	Monitor policy of UN/ECE Advisory Group Participate in IACC actions Use the TRIPS of WTO Monitor the actions of the WIPO Participate in multilateral organizations Lobby for stronger global IPR protection
Targeted at pirates	**Internal—company based**
Complete "competition analysis" of pirates Use surveillance program in retail and Internet venues Warn counterfeiters of legal action Institute civil and criminal actions Seek injunctions against counterfeit goods Develop supplier quality assurance program Compartmentalize the outsourced production process Monitor purchases of key components Understand inputs and outputs of "illicit actors" Aggressively cut prices Use covert actions	Develop IP protection strategy Establish brand integrity team Conduct market studies to determine counterfeit penetration and understand consumer behavior Develop company IP data gathering and monitoring system Educate employees about IP protection strategy Employ private investigators Use acquisition and/or joint venture strategy Establish factories in lower cost countries Develop cost–benefit analysis of IP protection program Analyze best practices of other firms

Sources: Adapted from Bush et al. 1989; Globerman 1988; Green and Smith 2002; Chaudhry and Walsh 1996; Cordell et al. 1996; Davison 2011a, b; Harvey 1987; Olsen and Granzin 1993; Wee et al. 1995; Wald and Holleran 2007; Philip Morris and Inc 2003; Kolsun and Montan 2002; Hopkins et al. 2003; Parloff 2006; Nia and Zaichkowsky 2000; Firth 2006; Fuchs and Zhou 2010; Chang 2011 and Staake and Fleisch 2008

Table 11.2 Most effective anticounterfeiting actions

IPR action	Directed at	Rating
Register trademarks/patents/copyrights	Governments	4.40
Encourage distributors to notify manufacturer	Distribution channel	4.07
Educate employees about counterfeit goods	Company internal	4.07
Educate channel members	Distribution channel	3.93
Warn distributors and retailers about possible penalties	Distribution channel	3.93
Obtain local police support	Pirates	3.87
Encourage enforcement of existing laws	Governments	3.80
Pursue injunctions against counterfeiters	Pirates	3.73
Monitor information sources for anticounterfeiting developments	Company internal	3.40
Monitor and investigate retailers and distributors	Distribution channel	3.33

Key: Scale: 5 = very effective; 4 = somewhat effective; 3 = neither effective nor ineffective; 2 = somewhat ineffective; 1 = very ineffective; 0 = did not use

to defend their brands. One of the major goals of our research has been to determine which actions were most useful when implemented by managers who were combating the counterfeit problem in terms of both frequency of use and effectiveness. Thus, we developed a questionnaire designed to gauge the strategies listed in Table 11.1 and responses were elicited from the US international business managers.

Frequency of Actions Used

Our research reveals that managers most frequently combat the counterfeiting problem by attempting to educate channel members, for instance, warning distributors and retailers of possible damages from selling counterfeits. A second highly used tactic was lobbying international organizations for stronger protection against pirates. A third frequently used action was developing a company enforcement team. Lastly, company-based tactics such as educating employees about copycats, implementing acquisition and joint venture strategies to minimize counterfeiting, and establishing factories in lower cost countries were also often used by managers.

Managers were generally unlikely to target actions at consumers. As has been shown in Chap. 5, consumers are quite ready to acquire counterfeit products and may not question the ethics involved in their illicit behavior. Managers in our studies also did not frequently lobby home or host governments. In our research, those who chose China as their number one problem country far more frequently developed company enforcement teams and lobbied the US government to fight counterfeit goods.

Effectiveness of Actions

The actions seen as most effective by the managers surveyed are shown in Table 11.2 below.

Table 11.3 Least effective anticounterfeiting actions

IPR action	Directed at	Rating
Acquisition/joint venture with counterfeiter	Company internal	0.36
Aggressively cut prices	Pirates	0.93
Provide financial incentives for distributors/retailers to reject counterfeits	Distribution channel	1.00
Offer site licenses (software)	Consumers	1.69
Stress the harmful effects of counterfeiting in advertisements	Consumers	2.13
Establish factories in lower-cost countries	Company internal	2.27
Participate in multilateral negotiations	International organizations	2.27
Solicit retailer/distributor suggestions for anticounterfeiting tactics	Distribution channel	2.33
Monitor the actions of the World Intellectual Property Organization (WIPO)	International organizations	2.40
Implement surveillance program to check products in stores	Distribution channel	2.47

Key: Scale: 5 = very effective; 4 = somewhat effective; 3 = neither effective nor ineffective; 2 = somewhat ineffective; 1 = very ineffective; 0 = did not use

Based on the sample of managers interviewed, the most effective action to take is basic—to register copyrights, trademarks, and patents. In conjunction with that seemingly obvious, yet critical, suggestion is the importance of focusing attention on the distribution channel. Four of the ten most effective actions are directed at distribution. Such actions involve monitoring and investigating both retailers and distributors, having distributors notify the manufacturer upon identification of counterfeit goods in the marketplace, educating channel members about counterfeit products, and warning distributors and retailers about possible penalties. Managers also use local police and the legal system to fight against pirates, encouraging governments to enforce existing laws rather than lobbying for new ones. Information gathered from the managers polled highlights the importance of educating within the company and of monitoring information sources for anticounterfeiting developments. Other strategies that rated somewhat effective include participating in activities sponsored by the International Anti-Counterfeiting Coalition (IACC), heightening the awareness of local law enforcement officers, developing a company enforcement team, and lobbying for stronger global intellectual property protection.

Some actions were reported to be quite *ineffective*, and are listed in Table 11.3 below. The results of this survey clearly indicate that managerial opinion differed significantly from many of the suggestions put forth by previous authors [see Table 11.1]. These managers believe that forming joint ventures, making acquisitions of pirates, or aggressively cutting prices are highly ineffective strategies. Soliciting retailer/distributor suggestions, rewarding members of the distribution channel for rejecting counterfeits, and checking products in stores are also reportedly unsuccessful. Stressing harmful effects in advertising is also regarded as ineffective by the managerial respondents. Some international activities, such as monitoring the WIPO, also ranked poorly for effectiveness.

Organizing to Fight Counterfeit Product

In order to fight against counterfeit products a company must look at its entire supply chain. The Economist Intelligence Unit (2006) puts it in a colorful way, "the problem…needs to be addressed along the entire slippery, serpentine global supply chain, through every jurisdictional loophole from manufacturing to retail sale." For example after experiencing serious problems, New Balance is monitoring its supply chain carefully, checking out contractors, writing strong audit clauses into contracts, and enforcing the contracts. It is also embedding encrypted information in security tags and monitoring the number of tags it gives to its suppliers (Parloff 2006).

An illustrative example is provided by Wald and Holleran (2007). They describe the challenge faced by Johnson and Johnson's Medical Device and Diagnostics (MD&D) Business. At first managers believed they had a gray market problem and they began to investigate. Their findings indicated that counterfeit surgical mesh had found its way into their supply chain. With the help of Ernst & Young, the company identified three factors which exacerbated the counterfeit problem: MD&D's business culture, business design and practices, and finally information and reporting. The business culture was predicated on a highly decentralized model. This meant that each operating and regional company was dealing with counterfeiting alone using different brand protection policies and strategies. The business design meant no single person or group at MD&D was responsible for protecting their brands or products and there was no analysis of illegal global activities. There was no single supply chain strategy and an incomplete process for reviewing suppliers, manufacturers, and distributors. In addition the business design did not allow for sharing of data. The lack of an effective information system meant the company could not be sure where the product was being used after flowing through the entire distribution channel.

To respond to these factors MD&D established a brand protection policy, developed an organization to address this issue across the entire business, and created a market monitoring program. The policy addresses the protection of intellectual property, product protection, supply chain standards, incident reporting, and enforcement. The organization was charged with addressing accountability and includes a vice president and several senior executives. Possible counterfeiting incidents are investigated by operating companies but they also report findings to corporate security. This gives corporate executives a better idea of possible global problems. The company has also developed product protection plans for at-risk products that include overt and covert anticounterfeiting technologies. As part of the market monitoring program, representatives of the company are buying products in markets and from the Internet. The net result of these actions is a much more effective anticounterfeiting program.

Firth (2006) advises that when it comes to IP protection "much more than an ounce of prevention is necessary today." He recommends a thorough review and updating of all company operations and internal policies, the development of a corporate IP protection strategy, and the use of offensive and defensive actions. The former include surveillance, education, and legal activity while the latter encompasses registering patents and trademarks and regularly reviewing IP security. Lian Hoon Lim, a Hong Kong consultant for A.T. Kearney, recommends a "portfolio approach" using a combination of secrecy, research about local partners, new technology and business strategies as well as legal enforcement of patent and trademark rights (Associated Press 2006).

Recommended Action Program

First, it is clear that the problem of counterfeiting will pervade global markets for some time. While governments and international organizations are focusing some additional attention on IPR, the owners of intellectual property must take responsibility to act on their own. Success comes from taking this problem seriously, regardless of whether one is the CEO of a $50 billion corporation or President of small startup. Based on our analysis of managerial perceptions of this global problem and information extracted from previous publications on this topic we strongly recommend managers construct an action plan based on the one described in Fig. 11.3. Of course the plan must be adapted so that it is relevant for a particular industry and a particular market. DNA tags will not be appropriate countermeasures for illegal downloading of music or movies. And urging the passage of new laws, in our opinion, will not have much effect in China. Figure 11.3 is a base that managers can work from to develop their specific plan. Although the actions in the figure appear sequentially, managers should be clear that this is an iterative process. Each part of the program is affected by all of the others.

1. *Develop IP protection strategy*. We have seen how important it is to have an overall strategy to protect valuable intellectual property rights. This is a key responsibility of top management and must involve many if not all of the company's functions. Davison (2010) says "anti-counterfeiting should be controlled by someone senior enough to see the connections across the company." The policy should be clearly communicated throughout the organization and also to contractors, distributors, retailers as well as government officials. Before implementing the policy in every country, a cost–benefit analysis should be completed so that the proper controls can be put in place for specific products in specific places. For pharmaceuticals, Davison (2010) advises that patient safety, revenue defense, legal compliance, and the cost of the program must be taken into account in deciding how the program should be designed and implemented. The company must establish a budget for protecting its intellectual property, for both the required human resources as well as the operating expenses. One knowledgeable attorney stressed the importance of a budget line for this program and employing a CFO who believes anticounterfeiting activity is critical to the brand. To quote her, "the company must commit to the effort" (Croxon 2007).

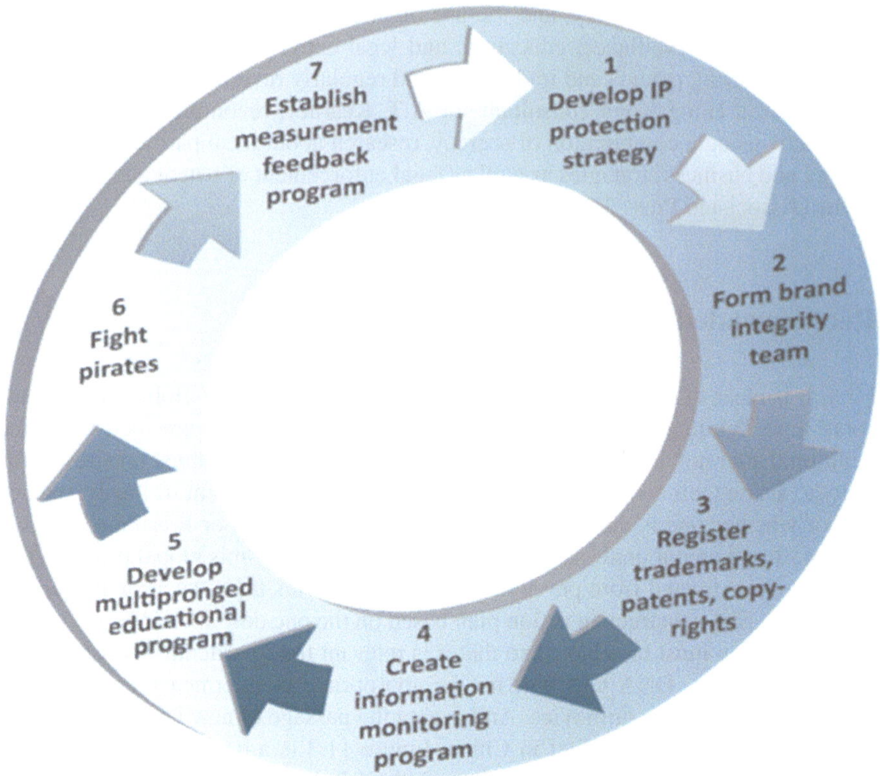

Fig. 11.3 Recommended action plan

2. Establish a formal and/or informal brand integrity team. Some firms have large sophisticated antipiracy organizations. According to Barboza and Lohr (2007) Microsoft's 75-member team was tracking a Chinese counterfeiting syndicate for more than 6 years before effecting a particularly large seizure of counterfeit software. On the other hand, for ABRO industries, an automotive and industrial parts distributor, protecting copyrights is the responsibility of the CEO (Morton 2011). Stopfakes.gov, a website developed by the United States Patent & Trademark Office, is intended to help small businesses protect their rights (Why protect intellectual property? 2007).
3. *Manage the registration of all copyrights, trademarks, and patents in key markets*. This recommendation is a little more complicated than it seems. Requirements vary for trademarks, patents, and copyrights. Although 174 countries belong to the Paris Convention ("Contracting Parties," n.d.), all of which recognize patent claims made in a firm's home country, it is necessary to register patents in various jurisdictions. It is possible to obtain patent protection in all 27 member countries of the EU by filing one application. In addition, by filing one patent application

with the United States Patent and Trademark Office (USPTO), US applicants can also concurrently apply for protection in up to 144 countries. The Stopfakes (2012) website advises IP holders they can apply for trademark registration in any of the countries that have joined the Madrid Protocol by filing a single application, called an "international application," with the International Bureau of the World Property Intellectual Organization (WIPO), through the USPTO. This should allow applicants to seek protection in 85 countries. According to the US Commercial Service (Stopfakes.gov 2012), no international copyright exists. The service recommends registration of copyrights in the United States as well as any country where a firm will be doing business. WIPO provides lists of countries and their copyright rules.

The company must set up a system to determine where its IP must be registered and when the registrations need to be renewed. ABRO has 1,150 registrations in 160 countries with 141 additional registrations pending in nine other countries (Morton 2011). Unfortunately according to the US patent and trademark office only 15% of small companies doing business internationally are even aware that they needed to file for IP protection. Guitar maker C. F. Martin lost its trademark in China by failing to register. Counterfeiters beat them to it (Mallinder 2011).

4. *Create a monitoring program to quickly funnel any information about counterfeits to a central information repository*. This program should review any IP developments in home and host markets, as well as those implemented by relevant international organizations, such as the IACC. As was noted in our study, the IACC was perceived as the most effective international organization to monitor future anticounterfeiting measures, as opposed to the TRIPS in the WTO. This information should be reviewed on a regular basis by top management to monitor conditions, and to adapt tactics to the latest pirate actions.
5. *Develop a multipronged education program, with actions directed at employees, the distribution channels, contract manufacturers, local law enforcement, and international organizations*. Educating employees and channel members, as well as local law enforcement, is crucial. As recommended in the *China Business Review* (Alibaba 2006) employees must believe that there is no "good" counterfeiting. Especially in China, employees frequenting markets where counterfeit products are sold "perpetuates the [counterfeit] industry and sends a wrong message to PRC authorities." Local management, marketing, and sales people should let various audiences know of the threats resulting from counterfeit products. A firm should emphasize to contract manufacturers, distributors, and retailers that it will take action to protect its intellectual property. And any actions taken should be widely publicized to all. Educating the local police while building good relations will help pave the way for effective action when necessary (Croxon 2007; Chang 2011). Enforcement officers should understand product specifics including packaging, unique features, and authentication techniques embedded by the manufacturer. They should also be familiarized with common counterfeit variants which have appeared in the market. Close cooperation is an ongoing effort which will pay significant dividends.

6. *Take action against pirates on every level—retailers, distributors, and manufacturing sources pursuing injunctions and cooperating with local law enforcement.* Management must be willing to take action against IPR violators. This means using all tools available including law enforcement at various levels (from national Customs officials to local police), other government agencies and the courts as well as trade associations. As described in Chap. 9, the cooperation developed with law enforcement officials in China has helped firms fight the widespread counterfeiting in that country.

   A decade ago, ISD, a marketer of premium imported Scotch whiskey, faced a major problem in Thailand after several deaths were attributed to the consumption of counterfeit whiskey marketed using their brand. The company employed multiple actions including identifying and punishing retail outlets, destroying the pirates' production facilities, lobbying for stricter penalties in the Thai legal system, and obtaining local police support for "sting" operations. ISD even hired a "dream team" of former Scotland Yard and British military commandos to lead their operations (Green and Smith 2002). The cooperation pattern for law enforcement in China was discussed in depth in Chap. 9. Some firms are employing new strategies including applying for injunctions in US courts to close down for violating websites or seize counterfeiters' overseas bank accounts (Ritter 2011; Reuters 2011).

   A recent example of a sting operation with law enforcement in several countries is Operation Barrel (October 2011). This joint operation targeted illicit tobacco products (and synthetic drug precursors) transported by rail. The multi-country investigation resulted in the seizure of two million cigarettes in its first joint operation. It was noted that the use of EU-funded scanning devices on the border between Poland and the Ukraine was instrumental for detecting the illicit tobacco (twenty-four EU Member States; and four other countries (Croatia, Turkey, Norway, and Switzerland); and the European Anti-Fraud Office (OLAF) of the European Commission (Operation Barrel, 2012)).
7. *Develop an evaluation and feedback system.* Fighting counterfeiters is a dynamic task. The strategies that work today may not work tomorrow. As long as there is demand, pirates will adapt to keep their operations going. The measurement of success should not rely solely on the number of seizures made at the minimum cost. Focusing only on seizures leads the firm toward easy targets such as warehouses while the source factories may be forgotten and the key players can continue undisturbed (Alibaba 2006). Hopkins et al. (2003) recommend that in addition to financial measurements, a company also look to nonfinancial measurements such as brand degradation and recovery, public relations, and government cooperation. While these items are difficult to measure, efforts should be made to assess success in each of these areas. Fuchs and Zhou (2010) offer a precise approach to calculating the costs and benefits for an anticounterfeiting program which takes into account short, medium, and long-term losses vs. specific costs for anticounterfeiting programs instituted in various departments. In an example they show that expenses amount to far less than potential damages caused by chronic counterfeiting. The lesson learned here is that all financial and

nonfinancial measurements should be combined to give management a clear idea of the success or shortcomings of their anticounterfeiting program.

Conclusions

The problem of counterfeit goods has received an inordinate amount of attention. Governments and international organizations are mounting antipiracy actions with regularity. Nevertheless, it is incumbent upon firm management to recognize the seriousness of this problem. Firms must take an active stance to prevail over an increasingly threatening intellectual property environment. A firm of any size can mount an effective anticounterfeiting program.

In this chapter we have reported on the extensive advice given by many authors. While much of this advice is useful, very little is based upon primary research with the managers charged with the responsibility for protecting company IPR. This chapter summarizes all the suggestions made in Table 11.1 and then reports upon the effectiveness of the recommended actions. The managers we interviewed first recommend registering trademarks, patents, and copyrights in all the relevant jurisdictions. The most effective actions seem to be those aimed at the distribution channel including asking distributors to notify the manufacturer of counterfeit product, educating and warning channel members about possible penalties, and monitoring/investigating retailers and distributors. Also effective are educating employees, obtaining local police support, and pursuing injunctions as well as setting up an information system. A critical step is to establish an overall IP strategy and plan involving nearly all functional and geographic divisions.

The least effective actions were often related to consumers such as advertising the harmful effects of counterfeiting. Acquiring or forming joint ventures with counterfeiters is seen as particularly ineffective as is cutting prices. The only international organization that has established a level of effectiveness with these respondents is the IACC. Based on the findings of our studies as well as the recommendations of those involved in fighting pirates on a day-to-day basis we have developed a suggested action program. We believe this program can be instituted by large or small firms based on a careful cost–benefit analysis and will serve to measurably improve the effectiveness of company anticounterfeiting actions.

Chapter 12
The Future: Will the Piracy Paradox Persist?

Introduction

The piracy paradox means that, although there has been attention paid to fighting counterfeit goods by journalists, scholars, governments, and associations, sales of pirated product continue to grow rapidly. Before looking at the future of this pernicious problem, it is important to review the past. As we have seen there have been any number of articles in the popular and business press focusing on counterfeit trade. In addition some books have been published reviewing the piracy problem. However few have addressed the issue using a comprehensive, research-based approach. This book has looked at the full scope of the counterfeit product problem, describing both historical and cultural origins for the growth of counterfeit product and recommending a specific corporate action program to protect a firm's IPR. This final chapter summarizes all the findings presented in this book, looks to the future, and recommends areas for additional research.

The Growth of Counterfeit Trade

Product counterfeiting probably goes back many millennia. As soon as inventor's marks began to appear in China approximately 5,000 years ago, the opportunity for product counterfeiting was created. In the Aztec Empire, pirates developed ways of selling inferior cacao beans. Based on archaeological findings, Roman Empire oil lamps marked FORTIS were probably copied more than 2,000 years ago. One of the earliest legal actions related to trademark infringement dates back to the late 1500s. The early history of the United States is replete with significant product copying including the first water-powered cotton spinning mill and unauthorized editions of Charles Dickens' novels.

As described extensively in Chap. 2 developing a reliable estimate of the size of the counterfeit market is nearly impossible. It does appear that this market has been

P. Chaudhry and A. Zimmerman, *Protecting Your Intellectual Property Rights*, Management for Professionals, DOI 10.1007/978-1-4614-5568-4_12,

growing rapidly. In 1982 worldwide annual sales of pirated product were estimated at only \$5.5 billion. In 1984 this figure had grown to over \$25 billion. Currently many sources believe the total is over \$500 billion. A careful review of these calculations of the size of the counterfeit market, however, seems to lead back to a few sources who themselves refer to their estimates as assumptions. Respected organizations who have attempted to develop a meaningful estimate of counterfeit product sales generally find it impossible. As we have seen the amount of counterfeit product intercepted by Customs Services around the world represents less than 1% of the total volume of goods flowing on global trade routes. Most recently, the OECD estimated the volume of *tangible* counterfeit products at about \$250 billion, larger than the GDPs of 150 countries and this number has been repeated by many media outlets. Yet the OECD itself questions the reliability of its estimate.

A decade ago specific product categories were named most vulnerable to counterfeiting. These seemed to be highly visible brand name products, prestige products, high-tech products, and pharmaceuticals. Recent research shows no product is immune to product piracy. A large percentage of computer software appears to be pirated. Counterfeit footwear, wearing apparel, watches, handbags, computers, DVDs, software, music, cigarettes, and consumer electronics are among the products most frequently seized by the US and EU Customs Services. However recent studies show even military components have been counterfeited. Illicit drugs are particularly worrying since their use can result in unwarranted side effects or even death.

Many stakeholders are negatively affected by phony products including consumers, home and host country governments and workers, wholesalers and retailers and especially owners of the trademarks, copyrights and patents violated. Beneficiaries include satisfied consumers but also terrorists.

In Chap. 2 the driving forces for the growth of the counterfeit goods market have been described. These include low-cost technology allowing small investment for sophisticated production equipment, globalization and the resulting lower trade barriers, consumer complicity, expansion of channels and markets especially the Internet, powerful worldwide brands, weak international and national enforcement, and high tariffs and taxes.

Source Countries

Although the OECD says that product counterfeiting takes place in just about all countries, China is the leading source of pirated product. Over the years, about 80% of counterfeit product seized by Customs authorities in the United States and the EU originates in China. For 2011, 62% of US seizures are from China but Hong Kong's share rose to 18%. Many other countries are named in various studies including Russia, India, South Korea, Turkey, and Taiwan. The USTR continues to single out Paraguay for special attention and designates it for Section 306 Monitoring. The agency has placed 13 countries on the Priority Watch List and another 26 on the Watch List. Chapter 3 includes detailed descriptions of the most important countries for counterfeit goods. In addition markets within countries such as Yiwu and Beijing's Silk Street Market in China and several locations in Argentina, Mexico, Russia, Thailand, India, the Philippines, and Indonesia are described. One location, on the border of Brazil, Paraguay, and Argentina, portrayed as the largest illicit market in the Western Hemisphere, is called Ciudad del Este. USTR also has started to identify "virtual markets" for counterfeit goods. A list of these is provided in Chap. 3.

The IPR Environment

This book has described the basic drivers of the intellectual property rights environment in a particular country. These include the level of consumer complicity, the level of pirate activity, and the level of host country enforcement. In our opinion, these three factors more than anything else work to determine the IPR atmosphere. As we have seen consumers are only too willing to purchase counterfeit product. The second factor relates to the capabilities of pirates in country. In some cases there may be a favorable business environment for the pirates, such as their known linkages to organized crime to finance and support their illicit manufacturing and trafficking of fake goods. However, in a few countries, an atmosphere based on cultural taboos or other impediments may keep pirates from establishing a foothold. Looking at the final factor, it is clear that regulations alone, while important, cannot stop product counterfeiting. The most important factor here is local enforcement including suitable penalties for violation of IPR rights. Chapter 4 lays out this model and also describes research conducted by the authors investigating managerial insights into the efficacy of various anti-counterfeiting tactics and managers' willingness to make future commitments in protective vs. non-protective IPR environments. Managers used tailor-made actions to combat pirates where counterfeiting activity was highest but did not change their strategies in markets where consumers were more complicit vs. less complicit. Managers used more counterfeiting actions where local law enforcement was better but it appears they believe employing many measures where enforcement is low will not yield the required results. Our research also revealed that despite a poor IPR environment, especially in China, managers expected to increase their future investment commitment, indicating that the strategic importance of a particular market overwhelms IPR considerations.

Consumer Complicity

One of the key drivers of the IPR environment is consumer complicity. A very large percentage of consumers are willing to purchase pirated product. They perceive purchasing counterfeit product as a victimless crime. In fact some studies show that additional education makes consumers more likely to purchase counterfeit software. Attitudes vary by culture, for instance in China centuries of collectivism have a significant effect on attitudes toward the ownership of intellectual property and do not create a barrier to purchasing copied products. Research conducted by one author identified intrinsic as well as an extrinsic determinants of consumer complicity. Product attributes contribute to consumer willingness to purchase these products. In particular appearance, image, purpose, and the perceived quality have been found to affect the purchase intention of consumers. Consumers might be able to tell that products are not genuine. Major factors contributing to this recognition can be a low price, buying location and poor packaging or printing. However, as demonstrated in Chap. 6, some fakes, such as pharmaceuticals are confusingly similar to the genuine product, and manufacturers can employ authentication technology to allow consumers to validate the legitimacy of the good.

Antipiracy Marketing Techniques

Advertising is being directed at consumers to try to alter their feelings about the acceptability of purchasing counterfeit product. These ads are based on social marketing concepts. Chapter 6 reviews the bases of social marketing (demarketing) concepts and an agenda to change public judgment and recommends a communications framework for an antipiracy campaign. Here several advertisements are shown using various techniques including peer pressure, fear of prosecution, negative association to pirates, whistleblowing, and reward. Finally we include a discussion of "bottom-up" media outlets, such as blogs, that justify the use pirated product.

Actions by the EU and the US Governments

The European Union and the US government are both taking the piracy problem seriously. This is the focus of Chap. 7. In the US, the Department of Homeland Security plays a major role in protecting IPR rights. Also involved are the US Department of State, the US Department of Commerce (International Trade Administration and Commercial Law Development), several divisions of the US Department of Justice, the FBI, and the US Agency for International Development, USTR, the US Patent and Trademark Office and the Copyright Office of the Library of Congress. The government uses the STOP! as an umbrella program designed to integrate the various government agencies involved with the anti-counterfeiting effort. As shown in Chap. 7, many of the new government-led initiatives have been established within the past decade and one may question how effective these agencies and/or legislation have reduced the profit incentives of counterfeit trade. On the contrary, the estimates of illicit trade show double-digit (if not triple-digit) percent growth from year to year based on both US and EU seizure statistics.

The EU has nine directives in effect governing some aspect of intellectual property rights. The relative recency of the directive establishing minimum enforcement of IPR standards and the advent of 12 new member states since 2004 seems to mean there may be difficulties in implementation within the EU as well. It is expected that major differences in enforcement will prevail within the 27 member states. In the past, the United States and the EU have agreed on a joint action strategy. Despite all this increased protection of intellectual property rights by way of both new government agencies and legislation, many observers believe IPR owners must continue to be vigilant in protecting their own rights through company-directed measures.

Government and Industry Led Operations

In addition to the many government agencies described in the United States and the EU, there are a large number of multilateral organizations looking to help secure a better IPR environment. These include TRIPs, part of the World Trade Organization, WIPO from the UN, the World Health Organization, OECD, and Interpol to name a few. However, as shown in chaps. 4 and 11 our research indicates managers do not see participating in these organizations as particularly effective. This leads us to speculate about the effectiveness of these multilateral agencies to prohibit the growth of the fake trade. It appears that there is a similarity here to our assertion about the Stop Fakes! and EU Enforcement Directive. The development of these supranational agencies has not diminished the escalation of counterfeits. In fact, we have seen a rise of fake product offerings in nontraditional goods, such as pharmaceuticals and cigarettes that shows not only growth in the trade, but also product diversification.

A number of business associations also address the IPR problem, for example the International Anti-Counterfeiting Coalition (IACC), the Business Software Alliance (BSA), the Motion Picture Association (MPA), the Recording Industry Association of America (RIAA), and the International Federation of Phonographic Industry (IFPI). Some of these associations are focused on one particular industry and some are more effective than others. As described in Chap. 4, several managers in our research found the IACC somewhat effective. Several of our sources of information are these business associations since they provide a wealth of data. However, one must also recognize a possible bias in their data, as discussed in Chap. 10, regarding the overestimation of the size of the Internet piracy market for the movie industry. In 2008, the MPA significantly decreased the estimated size of the market lost to counterfeits through the Internet to appease criticism from several sources that questioned the validity of their data collection.

China

As we have seen China is the key supplier of counterfeit product. In this country just about every product is being pirated, sold, and exported. Chapter 9 briefly reviews the unprecedented growth of the Chinese economy which has risen from subsistence and now stands second largest in the world. As might be expected with this rapid growth have come rapid increases in exports. And globalization has allowed a concomitant growth in exported counterfeit product.

To understand the attitudes toward intellectual property in this country, one needs to look at the history of China starting over 2,000 years ago. Confucianism required the control of information and the idea that the best current inventions are based on shared work from the past. These basic cultural precepts dovetailed well with Communism and worked against respect for individual or firm intellectual property rights. Although China, reacting to heavy prodding from the United States, has enacted acceptable IPR legislation, enforcement continues to be a problem. Many programs have been launched by the Chinese central government to stamp out piracy but the competing interests of local and national government agencies makes actual enforcement inconsistent. Recently a new State Council-level leadership structure has been formed chaired by a Vice Premier to continue the fight against counterfeit products. While there is some evidence that attitudes may be changing in China, we continue to believe firms must take their own initiatives to protect their valuable intellectual property in this important market.

The Internet

As previously stated the Internet is ideal for distributing pirated products. Some web suppliers are quite sophisticated. The Internet is seen as the third largest market for distributing counterfeit products of every kind from software and music to pharmaceuticals. Trading on this virtual marketplace of more than 2 billion consumers is by its nature unregulated. Here again, measuring the amount of counterfeit products sold is nearly impossible, although many industry associations say their members are feeling the effects of unauthorized Internet sales. The US government has launched a number of specialized operations aimed at reducing online piracy of products like computer games but consumers do not see the harm in downloading copyrighted material from the Internet. In some cases groups, such as the infamous warez, release pirated products as a matter of pride, not for profits. This type of intrinsic motivation led to the passing of the No Electronic Theft (NET) Act in the United States. Under this legislation, it became a federal crime to reproduce, distribute, or share copies of electronic copyrighted works such as songs, movies, games, or software programs, even if the person copying or distributing the material acts without commercial purpose and/or receives no private financial gain. The Digital Millennium Copyright Act was tested in the US court system.

In 2008, a US Court found that eBay had not violated Tiffany's trademarks by failing to adequately police what is on sale on its website. But, just 2 weeks earlier, a French court fined eBay €40 million for failing to protect the IPR of Louis Vuitton and other brand holders. The proposed Commercial Felony Streaming Act (S. 978) in the United States will provide another measure to curb the theft of digital content on the Internet—this bill targets criminals that profit from streaming, not consumers uploading their "lip-syncing" performances on YouTube. As discussed in Chap. 10, litigation will continue to test the enforcement of intellectual property rights in a virtual environment and the two divergent rulings against eBay create more confusion. The probable future litigation against additional Internet-based firms like YouTube.com is inevitable. Overall, the Internet creates special problems for IP managers.

Management Actions

Despite the actions of governments, multilateral organizations and associations, it is clear that owners of intellectual property must develop their own action plans to protect their rights. For more than 20 years much has been written about protecting IPR. Many authors have included very specific recommendations of actions firms should take to ensure their IPR is not being violated. The authors of this book have conducted research with corporate managers to see which of the recommended actions are useful and which are ineffective. Based on this research, in Chap. 11 we have recommended a specific action plan for both large and small firms that can be used to fight counterfeiting of their product. The use of interesting technology, such as labels with unique cryptographic signatures, and consumer-targeted authentication technology hold promise for making unauthorized product copying much more difficult—we are no longer talking about the pirate's ability simply to make a fake hologram to mislead the consumer. But, as noted in our work on counterfeit cigarettes, the pirates are very nimble players and can quickly circumvent new anti-counterfeiting technologies designed to fool the consumer. In this chapter we also emphasized the importance of special packaging which is frequently changed as an anti-counterfeiting weapon.

The most effective anti-counterfeiting actions include first, registering trademarks and patents; urging distributors to notify manufacturers of pirated product; educating and warning distributors and retailers; pursuing injunctions against pirates; educating employees; encouraging enforcement and obtaining local police support; and setting up an information monitoring system to watch for signs of violations. The recommended seven-step plan begins with developing an IP protection strategy, then forming a brand integrity team which takes responsibility for registering trademarks, patents, and copyrights, developing an information monitoring program and designing education and action plans as well as developing measurement and feedback mechanisms.

Future Research

As we have established in previous chapters, several articles have been written about the continuing problem of counterfeit product but very few studies have been based on a carefully constructed research design with survey work (that is, to measure managerial perceptions, consumer complicity behavior across country markets, and the like). Obviously it is quite difficult to conduct research about a subject where individuals are working outside the law to reap significant profits. The pirates are hardly willing to talk about their operations. On the other side, those charged with protecting corporate IPR are also reluctant to discuss their most successful strategies. In some of our survey work, managers simply stated that their firm's anti-counterfeiting tactics were proprietary. Thus, we found a paradox in our research efforts designed to increase the general knowledge of the effectiveness of an array of anti-fake techniques, since several firms were not willing to share their expertise. Other companies, in nontraditional counterfeit goods, such as pharmaceuticals, are struggling with the public relations issues that they face with the growth of counterfeit prescription drugs—the fear can be brand dilution and/or switching if the populous is made more aware of the illicit trade in this industry. However, as discussed in Chap. 6, some pharmaceutical firms, such as Pfizer are taking a very proactive stance on educating the consumer about fakes with video postings at their company site on YouTube. These are probably some of the reasons why insignificant research has been completed in this area. While more empirical research is required, the major barrier to replication of this type of study will be to garner a reasonable sample size to build on the results gathered. Nevertheless we present a number of open questions we believe may lend themselves to future research:

1. *The true size and growth of the counterfeit product market.* A coordinated effort based on more than hearsay or extrapolations from very small seizure statistics is required to establish a more reliable baseline to estimate the growth of counterfeit trade.
2. *The determining factors of the IPR environment.* It is possible that other factors in addition to the level of consumer complicity, pirate activity, and host country enforcement determine the intellectual property rights environment of a particular country market. Thus, in our efforts to standardize a model that captures the main variables of a "global" IPR environment, we may be excluding other factors that correlate with this illicit trade, such as a specific country's level of economic development and/or its inhabitants access to technology.
3. *The validity of the variables used in the IPR conceptual framework.* The exact relationships between the IPR environment, the level of the firm's market commitment and subsequent IPR actions targeted at consumers, distribution channels, home and host governments. We found mixed support for this model in our study discussed in Chap. 4. Thus, the model needs to be examined using more sophisticated hypothesis testing with a larger

sample size to establish the scale items used in the model and their probable interrelationships.

4. *The context of measuring the protection of intellectual property rights.* The need for more specific market research that varies a study design by either product category (such as fake movies vs. counterfeit pharmaceuticals), shopping environment (such as physical vs. Internet markets), and/or espoused values of the consumers willing to engage in the counterfeit trade (such as idealism vs. relativism) is required to augment our understanding of "context" that shapes the problem across country markets. Our recent published work of consumers in Brazil, Russia, India, China (BRIC), and the United States was a start at answering such questions as whether the consumer feels more ethical concerns for a fake pharmaceutical available through the Internet? And, how does a complicit consumer across these distinct country markets perceive the effectiveness of demarketing communications?
5. *The need to establish whether market segmentation variables can profile a complicit consumer.* Previous research has established very weak linkages to demographic variables such as level of education, to predict a consumer's complicity to purchase counterfeit products. Even the motion picture industry has the broad market segment of male, aged 16–24 and living in an urban environment to profile its "typical" user of fake movies. In an age of "zip code" market segmentation and "mobile marketing" can we somehow find a way to develop better segmentation variables that will allow firms to target their actions in a more effective manner? As discussed in Chap. 5, our recent work using BRIC and US consumers created a consumer complicity index to segment based on non-demographic variables, such as their willingness in the past (and future) to obtain counterfeits in both virtual and physical markets. Also, the current work in this area has been conducted via convenience samples in one country market—thus the question of how these variables change in across country markets is just starting to be addressed in other studies, like the 2009 BASCAP study.
6. *The plausibility of social marketing campaigns to change consumer behavior in counterfeit goods.* The social marketing literature has been established in terms of decreasing consumption of such products as alcohol and there are parallels that can be made between a MADD drunk driving campaign and fake pharmaceuticals—the fear is the same—severe health risk.
7. *The effectiveness of multilateral and national agencies and the recent legislation designed to combat the growth of counterfeit trade.* The legal community has published articles that address litigation for such legislation as the Digital Millennium Copyright Act. However, there is a complete lack of pragmatic work that even questions the "cause and effect" relationship of the agencies and/or the legislation designed to deter pirates. For example, did the DMCA of NET Act established in the United States really deter the warez groups? Did the TRIPs within the WTO trickle down to grass roots enforcement of intellectual property rights at the country-specific level or does this type of supranational organization remain as the focal point of global policymakers alone?

The Outlook

Looking at the underlying reasons for the growth of counterfeit product sales around the world described in this book, it is difficult to envision a scenario which will negatively impact these driving forces. The price-performance ratio of technology continues to decline, meaning pirates can get the production and communications equipment they need at ever lower costs. Trade barriers continue to fall and it does not seem like the number of free trade zones and ports will be declining anytime soon. And the free flow of financial resources appears to be growing. Our research on consumer complicity reinforces the idea that consumers do not see much harm in purchasing counterfeit product. In our study discussed in Chap. 4, advertising attempting to change this perception was judged relatively ineffective by managers involved in fighting the counterfeit problem. The Internet will continue to grow, and despite the French court finding against eBay, it is apparent that this medium seems almost ideally suited to the distribution of pirated product. The growth of relative affluence in newly emerging countries like China and India will increase the demand for well-recognized brands. But many consumers will not be able to afford to purchase a legitimate product. This will also be a force for the continued increase in sales of counterfeit goods. Managers surveyed by the authors generally do not see international bodies as particularly effective in slowing down the growth of pirated product. In addition, enforcement of local laws is uneven at best. Since other considerations often are far more important in multilateral negotiations, the enforcement of IPR rights in many countries will probably not improve much. Judging by US history, it is possible that indigenous manufacturers will demand improved enforcement of IPR laws in these newly emerging markets and that could significantly slow local pirate activities.

The European Patent Office (EPO) has been conducting a project attempting to assess the future of intellectual property (EPO 2011). This 30-year-old organization includes 38 nations. The project is focused on the worldwide IP environment and is based on expert development of proposed scenarios. The EPO project sees five basic driving forces affecting the IP environment over the next 15 years. They define these as power, global jungle, rate of change, systemic risks, and knowledge paradox. The first driving force, power, recognizes that power is moving from established authority such as governments to new organizations including multinational corporations, societal and international organizations, special interest movements, and regional trading blocs. For the global jungle they see globalization as an integrator of national economic systems and a "flattening of the world." Rate of change relates to the tension between the rate of change in technology and long-term cycles for political and legal institutions. Systemic risks focus on the risks created by global interdependence including pressures caused by population that may result in cultural conflicts and even the rise of terrorism. The knowledge paradox focuses on the tension between monopoly ownership of intellectual property, the speed of technological obsolescence and the accessibility of information, making counterfeiting easier. The EPO recognizes the problems of "heavy-handed IPR enforcement." For example, the recent outcry over the attempt to implement ACTA seems to show there are limits to acceptable restrictions in the Internet world.

As a result of this analysis the EPO has created four possible scenarios. In the first called "Market Rules," multinational corporations hold the power and they can build major IP portfolios where the market will determine the results of the system. The second called "Whose Game" sees geopolitics as the dominant driver and enforcement of IP becomes very difficult and fragmented. The third they have named "Trees of Knowledge" where society is the key force. In this case society loses trust for the IP system and therefore that system erodes. A loose knowledge movement echoing the environmental movement comes about with the idea that knowledge is a common good. Finally there is "Blue Skies" where the key is technology. In this scenario complex new technologies force changes in the classic IP system. The EPO sums up by reminding us that there are "fundamental changes in the way in which knowledge is being produced and used within the global society." Their questions attempt to identify the best way to adapt to these changes.

Based on the knowledge we have gathered for the creation of this book it is difficult to predict the future of the intellectual property rights environment. It only seems safe to say that vigilance on the part of IPR owners will be required for the foreseeable future—*the piracy paradox persists.*

References

A crime with huge profits, low penalties. (2012, January 7). *ABC News*. Retrieved June 9, 2012, from http://abcnews.go.com/Business/story?id=89874&page=1#.UKLB_2e1nmB.

A Fistful of Fakes. (2012). *Supplement magazine to The Financial Times*. Fondation de la Haute Horlogerie. Cited March, 2012.

Abbott, G. W. Jr. & Sporn, L. S. (2002). *Trademark counterfeiting*. New York: Aspen Law and Business: § 1.03 [A] [2].

About VeRo. (2012). *An overview of the Verified Rights Owner program at Ebay*. Retrieved June 16, 2012, from http://pages.ebay.co.uk/vero/about.html.

ACTA Up. (2012). *Economist*, 402.8771, 62. Retrieved June 1, 2012, from Business Source Complete, from http://www.economist.com/node/21547235.

Administration's White Paper on Intellectual Property Enforcement Legislative Recommendations. (2011, March). A report from the Executive Office of the President of the United States. Retrieved July 1, 2011, from http://www.whitehouse.gov/sites/default/files/ip_white_paper.pdf.

Alford, W. P. (1995). *To steal a book is an elegant offense*. Stanford, CA: Stanford University Press.

Allen, E. (2011). *The illicit trade in tobacco products and how to tackle it*. Washington, DC: International Tax and Investment Center.

Allen, W. (2010). Counterfeits proliferate. *Packaging Digest*, pp. 34–35. Retrieved January 7, 2012, from www.packagingdigest.com.

Al-Rafee, S., & Cronan, T. P. (2006). Digital piracy: Factors that influence attitude toward behavior'. *Journal of Business Ethics, 63*(3), 237–259.

Amcor. (2011a, July 22). Submission by Amcor to the Australian Government on the Australian Act, Submission No. 42. Retrieved March 13, 2012, from http://www.aph.gov.au/house/committee/haa/billtobaccopackage/subs/sub42.pdf.

Amcor Ltd. (2011b). *Inquiry on the tobacco plain packaging bill.* Retrieved January 25, 2012, from http://www.aph.gov.au/house/committee/haa/billtobaccopackage/subs/sub42.pdf.

Amcor. (2012). Retrieved March 28, 2012, from http://www.amcor.com.

Andreasen, A. R. (2005). *Social marketing in the 21st century*. Thousand Oaks, CA: Sage.

Anti-Counterfeiting Amendments of 2003. (2004). *Hearing before the subcommittee on courts, the internet, and intellectual property of the committee on the judiciary house of representatives 108th congress, 2nd session*. Retrieved July 27, 2007, from http://commdocs.house.gov/committees/judiciary/hju91752.000/hju91752_0.HTM.

Asanghanwa, E. (2008). *Product counterfeiting made easy. And why it's so difficult to prevent.* Retrieved May 27, 2008, from http://www.rsaconference.com/uploadedFiles/RSA365/Security_Topics/Deployment_Strategies/White_Papers/Atmel/doc5280.pdf.

P. Chaudhry and A. Zimmerman, *Protecting Your Intellectual Property Rights*, Management for Professionals, DOI 10.1007/978-1-4614-5568-4,

Associated Press. (2006). *China's anti-piracy war: Companies fight back. MSNBC.* Retrieved January 14, 2008, from http://www.msnbc.msn.com/id/13617623/.

A.T. Kearney, Inc. (2005). *The counterfeiting paradox.* Retrieved September 18, 2007, from http://www.atkearney.com/shared_res/pdf/Counterfeiting_Paradox.pdf.

Bajaj, V., & Pollack, A. (2012, March 12). India orders Bayer to license a patented drug. *New York Times.* Retrieved May 28, 2012, from http://www.nytimes.com/2012/03/13/business/global/india-overrules-bayer-allowing-generic-drug.html.

Baker, J. (2011, November 22). Business software alliance withdraws support for stop online piracy act. *PCWorld Business.* Retrieved February 13, 2012, from http://www.pcworld.com/businesscenter/article/244501/business_software_alliance_withdraws_support_for_stop_online_piracy_act.html.

Baker, S., & Green, H. (2008, June 2). Beyond blogs: What business needs to know. *Business Week*, pp. 44–50.

Barboza, D. (2007, July 7, 8). China's new concern: Exploding phones. *International Herald Tribune*, p. 1.

Barboza, D., & Lohr, S. (2007, July 25). FBI and Chinese seize $500 million of counterfeit software. *New York Times*, p. C1.

Barker, A. (2012). EU reform: Wrangle over patent court site nears end. *Financial Times.* Retrieved on August 1, 2012, from http://www.ft.com/cms/s/0/c5da3922-b313-11e1-83a9-00144feabdc0.html#axzz2BxOXIlhJ.

Barry, K. (2007). *Counterfeits and counterfeiters: The ancient world.* Retrieved September 11, 2007, from http://www.ancient-times.com/newsletters/n13/n13.html.

BASCAP. (2009). *Research report on consumer attitudes and perceptions on counterfeiting and piracy.* (2009, November). A report prepared by the Business Action to Stop Counterfeiting and Piracy (BASCAP). Retrieved June 1, 2012, from http://www.iccwbo.org/uploadedFiles/BASCAP/Pages/BASCAP-Consumer%20Research%20Report_Final.pdf.

Bate, R. (2010). India's fake drugs are a real problem. *Wall Street Journal.* Retrieved May 19, 2012, from http://online.wsj.com/article/SB10001424052748703315404575249901511960396.html.

Battersby, G. J. (2011). Coping with infringements and counterfeits. *The Licensing Journal,* 19–25.

BBC. (2005). *Internet piracy trio sent to jail.* Retrieved May 1, 2007, from http://news.bbc.co.uk

BBC. (n.d.). *Immigration and emigration—Industrial espionage.* Retrieved November 23, 2007, from http://www.bbc.co.uk/legacies/immig_emig/england/derby/article_2.shtml.

Benson, T. (2004, August 17). Brazil starts to crack down on counterfeit goods. *New York Times*, p. W1.

Berntsen, M. C. (2010). Knowledge and misfeasance: Tiffany v. Ebay and the knowledge requirement of contributory trademark infringement. *16 Boston University Journal of Science and Technology Law 102.* Winter.

Best Global Brands 2011. (2011). Retrieved May 24, 2012, from http://www.interbrand.com/en/best-global-brands/best-global-brands-2008/best-global-brands-2011.aspx/.

Bialik, C. (2007, October 19). Efforts to quantify sales of pirated goods lead to fuzzy figures. *Wall Street Journal*, p. B1.

Bian, X., & Moutinho, L. (2009). An investigation of determinants of counterfeit purchase consideration. *Journal of Business Research, 62*(3), 368–378.

Bian, X., & Veloutsou, C. (2007). Consumers' attitudes regarding non-deceptive counterfeit brands in the UK and China. *Journal of Brand Management, 14*(3), 211–222.

Bloch, P. H., Bush, R. F., & Campbell, L. (1993). Consumer 'accomplices' in product counterfeiting: A demand-side investigation. *Journal of Consumer Marketing, 10*(4), 27–36.

Bogdanich, W. (2007, December 17). Free-trade zones ease passage of counterfeit drugs to U.S. *New York Times*, p. A1.

British filmmakers seeking major crackdown on piracy. (2004). *DVD Intelligence News Desk Archive.* Retrieved June 15, 2008, from http://www.dvdintelligence.com/news_desk/editorials/FIGHTING%20PIRACY/pira_filmmakers.htm [ad copy in 6.13].

Bruner, G., James, K., & Hensel, P. (2001). *Marketing scales handbook: A compilation of multiitem measures* (Vol. 3). Chicago: American Marketing Association.

Bufalino, A. J., Moreno, C. P., & Villeneuve, A. (2010, September 5). Internet merchants owe a greater duty of care to their European Clients—Louis Vuitton v. eBay [France] in contrast see Tiffany v. eBay [NY, US]. *National Law Review.* Retrieved June 5, 2012, from http://www.natlawreview.com/article/internet-merchants-owe-greater-duty-care-to-their-european-clients-louis-vuitton-v-ebay-fran.

Bush, R., Bloch, P., & Dawson, S. (1989). Remedies for product counterfeiting. *Business Horizons, 32*(1), 59–65.

Business Software Alliance. (2010). *Piracy impact study: The economic benefits of reducing software piracy.* Retrieved April 1, 2012, from http://portal.bsa.org/piracyimpact2010/studies/piracyimpactstudy2010.pdf.

Business Software Alliance. (2011a, November 15). *At summit meeting, global software industry executives advocate steps to grow India's IT sector.* Retrieved November 29, 2011, from http://www.bsa.org/country/News%20and%20Events/News%20Archives/en/2011/en-10262011-smithbill.aspx.

Business Software Alliance. (2011b, October 26). *House bill shines light on growing problem of online piracy.* Retrieved November 29, 2011, from http://www.bsa.org/country/News%20and%20Events/News%20Archives/en/2011/en-11152011-gss.aspx.

Business Software Alliance. (2011c, November 21). *China's new commitments to strengthen IP protection and tackle software piracy offer promise of needed progress.* Retrieved November 29, 2011, from http://www.bsa.org/country/News%20and%20Events/News%20Archives/en/2011/en-11212011-jcct.aspx.

Business Software Alliance. (2011d). *Eighth annual BSA global software piracy study.* Retrieved November 29, 2011, from Business Software Alliance Web site: http://www.bsa.org.

Business Software Alliance. (2011e, May 12). *Emerging markets drive software piracy to a record $59 billion in 2010, BSA reports.* Retrieved November 29, 2011, from http://www.bsa.org/country/News%20and%20Events/News%20Archives/global/05062011-idc-globalpiracystudy.aspx.

Business Software Alliance. (2012). *Shadow market: 2011 BSA global software piracy study.* Retrieved May 18, 2012, from http://portal.bsa.org/globalpiracy2011/downloads/study_pdf/2011_BSA_Piracy_Study-Standard.pdf.

Business Software Alliance. (n.d.a.). *Smart about software: Software strategies for small businesses.* Retrieved November 29, 2011, from http://www.bsa.org/country/News%20and%20Events/Campaigns.aspx.

Buzzeo, R. (2005, October 4). Counterfeit pharmaceuticals and the public health. *The Wall Street Journal*, p. A20.

Capaccio, T. (2012, May 22). China counterfeit electronics found in weapons, U.S. panel says. *Bloomberg.* Retrieved June 5, 2012, from http://www.sfgate.com/cgi-bin/article.cgi?f=/g/a/2012/05/22/bloomberg_articlesM4DTXZ6KLVR701-M4F3M.DTL.

Cardwell, R., & Ghazalian, P. L. (2012). The effects of the TRIPS agreement on international protection of intellectual property rights. *International Trade Journal, 26*(1), 19–36.

Castle, S. (2007, July 10). The spread of tainted products from China. *International Herald Tribune*, p. 1.

CBS News. (2006). *A place where crime does pay.* Retrieved November 23, 2007, from http://www.cbsnews.com/stories/2006/03/06/eveningnews/printable1375945.shtml.

Chang, J. (2011). Personal interview. *Shanghai*, January 5, 2011.

Chang, J. (2012). Personal interview. *Telephone*, June 7, 2012.

Chaudhry, P. (2006). Changing levels of intellectual property rights protection for global firms: A synopsis of recent U.S. and EU trade enforcement strategies. *Business Horizons, 49*(6),463–472.

Chaudhry, P. (2012). Curbing consumer complicity for counterfeits in a digital environment. *Journal of Business & Technology Law, 7*(1), 23–34.

Chaudhry, P., & Stumpf, S. (2010). Consumer complicity with counterfeits: Fight of flight—Adressing the intellectual property issues in international trade. *Global Trade and Customs Journal, 5*(9), 347–357.

Chaudhry, P., Chaudhry, S., Stumpf, S., & Sudler, H. (2011a). Piracy in Cyber Space: Consumer complicity, pirates and enterprise enforcement. *Enterprise Information Systems, 5*(2), 255–271.
Chaudhry, P., Cordell, V., & Zimmerman, A. (2005). Modelling anti-counterfeiting strategies in response to protecting intellectual property rights in a global environment. *The Marketing Review, 5*(Spring), 59–72.
Chaudhry, P., Hill, R., Stumpf, S., & Yalcinkaya, G. (2011b). Consumer complicity across emerging markets. In M. Sarstedt, M. Schwaiger, C. R. Taylor (Eds.), *Measurement and research methods in international marketing (Advances in international marketing)* (Vol. 22, pp. 223–239). Bingley: Emerald Group Publishing Limited.
Chaudhry, P., Peters, J., Zimmerman, A., & Cordell, V. (2009). Evidence of managerial response to the level of consumer complicity, pirate activity, and host country enforcement of counterfeit goods: An exploratory study. *Multinational Business Review, 17*(4), 21–44.
Chaudhry, P., & Stumpf, S. (2007). Product counterfeiting in China: Managerial perceptions of supplier and buyer interest in counterfeit goods and the probable effectiveness of corporate anti-counterfeiting actions. In *Challenges in management—Yearbook of the graduate school of business administration. Zürich, 14*. Berlin: Springer.
Chaudhry, P., & Stumpf, S. (2010). Consumer complicity with counterfeits: Fight of flight—Adressing the intellectual property issues in international trade. *Global Trade and Customs Journal, 5*(9), 347–357.
Chaudhry, P., & Stumpf, S. (2011). Consumer complicity with counterfeit products. *Journal of Consumer Marketing, 28*(2), 139–151.
Chaudhry, P., & Walsh, M. (1995). Intellectual property rights: Changing levels of protection under GATT, NAFTA and the EU. *Columbia Journal of World Business, 30*(2), 80–92.
Chaudhry, P., & Walsh, M. (1996). An assessment of the impact of counterfeiting in international markets: The piracy paradox persists. *Columbia Journal of World Business, 31*(3), 34–49.
Chaudhry, P., & Zimmerman, A. (2009). *The economics of counterfeit trade*. Heidelberg: Springer. Retrieved January 20, 2012.
Chaudhry, P., Zimmerman, A., Peters, J., & Cordell, V. (2009b). Preserving intellectual property rights: Managerial insight into the escalating counterfeit market quandary. *Business Horizons, 52*(1), 57–66.
Chinese authorities find 22 fake Apple Stores, *BBC News: Technology*. (August 21, 2011). Retrieved March 25, 2012, from http://www.bbc.co.uk/news/technology-14503724.
Chinese consumers are falling out of love with fakes. (2012, January 14). *The Economist*, p. 67.
Chiu, H. C., Hsieh, Y. C., & Wang, M. C. (2008). How to encourage customers to use legal software. *Journal of Business Ethics, 80*(3), 583–595.
Choate, P. (2005). The golden covenant. *The New York Times*. Retrieved November 23, 2007, from http://www.nytimes.com/2005/07/10/books/chapters/0710–1st-choate.html?pagewanted=print.
Chow, D. C. K. (2005). *Intellectual property protection as economic policy: Will China ever enforce its IP laws?* Statement before Congressional-Executive Commission on China. Retrieved January 25, 2008, from http://www.cecc.gov/pages/roundtables/051605/Chow.php.
CIA World Factbook 2012. (2012). Retrieved April 20, 2012, from https://www.cia.gov/library/publications/the-world-factbook/rankorder/2001rank.html.
Cloak, T. (2007). The digital titanic: The sinking of YouTube.com in the DMCA's safe harbor. *Vanderbilt Law Review, 60*(5), 1561.
CNBC. (2007). *In Paraguay, piracy bleeds U.S. profits, aids terrorists*. Retrieved November 23, 2007, from http://www.cnbc.com/id/21082897/site/14081545/page/2/.
CNN. (1997). *Reformer with an iron fist*. Retrieved January 30, 2008, from http://www.cnn.com/SPECIALS/1999/china.50/inside.china/profiles/deng.xiaoping/.
Commuri, S. (2009). The impact of counterfeiting on genuine-item consumers' brand relationships. *The Journal of Marketing, 73*(3), 86–98.
Companies. U.S. & Foreign Commercial Service and U.S. Department of State. (n.d.). Retrieved May 24, 2012, from http://export.gov/worldwide_us/index.asp.

Container Shipping: Successful Turnaround. (March 28, 2011). Deutsche Bank, p.2, Table 3, Retrieved March 25, 2012, from http://www.dws-investments.com/EN/docs/research/container_shipping.pdf.

Cordell, V. V., Wongtada, N., & Kieschnick, R. (1996). Counterfeit purchase intentions: Role of lawfulness attitudes and product traits as determinants. *Journal of Business Research, 35*, 41–53.

Counterfeit drugs—New technology to combat counterfeit. (2012, February 12). Retrieved June 20, 2012, from https://its-true.de/en/news/news.html.

Counterfeit goods are linked to terror groups. (2007). *International Herald Tribune*. Retrieved July 16, 2007, from http://www.iht.com/articles/2007/02/12/business/fake.php.

Counterfeit sneakers seized in Germany. (2006). Retrieved July 17, 2007, from http://www.blog-toplist.com/sports/blogdetails-1536–5.html.

Counterfeiting in the United States: Consumer Behaviors and Attitudes. (2007). A report prepared by both the U.S. Chamber of Commerce and Gallup Consulting. Retrieved June 11, 2012, from http://www.theglobalipcenter.com/sites/default/files/reports/documents/uschambergallupcon-sumerperceptions.pdf.

Counterfeiting: Changes foreign companies can and should make. Alibaba.com website. (2006). Retrieved December 18, 2007, from http://resources.alibaba.com/article/4115/Counterfeiting_changes_foreign_companies_can_and_should_make.htm

Counterfeiting: The industry is on the wrong track. (2009, June 24). *Best in packaging.* Retrieved March 28, 2012, from http://bestinpackaging.blogspot.co.uk/2009/06/counterfeiting-industry-is-on-wrong.html.

Court confirms DMCA 'good faith' web site shut down rights (sic). (2003). *The Register.* Retrieved May 1, 2008, from http://www.theregister.co.uk/2003/05/30/court_confirms_dmca_good_faith/.

Court Jails Pirate Bay Founders. (2009, April 17). *BBC News*. Retrieved June 16, 2012, from http://news.bbc.co.uk/1/hi/8003799.stm.

Cronan, T. P., & Al-Rafee, S. (2008). Factors that influence the intention to pirate software and media. *Journal of Business Ethics, 78*(4), 527–545.

Croxon, S. (2007). Personal interview. *London*, October 19, 2007.

Curtis, W. E. (1889). *Trade and transportation between the United States and Spanish America* (pp. 287–289). Washington, DC: Government Printing Office.

Davison, M. (2010). Obstacles to implementing an effective anti-counterfeit strategy: Can they be overcome? *Pharmaceutical Technology Europe.* Retrieved June 1, 2012, from http://www.pharmatech.com/ptedigital0710.

Davison, M. (2011a). DRASTIC technologies for on-pack authentication. *Pharmaceutical Processing, 26*(3), 18–19. Retrieved June 1, 2012, from http://www.highbeam.com/doc/1G1-256212714.html.

Davison, M. (2011b). *Pharmaceutical Anti-Counterfeiting: Combating the Real Danger from Fake Drugs*, p. 132.

Deng, S., & Townsend, P. (1996). A guide to intellectual property rights in Southeast Asia and China. *Business Horizons, 39*(6), 43–51.

Department of Commerce. (2011). Retrieved November 29, 2011, from http://www.commerce.gov/news/fact-sheets/2011/11/21/22nd-us-china-joint-commission-commerce-and-trade-fact-sheet.

Di, H. (2011, November 6). Fake goods target of aggressive campaign. *Global Times*. Retrieved May 8, 2012, from http://www.globaltimes.cn/DesktopModules/DnnForge%20-%20NewsArticles/Print.aspx?tabid=99&tabmoduleid=94&articleId=682662&moduleId=405&PortalID=0.

Doms, M. (2003). Communications equipment: What has happened to prices? *Federal Reserve Bank of San Francisco*. Retrieved December 19, 2007, from http://www.frbsf.org/publications/economics/papers/2003/wp03–15bk.pdf.

Dunlop, T. (2012, March 12). China's faux Bordeaux stirs wine market. *Reuters*. Retrieved April 20, 2012, from http://www.reuters.com/article/2012/03/12/us-china-wine-fake-idUSBRE82B07E20120312.

DuPont anticounterfeiting solutions. (2012). Retrieved June 1, 2012, from http://www2.dupont.com/Authentication/en_US/index.html.

DuPont fights against counterfeit products. (2007). Retrieved December 21, 2007, from http://ap.stop.dupont.com/Media_Center/en_RU/news_events/article20070516.html.

EBay protects intellectual property through its VeRO program. (n.d.). Retrieved April 1, 2008, from http://pages.ebay.com/help/tp/programs-vero-ov.html.

Ebay. (2012). About VeRo programme. Retrieved on June 5, 2012, from http://pages.ebay.co.uk/vero/about.html.

ECN. (2012). *Partnership to create nanotechnology-driven anti-counterfeiting technology.* Retrieved June 4, 2012, from http://www.ecnmag.com/news/2012/01/partnership-create-nano-technology-driven-anti-counterfeiting-technology.

The Economist Intelligence Unit. (2006). *Market indicators & forecasts.* Retrieved November 10, 2007, from www.eiu.com.

Economist Intelligence Unit. (2012). http://www.eiu.com.

Eisend, M., & Schuchert-Güler, P. (2006). Explaining counterfeit purchases: A review and pre-view. *Academy of Marketing Science Review, 6*(12), 1–25.

Engleman, E. (2011, June 16). Illegal video streaming elevated to felony under Senate bill. *Bloomberg*. Retrieved June 16, 2012, from http://www.bloomberg.com/news/2011-06-16/illegal-video-streaming-elevated-to-felony-under-senate-measure.html.

Epstein, Z. (2012, June 15). Found of illegal movie streaming site sentenced to 4.5 years in jail, $4.7 million fine. *Yahoo News!* Retrieved June 16, 2012, from http://news.yahoo.com/founder-illegal-movie-streaming-sentenced-4-5-years-202537619.html.

Ereli, A. (2004). *United States announces programs to fight billions lost to intellectual property theft*. Retrieved August 1, 2005, from http://www.usstate.gov.

European Commission. (2004). Directive 2004/48/EC of the European Parliament and of the Council of 29 April 2004 on the Enforcement of Intellectual Property Rights. *Official Journal of the European Union*. Retrieved July 1, 2005, from http://www.europa.eu.int.

European Commission. (2004). EU strengthens fight against piracy and counterfeiting beyond its borders. Retrieved on November 5, 2006, from http://trade.ec.europa.eu/doclib/docs/2004/december/tradoc_119906.pdf.

European Commission. (2005). *Customs: Commission launches action plan to combat counterfeiting and piracy*. Retrieved December 18, 2005, from http://europa.eu.int.

European Commission. (2006). *Russia*. Retrieved December 28, 2008, from http://trade.ec.europa.eu/doclib/docs/2006/october/tradoc_130411.pdf.

European Commission. (2008). U.S. customs and border protection and European commission announce first joint operation combating counterfeit goods. Retrieved on May 1, 2012, from http://ec.europa.eu/taxation_customs/resources/documents/common/whats_new/ec_us_joint_operation_en.pdf.

European Commission. (2010a). *Report on EU customs enforcement of intellectual property rights: Results at the EU border.* Retrieved June 15, 2012, from http://ec.europa.eu/taxation_customs/resources/documents/customs/customs_controls/counterfeit_piracy/statistics/statistics_2010.pdf.

European Commission. (2010b). *Operation Sirocco 40 million cigarettes seized in joint customs operation*. Retrieved January 13, 2012, from http://europa.eu/rapid/pressReleasesAction.do?reference=IP/10/1275&format=HTML&aged=0&language=EN&guiLanguage=en.

European Commission. (2011a). *Taxation and customs union. Report on EU customs enforcement of intellectual property rights: Results at the EU border—2010*. Retrieved May 24, 2012, from http://ec.europa.eu/taxation_customs/resources/documents/customs/customs_controls/counterfeit_piracy/statistics/statistics_2010.pdf.

European Commission. (2011b). *OLAF and Chinese authorities join forces to fight cigarette smuggling from Asia*. Retrieved January 13, 2012, from http://ec.europa.eu/anti_fraud/press_room/pr/2011/18_en.html.

European Commission. (2011c). *Taxation and customs union*. Retrieved January 6, 2012, from http://ec.europa.eu/taxation_customs/resources/documents/customs/customs_controls/counterfeit_piracy/statistics/statistics_2010.pdf.

European Commission. (2011d, April 13). *Commission proposes unitary patent protection to boost research and innovation.* Retrieved June 25, 2012, from http://europa.eu/rapid/pressReleasesAction.do?reference=IP/11/470&format=HTML&aged=0&language=EN&guiLanguage=en.

European Commission. (2012). Enforcement of intellectual property rights. Retrieved on September 22, 2012, from http://ec.europa.eu/internal_market/iprenforcement/index_en.htm.

European Commission. (2012). Enforcement of intellectual property rights. Retrieved on September 30, 2012, from http://ec.europa.eu/internal_market/iprenforcement/index_en.htm.

European Commission. (2012). Commission initiatives for combating counterfeiting and other IPR infringements. Retrieved November 10, 2012, from http://ec.europa.eu/taxation_customs/customs/customs_controls/counterfeit_piracy/commission_initiatives/index_en.htm.

European Patent Office. (2011). *Scenarios for the future.* Retrieved June 6, 2012, from http://www.epo.org/news-issues/issues/scenarios.html.

European Union, Taxation and Customs Union. (2011, July). *Report on EU customs enforcement of intellectual property rights. Results at the EU border—2010.* Retrieved April 20, 2012, from http://ec.europa.eu/taxation_customs/resources/documents/customs/customs_controls/counterfeit_piracy/statistics/statistics_2010.pdf.

Europol. (2011). *OCTA 2011. EU organized crime threat assessment.* Retrieved January 12, 2012, from www.europol.europa.eu.

Evans, D. L. (2004). *Evans: Strategy targeting organized piracy cracks down on pirates who steal from American workers.* Retrieved August 1, 2005, from http://www.commerce.gov/opa/press/Secretary_Evans/2004_Releases/October/04_Evans_IPRPressConference_Release.htm.

Executive Office of the President of the United States. (2011a, June) *2011 U.S. intellectual property enforcement coordinator joint strategic plan.* Retrieved March 1, 2012, from http://www.whitehouse.gov/sites/default/files/omb/IPEC/ipec_anniversary_report.pdf.

Executive Office of the President of the United States. (2011b, March). *Counterfeit Pharmaceutical Inter-agency Working Group report to the Vice President of the United States and to Congress.* Retrieved June 25, 2012, from http://www.whitehouse.gov/sites/default/files/omb/IPEC/Pharma_Report_Final.pdf.

Executive Office of the President of the United States. (2012, March/April). *Intellectual Property Spotlight.* Retrieved June 25, 2012, from http://www.whitehouse.gov/sites/default/files/omb/IPEC/spotlight/ipec_spotlight_mar_apr_spotlight_2012.pdf.

Export.gov. (2011). *Doing business in China.* Retrieved June 8, 2012, from http://export.gov/china/doingbizinchina/index.asp.

Faison, S. (1995, May 17). Fighting piracy and frustration in China: Counterfeit goods flourish in a legal system that is often outwitted. *New York Times*, p. D1.

Faucon, B., & Whalen, J. (2012, April 5). Fake Avastin took murky path to U.S. *The Wall Street Journal.* Retrieved June 13, 2012, from http://online.wsj.com/article/SB10001424052702303302504577323500453577094.html.

FDA. (2012). *Compliance policy guide CPG Sec. 400.210, Radiofrequency identification feasibility studies and pilot programs for drugs November 2004.* Retrieved June 4, 2012, from www.fda.gov/downloads/ICECI/ComplianceManuals/CompliancePolicyGuidanceManual/UCM246448.doc.

Field, A. M. (2007, April 30). Pirates of the supply chain. *Journal of Commerce.* Retrieved June 1, 2012, from www.joc.com.

Finlay, B. (2011, February). *Counterfeit drugs and national security.* Retrieved June 14, 2012, from http://www.stimson.org/images/uploads/research-pdfs/Full_-_Counterfeit_Drugs_and_National_Security.pdf.

Firth, G. (2006). IP protection best practice tips. *The China Business Review, 33*(1), 18–25.

Fisher, K. (2007). *BSA announces $1 million reward for piracy snitches.* Retrieved June 1, 2008, from http://arstechnica.com/news.ars/post/20070702-bsa-announces-1-million-award-for-piracy-snitches.html.

Fiveash, K. (2008). US, EU seize counterfeit computer goods. Retrieved on October 1, 2009, from http://www.theregister.co.uk/2008/02/22/us_eu_ipr_enforcement_seize_goods/.

Forsyth, D. R. (1980). A taxonomy of ethical ideologies. *Journal of Personality and Social Psychology, 39*(1), 175–184.

Fowler, G. (2006, May 31). Disney fires a broadside at pirates. *The Wall Street Journal*, p. B3.

Frontier Economics. (2011). *Estimating the global economic and social impacts of counterfeiting and piracy*. London: Frontier Economics, February 2011. http://www.iccwbo.org/uploaded-Files/BASCAP?Pages/Global%20Impacts%20-%20Final.pdf.

Fuchs, H. J., & Zhou, S. (2010). Why anti-counterfeiting programmes pay. *Managing Intellectual Property, 196*, 20–23. Retrieved June 4, 2012, from http://www.managingip.com/Article/2383108/Why-anti-counterfeiting-programmes-pay.html.

Geist, M. (2012). Canada a pirate's paradise? Way overboard. Retrieved November 13, 2012, from http://www.huffingtonpost.ca/michael-geist/counterfeit-canada-_b_1585379.html.

Gentleman, A. (2007). Indian law on generic drugs is upheld. *International Herald Tribune*. Retrieved December 27, 2007, from http://www.iht.com/bin/print.php.

Gentry, J. W., Putrevu, S., & Shultz, C. J., II. (2006). The effects of counterfeiting on consumer search. *Journal of Consumer Behaviour, 5*(3), 245–256.

Genuario, L. (2006, March). Fight counterfeits—A four-tiered approach to help fight against the global problem of counterfeiting. *Beauty Packaging Magazine*. Retrieved March 28, 2012, from http://www.beautypackaging.com/articles/2006/03/fight-counterfeits.

Gilbert, W. S., & Sullivan, A. (1960). *The complete Gilbert and Sullivan*. New York: Black Dog and Leventhal Publishers.

Gillard, L. (1990, January). Wheelers and dealers of Renaissance Europe. *UNESCO Courier*, pp. 32–35.

Global Financial Integrity. (2011, February). *Transnational crime in the developing world*. Retrieved March 23, 2012, from http://www.gfintegrity.org/storage/gfip/documents/reports/transcrime/gfi_transnational_crime_web.pdf.

Globerman, S. (1988). Addressing international product privacy. *Journal of International Business Studies, 19*(3), 497–504.

Goles, T., Jayatilaka, B., Beena, G., Parsons, L., Chambers, V., Taylor, D., et al. (2008). Softlifting: Exploring determinants of attitude. *Journal of Business Ethics, 77*(4), 481–499.

Government has a fine line to walk. (2007). Editorial, *Bangkok Post*. Retrieved December 21, 2007, from http://www.readbangkokpost.com/business/pharmaceuticals/intellectual_property_or_savin_3.php#article2.

Green, M. D. (2011). *Perspectives: Counterfeit drugs*. Centers for Disease Control and Prevention. Retrieved February 3, 2012, from http://wwwnc.cdc.gov/travel/yellowbook/2012/chapter-2-the-pre-travel-consultation/perspectives-counterfeit-drugs.htm

Green, R. T., & Smith, T. (2002). Executive insights: Countering brand counterfeiters. *Journal of International Marketing, 10*(4), 89–106.

Grendi, E. (1994). Counterfeit coins and monetary exchange structures in the Republic of Genoa during the 16th and 17th centuries. In E. Muir & G. Ruggiero (Eds.), *History from crime* (pp. 170–205). Baltimore, MD: Johns Hopkins University Press.

Griffin, J. (2012). *High-risk products: Know when you may be in a counterfeit situation*. Retrieved May 18, 2012, from http://www.counterfeitscankill.com/news/?fa=show&id=3338&cms=1

Gross, M. (2004). *IPSOS piracy poll*. Retrieved June 8, 2008, from http://www.ipsos-na.com/news/pressrelease.cfm?id=2452.

Grover, R. (2006, April 3). The word in Hollywood, "download." *Business Week*, p. 15.

Gupta, P. B., Gould, S. J., & Pola, B. (2004). To pirate or not to pirate: A comparative study of the ethical versus other influences on the consumer's software acquisition—mode decision. *Journal of Business Ethics, 55*(3), 255–274.

Halliday, J. (2010, November 26). Pirate Bay co-founders lose appeal. *The Guardian*. Retrieved March 1, 2012, from http://www.guardian.co.uk/technology/2010/nov/26/pirate-bay-founders-appeal.

Harvey, M., & Ronkainen, I. (1985). International counterfeiters: Marketing success without the cost and the risk. *Columbia Journal of World Business, 20*(3), 37–45.

Harvey, M. G. (1987). Industrial product counterfeiting: Problems and proposed solutions. *The Journal of Business and Industrial Marketing, 2–4*, 5–13.
Hattersley, J. R. (2006). *Covert and invisible data mark reading*. Retrieved May 27, 2008, from http://www.spiritdatacapture.co.uk/PDF/CaseStudies/Covert_and_invisible_mark_reading.pdf
Havocscope Statistics. (2012). Retrieved May 24, 2012, from http://www.havocscope.com/.
Heelys, Inc. (2007a). *Form 10-K for HEELYS, Inc*. Retrieved July 17, 2007, from http://biz.yahoo.com/e/070315/hlys10-k.html.
Heelys, Inc. (2007b). *Heelys, Inc. reports fiscal 2007 first quarter financial results*. Retrieved July 17, 2007, from http://investors.heelys.com/releasedetail.cfm
Hirschman, E., & Holbrook, M. (1982). Hedonic consumption: Emerging concepts, methods and propositions. *The Journal of Marketing, 46*(3), 92–102.
Holbrook, M., & Hirschman, E. (1982). The experiential aspects of consumption: Consumer fantasies, feelings, and fun. *The Journal of Consumer Research, 9*(2), 132–140.
Hopkins, D. M., Kontnik, L. T., & Turnage, M. T. (2003). *Counterfeiting exposed: Protecting your brand and customers*. Hoboken, NJ: Wiley.
Horwich, L. (2006, May 18). New study piques industry interest in movie piracy. *Back Stage East, 47*(20), p. 3 and 48.
How to catch a pirate. (2006, February 27). *Economist Intelligence Unit, Business China*, pp. 6–7.
Husted, B. W. (2000). The impact of national culture on software piracy. *Journal of Business Ethics, 26*(3), 197–211.
ICE announces results of 'Operation Strike Out'. (2011, October 31). Retrieved June 15, 2012, from http://www.ice.gov/news/releases/1110/111031washingtondc.htm.
IFPI. (2012). *FPI welcomes court ruling finding vKontakte liable for copyright infringement.* Retrieved May 24, 2012, from http://www.ifpi.org/content/section_news/20120518.html.
IIPA. (2012a). *Chart of countries special 301 placement.* Retrieved May 24, 2012, from http://www.iipa.com/pdf/2012SPEC301HISTORICALCHART.pdf.
IIPA. (2012b). *IIPA country reports.* Retrieved May 24, 2012, from http://www.iipa.com/countryreports.html.
Imitating property is theft. (2003, May 17). *The Economist*, pp. 52–54.
Intellectual property and the development aspects of the WTO's Doha round negotiations. (2011, April 11). Retrieved June 20, 2012, from http://sydney.edu.au/news/law/457.html?eventid=7340.
International AntiCounterfeiting Coalition. (2007). *Get real-the truth about counterfeiting.* Retrieved December 28, 2007, from http://www.iacc.org/counterfeiting/counterfeiting.php.
International AntiCounterfeiting Coalition. (2012). *The truth about counterfeiting: Get real.* Retrieved June 15, 2012, from https://iacc.org/about-counterfeiting/the-truth-about-counterfeiting.php.
International customs operation "FAKE". (2005). Retrieved January 5, 2006, from http://ec.europa.eu/anti_fraud/fake/press/ip_en.pdf.
International Federation of the Phonographic Industry. (2005). *IFPI comment on European commission's launch of action plan to combat counterfeiting and piracy*. Retrieved November 11, 2005, from http://www.ifpi.org/content/section_news/20051012.html.
Internet piracy hurts individual creators, not just industries say the entertainment unions. (2005). Retrieved May 1, 2008, from www.musicunited.org/press/2005/0126.html.
Internet World Stats. (2011). Retrieved June 15, 2012, from http://www.internetworldstats.com/
INTERPOL. (n.d.). *Interpol's IP crime program*. Retrieved July 21, 2008, from http://www.interpol.int/Public/FinancialCrime/IntellectualProperty/Default.asp.
IPR enforcement report. (2009). *Commission of the European communities.* Retrieved May 24, 2012, from http://trade.ec.europa.eu/doclib/docs/2009/october/tradoc_145204.pdf.
It is patently absurd to try to lock up the Chinese copycats. (2005, July 19). *The Financial Times*, p. 19.
Jackson, E. (2012, February 19). Fake malaria drugs threaten treatment. *ABC News*. Retrieved May 21, 2012, from http://www.ABC.net.AU/correspondents/content/2012/s3434056.htm.

Jacobs, L., Coskun, S., & Jedlik, T. (2001). The nightmare of international product piracy: Exploring defensive strategies. *Industrial Marketing Management, 30*, 499–509.

Jieming, L. (2004). Retrieved April 11, 2008, from http://www.chinese-forums.com/archive/index.php/t-2509.html.

Jolly, D. (2012, February 5). A new question of Internet freedom. *New York Times*. Retrieved June 3, 2012, from www.nytimes.com/2012/02/06/technology/06iht-acta06.html?…all.

Joossens, L., Merriman, D., Ross, H., & Raw, M. (2010). The impact of eliminating the global illicit cigarette trade on health and revenue. *Addiction, 105*(9), 1640–1649. doi:10.1111/j.1360-0443.2010.03018.x.

Kahn, J. (2007a, July 9). In China's safety woes, echoes of US history. *International Herald Tribune*, p. 1.

Kahn, J. (2007b, July 11). Chinese execute ex-chief of food agency. *International Herald Tribune*, p. 1.

Kini, R. B., Ramakrishna, H. V., & Vijayaraman, B. S. (2004). Shaping of moral intensity regarding software piracy: A comparison between Thailand and U.S. students. *Journal of Business Ethics, 49*(1), 91–104.

Knapper, M. (2004). Europe cracks down on pirates. *Managing Intellectual Property*. Retrieved August 1, 2005, from Proquest Database.

Kohler, J., & Baghdadi-Sabeti, G. (2011). *The world medicines situation 2011: Good governance for the pharmaceutical sector*. A report prepared for the World Health Organization. Retrieved June 14, 2012, from http://www.who.int/medicines/areas/policy/world_medicines_situation/WMS_ch20_wGoodGov.pdf.

Kolsun, B., & Montan, N. V. (2002). Building a comprehensive anticounterfeiting program. In G. W. Abott & L. S. Sporn (Eds.), *Trademark counterfeiting* (pp. 7-1–7-94). New York: Aspen Law and Business.

Kotler, P., Roberto, N., & Lee, N. R. (2002). *Social marketing: Improving the quality of life*. Thousand Oaks, CA: Sage.

Kovács, L. (2005). *Stepping up action against counterfeiting and piracy*. Retrieved July 1, 2005, from http://ec.europa.eu/taxation_customs/resources/documents/speech-kovacs-counterf.pdf.

Kwok, S. K., Ting, S. L., Tsang, A. H. C., & Cheung, C. F. (2010). A counterfeit network analyzer based on RFID and EPC. *Industrial Management & Data Systems, 110.*(7), 1018–1037.

Kwong, K. K., Yau, O. H. M., Lee, J. S. Y., Sin, L. Y. M., & Tse, A. C. B. (2003). The effects of attitudinal and demographic factors on intention to buy pirated CDs: The case of Chinese consumers. *Journal of Business Ethics, 47*(3), 223–235.

Lague, D. (2006, May 1). Next step for counterfeiters: Faking the whole company. *New York Times*, p. C1.

Lawmakers: Counterfeit Electronics Flood Pentagon Supply. (2011, November 7). *USA Today*. Retrieved June 15, 2012, from http://www.usatoday.com/news/washington/story/2011-11-07/pentagon-counterfeit-electronics/51112630/1.

Leach, P. T. (2011, January 26). *Maersk upgrades 2011 growth forecast*. Retrieved June 15, 2012, from http://www.joc.com/maritime/maersk-changes-2011-forecast-container-growth.

Leidecker, J., & Bruno, A. (1984). Identifying and using critical success factors. *Long Range Planning, 17*(1), 23–32.

Leu, M. C. (2011). Authenticate this: Revamping secondary trademark liability standards to address a worldwide web of counterfeits. *Berkeley Technology Law Journal, 26*. Retrieved June 10, 2012, from http://papers.ssrn.com/sol3/papers.cfm?abstract_id=1808240.

Look for the silver lining. (2008, July 19). *The Economist*, p. 23.

Maddison, A. (2001). *The China/West European dichotomy, 1–2001 AD*. Retrieved January 29, 2008, from http://www.theworldeconomy.org/publications/worldeconomy/histostats-table08–3.pdf.

Maleske, M. (2012). *China aims to strengthen IP rights enforcement—U.S. officials question new initiatives' effectiveness*. Retrieved March 28, 2012, from http://www.insidecounsel.com/2012/02/01/china-aims-to-strengthen-ip-rights-enforcement?page=2.

Mallinder, L. (2011, July 30). Take back your own idea. *Business Without Borders*. Retrieved April 25, 2012, from http://www.businesswithoutborders.com/industries/importexport/take-back-your-own-idea/.
Marquand, R. (2002). China's pirate industry thriving. *The Christian Science Monitor*. Retrieved November 18, 2007, from http://www.csmonitor.com/2002/0109/p6s1-wosc.html.
Marron, D. B., & Steel, D. G. (2000). Which countries protect intellectual property? The case of software piracy. *Economic Inquiry, 38*(2), 159–174.
McNeal, G. (2012, February 14). NDAA may put defense contractors in prison for counterfeit parts. *Forbes*. Retrieved June 4, 2012, from http://www.forbes.com/sites/gregorymc-neal/2012/02/14/ndaa-may-put-contractors-in-prison-for-counterfeit-parts/.
McNeil, D. G., Jr. (2000, December 1). Selling cheap 'generic' drugs, India's copycats irk industry. *New York Times*, p. 1.
Mertha, A. (2005). *The politics of piracy: Intellectual property in contemporary China*. Ithaca, NY: Cornell University Press.
Microsoft. (2010). *Addressing global software piracy*. Retrieved May 29, 2012, from http://www.microsoft.com/en-us/news/presskits/antipiracy/docs/piracy10.pdf.
Mihm, S. (2007). A nation of outlaws—A century ago, that wasn't China it was us. *The Boston Globe*. Retrieved November 13, 2007, from http://www.boston.com/news/globe/ideas/articles/2007/08/26/a_nation_of_outlaws.
Mission to stop piracy. (2006). Retrieved May 23, 2006, from http://www.ip-video.gov.hk/eng/api/api08_e_BB.htm.
Moores, T. (2008). An analysis of the impact of economic wealth and national culture on the rise and fall of software piracy rates. *Journal of Business Ethics, 81*(1), 39–51.
Morris, J., & Stevens, P. (2007). Counterfeit medicines in LDCs: Problems and solutions. In P. Stevens (Ed.), *Fighting the diseases of poverty*. London: International Policy Press. Retrieved December 5, 2007, from http://www.fightingdiseases.org/images/pictures/Full_FightDisofPov.pdf.
Morton, P. (2011). *The "Abronization" of ABRO*. Retrieved May 15, 2012, from http://www.businesswithoutborders.com/industries/transportation/the-%E2%80%9Cabronization%E2%80%9D-of-abro/.
Mostert, F. (2008). *Counterfeits on ebay: Who is responsible?* Retrieved July 27, 2008, from http://www.ft.com.
Motion Picture Association of America. (n.d.). Types of content theft. Retrieved on July 5, 2012, from http://www.mpaa.org/contentprotection/types-of-content-theft.
MPAA explains pyramid of internet piracy. (2006, June 3). Retrieved June 20, 2012, from http://labnol.blogspot.co.uk/2006/06/mpaa-explains-pyramid-of-internet.html.
Muncy, J., & Vitell, S. J. (1992). Consumer ethics: An investigation of the ethical beliefs of the final consumer. *Journal of Business Research, 24*(4), 297–311.
Mutterperl, M. (2007, February 13). Taking back a fake world: Recommendations for combating the spread of global counterfeiting and piracy before it's too late. *Fulbright & Jaworski LLP Client Alert*. Retrieved March 25, 2012, from http://www.fulbright.com/index.cfm?fuseaction=publications.detail&pub_id=2586&site_id=494&detail=yes.
Naim, M. (2005). *Illicit: How smugglers, traffickers and copycats are hijacking the global economy*. New York: Doubleday.
National Intellectual Property Rights Coordination Center. (2011). *Intellectual property rights violations: A report on threats to United States interests at home and abroad*. Retrieved on June 30, 2012, from http://www.stopfakes.gov/news/national-ipr-center-releases-2011-ip-threat-report.
National Electrical Manufacturer's Association. (2005). *US Ambassador's roundtable on intellectual property rights in China*. Retrieved January 25, 2008, from http://www.nema.org.
National Electrical Manufacturers Association. (2012). *Authentication technologies for brand protection*. Retrieved June 1, 2012, from http://www.nema.org/gov/anti-counterfeiting/.
New measures to bolster customs enforcement of intellectual property rights. (2011). Retrieved on September 1, 2012, from http://www.worldcommercereview.com/publications/article_pdf/419.

Nia, A., & Zaichkowsky, J. L. (2000). Do counterfeits devalue the ownership of luxury brands? *The Journal of Product and Brand Management, 9*(7), 485–497.

Nill, A., & Shultz, C. J. (1996). The scourge of global counterfeiting. *Business Horizons, 39*(6), 37–42.

Noon, C. (2006). *Schultz' Starbucks wins China copyright case*. Retrieved July 17, 2007, from http://www.forbes.com/2006/01/02/schultz-starbucks-china-cx_cn_0102autofacescan01.html.

Nunes, J., Hsee, C., & Weber, E. (2004). Why are people so prone to steal software? The effect of cost structure on consumer purchase and payment intentions. *Journal of Public Policy & Marketing, 23*(1), 43–53.

Nurton, J. (n.d.). Shock around Europe as ACTA falls apart. *Managing Intellectual Property, 217*, 5. Retrieved June 1, 2012, from http://www.managingip.com/Article/2985886/Shock-around-Europe-as-ACTA-falls-apart.html.

OECD. (2007). *The economic impact of counterfeiting and piracy: Executive summary*. Retrieved May 3, 2012, from http://www.oecd.org/dataoecd/13/12/38707619.pdf.

Official chagrined by beanie babies. (1998, July 11). *New York Times*. Retrieved February 22, 2008, from http://query.nytimes.com/gst/fullpage.html?res=9C0DE5DA1431F932A25754C0A96E958260.

Olsen, J. E., & Granzin, K. L. (1993). Using channels constructs to explain dealers' willingness to help manufactures combat counterfeiting. *Journal of Business Research, 27*(2), 147–170.

Ono, S. (1999). *Overview of Japanese trademark law* (Chap. 2). Retrieved November 18, 2007, from http://www.iip.or.jp/translation/ono/ch2.pdf.

OpenCongress. (n.d.). *S.978 Commercial Felony Streaming Act*. Retrieved April 15, 2012, from http://www.opencongress.org/bill/112-s978/show.

Organization for Economic Cooperation and Development. (2007a). *The economic impact of counterfeiting and piracy*. Retrieved July 23, 2008, from http://www.oecd.org/document/4/0,3343,en_2649_34173_40876868_1_1_1_1,00.html.

Organization for Economic Cooperation and Development. (2007b). *The economic impact of counterfeiting and piracy*. Retrieved June 18, 2007, from http://www/oecd.org/dataoecd/11/38/38704571.pdf.

Organization for Economic Cooperation and Development. (2007c). *The economic impact of counterfeiting and piracy*. Retrieved November 20, 2007, from http://www.oecd.org/dataoecd/13/12/38707619.pdf2.

Organization for Economic Cooperation and Development. (2007d). *The economic impact of counterfeiting and piracy* (Part I: 146). Retrieved November 23, 2007, from http://www.oecd.org/dataoecd/36/36/39543399.pdf-3.

Organization for Economic Cooperation and Development. (2007e). *The economic impact of counterfeiting and piracy* (Part II: 30–79). Retrieved November 23, 2007, from http://www.oecd.org/dataoecd/36/35/39543408pdf-4.

Organization for Economic Cooperation and Development. (2009). *Magnitude of counterfeiting and piracy of tangible products: An update*. Retrieved May 22, 2012, from http://www.oecd.org/dataoecd/57/27/44088872.pdf.

Originalidade: Piratatofora. (2012). Retrieved May 28, 2012, from http://www.piratatofora.com.br/.

Pang, L. (2004). Piracy/privacy: The despair of cinema and collectivity in China. *Boundary 2, 31*(3), 101–124.

Parkinson, G. (2008). RFID—Rx for drug security? *Chemical Engineering Progress, 104*(2), 6.

Parloff, R. (2006). Not exactly counterfeit. *Fortune*. Retrieved December 28, 2007, from http://money.cnn.com/magazines/fortune/fortune_archive/2006/05/01/8375455/index.htm

Paster, B. G. (1969). Trademarks—their early history. *TMR, 59*, 551–572.

PBS. (2007). *Samuel Slater—American factory system. They made America*. Retrieved November 23, 2007, from http://www.pbs.org/wgbh/theymadeamerica/whomade/slater_hi.html.

Penz, E., & Stöttinger, B. (2008). Corporate image and product similarity—assessing major demand drivers for counterfeits in a multi-country study. *Psychology and Marketing, 25*(4), 352–381.

Peracchio, T. (2011, July 4). Ten strikes Bill S. 978 has YouTube users scared and outraged. *Examiner*. Retrieved June 15, 2012, from http://www.examiner.com/article/ten-strikes-bill-s-978-has-youtube-users-scared-and-outraged.

Perkins, J. (2009). Brand security's white knight—packaging. *GCI*, pp. 50–51. Retrieved January 7, 2012, from www.GCIMagazine.com.

Pfanner, E. (2008). Sweden accuses 4 of copyright offenses. *The New York Times*. Retrieved July 31, 2008, from http://www.nytimes.com.

Philip Morris International, Inc. (2003). *Counterfeit cigarettes—The global problem and proposed solutions*. Retrieved March 14, 2008, from http://philipmorrisinternational.com/global/downloads/obe/counterfeit_cigarettes.pdf.

Philip Morris to back EU counterfeit fight; $1 billion to help thwart smugglers. (2004). *The Washington Post*. Retrieved August 1, 2005, from http://www.washingtonpost.com/ac2/wp-dyn/A53375-2004Apr5?language=printer.

Phillips, D. J. (2007). Will Heelys stock price skate higher in 2007? *Seeking Alpha*. Retrieved July 17, 2007, from http://retail.seekingalpha.com/article/23246.

Pignal, S. (2012, February 22). Anti-piracy pact falters after protests. *Financial Times*. Retrieved March 1, 2012, from http://www.ft.com/intl/cms/s/0/7e8ccc24-5d73-11e1-8bb6-00144feabdc0.html#axzz1ol7SOEsk.

Porter, E. (2012, February 4). The perpetual war: Pirates and creators. *The New York Times*. Retrieved March 17, 2012, from http://www.nytimes.com/2012/02/05/opinion/sunday/perpetual-war-digital-pirates-and-creators.html?_r=2&ref=eduardoporter.

Power Sellers (2012). Auction Site Count. Retrieved June 12, 2012 from http://www.powersellersunite.com/auctionsitewatch.php.

PRC Central Government. (2012). *Office of the State Council issues agenda to combat IPR infringement...*Retrieved May 24, 2012, from http://www.gov.cn/zwgk/2012-05/18/content_2140684.htm.

Prendergast, G., Chuen, L. H., & Phau, I. (2002). Understanding consumer demand for nondeceptive pirated brands. *Marketing Intelligence and Planning, 20*(7), 405–416.

Project Strider—A national intellectual property crime threat assessment, 2005–2008. (2010). Royal Canadian Mounted Police (RCMP). Retrieved June 10, 2012, from publications.gc.ca/collections/collection.../PS64-79-2010-eng.pdf.

Punch, L. (2005). Bogus brands and the internet. *Internet Retailer*. Retrieved September 18, 2007, from http://www.internetretailer.com/article.asp?id=15631.

Quality Brands Protection Committee. (2006). *Annual membership survey*. Retrieved February 19, 2008, from http://www.qbpc.org.cn/en/about/references/QBPCrelated/survey/2006en/file

Quality Brands Protection Committee (QBPC). (2012). Unpublished survey.

Quam, D. (2002). *Testimony before the US China Economic and Security Review Commission*. General Counsel, International Anti-Counterfeiting Coalition. Retrieved January 18, 2002, from http://www.uscc.gov/textonly/transcriptstx/tesqua.htm.

Reuters, T. (2011). *Insight: Gibson Dunn helps Gucci target Chinese banks*. Retrieved May 21, 2012, from https://www.google.com/search?source=ig&hl=en&rlz=1G1GGLQ_ENUS366&q=Gibson+Dunn+helps+Gucci+target+Chinese+banks&oq=Gibson+Dunn+helps+Gucci+target+Chinese+banks&aq=f&aqi=&aql=&gs_l=igoogle.12...1823.1823.0.3423.1.1.0.0.0.0.76.76.1.1.0...0.0.kjUIDR5MQO8.

Ritter, K. (2011, September 21). Chanel files Internet trademark lawsuit in Vegas. *Bloomberg Business Week*. Retrieved May 21, 2012, from http://www.businessweek.com/ap/financialnews/D9PT3SI00.htm.

Rokicki, J. (1987). Advertising in the Roman Empire. *Whole Earth Review*. Retrieved December 4, 2007, from http://findarticles.com/p/articles/mi_m1510/is_1987_Spring/ai_4806053

Rosenthal, D. E. (1998). A comment on the 1998 special 301 annual review of the US trade representative. *The Journal of World Intellectual Property, 1*(5), 743–745.

Rust, R. L. I. (1999). A brief history of chocolate, food of the gods. *Athena Review, 2*(2). Retrieved November 16, 2007, from http://www.athenapub.com/chocolat.htm.

Salnik, V. (2011, May 9). Brands and counterfeit goods: The mythical standoff. *Pravda*. Retrieved May 24, 2012, from http://english.pravda.ru/business/companies/05-09-2011/118952-brands-0/?mode=print.

Sandoval, G. (2010). Federal rules on campus file sharing kick in today. Retrieved on July 7, 2012, from http://news.cnet.com/8301-31001_3-20009386-261.html.

Sandvine. (2011). *Global Internet phenomena report.* Retrieved May 1, 2012, from http://www.sandvine.com/downloads/documents/10-26-2011_phenomena/Sandvine%20Global%20Internet%20Phenomena%20Report%20-%20Fall%202011.pdf.

Santo, M. (2012, February 2). *Illegal video streaming sites seized ahead of first live-streamed Super Bowl.* Retrieved June 16, 2012, from http://www.examiner.com/article/illegal-video-streaming-sites-seized-ahead-of-first-live-streamed-super-bowl.

Sardon, V. (2007). *Dicey access to illegal market, but great prices.* Retrieved December 21, 2007, from http://news.monstersandcritics.com/business/features/printer_1326724.php

Schatz, A. (2012, January 18). What is SOPA anyway? A guide to understanding the online piracy bill. *The Wall Street Journal.* Retrieved February 1, 2012, from http://online.wsj.com/article/SB10001424052970203735304577167261853938938.html.

Schuchert-Güler, P., & Martin E. (2003). *Non-price determinants of German consumers' inclination to purchase counterfeit products.* Diskussionbeiträge des Fachbereichs Wirtschaftswissenschaft der Freien. Universität Berlin, Nr. 2003/9.

Schwarz, B., & Wong, V. (2006, October). Counterfeit cures. *Insight*, pp. 29–33. Retrieved January 14, 2008, from http://www.amcham-shanghai.org/NR/rdonlyres/9D628132–7DEA-432EB18B-C0E27AC73E37/2362/09.pdf.

Shah, A. (2010, November 10). Free-trade zones attract criminals. *New York Times.* Retrieved June 5, 2012, from http://www.nytimes.com/2010/11/11/world/middleeast/11iht-m11mtrade.html.

Short, P. (2000). *Mao: A life.* New York: Henry Holt.

Shultz, C., & Saporito, B. (1996). Protecting intellectual property: Strategies and recommendations to deter counterfeiting and brand piracy in global markets. *Columbia Journal of World Business, 31*(1), 18–28.

Sidebotham, S. E. (1986). *Roman economic policy in the Erythra Thalassa, 30BC–AD217.* Leiden: E.J. Brill.

Silverman, E. (2007). *India, Novartis, the WTO and patents.* Retrieved December 27, 2007, from http://www.pharmalot.com/2007/09/india-novartis-the-wto-and-patents.

Singer, J. (2011, September). *Changes to U.S. patent law: What happens next.* Retrieved June 25, 2012, from http://ipspotlight.com/2011/09/19/changes-to-u-s-patent-law-what-happens-next/

Sipo.gov.cn. (2012). Retrieved May 24, 2012, from http://english.sipo.gov.cn/.

Software Information Industry Association. (2005). *SIIA anti-piracy 2005 year in review.* Retrieved December 12, 2006, from http://www.siia.net.

Solomon, J. (2005, August 23). U.S. breaks up smuggling ring connected to Asia; besides phony $4.5 million, suspect contraband includes cigarettes, drugs, weapons. *The Wall Street Journal*, p. A9.

South Africa Web. (2012, April 12). *Empirical data indicates that South African grey market is especially strong in the computer and electronics consumer goods, with iPads, iPods, iPhones leading the pack.* Retrieved June 6, 2012, from http://www.southafricaweb.co.za/article/gray-market-south-africa.

Spink, J., & Li, G. (2012). *Chinese anti-counterfeit efforts in China.* Retrieved May 8, 2012, from http://a-cappp.msu.edu/files/Spink_China.pdf.

Staake, T., Thiesse, F., & Fleisch, E. (2008). Countering Counterfeit Trade. Berlin: Springer-Verlag.

Staake, T., Thiesse, F., & Fleisch, E. (2012). Business strategies in the counterfeit market. *Journal of Business Research, 65*(5), 658–665.

Statistics of customs detentions recorded at the external borders of the EU – 2010. (2011). *EUbusiness.* Retrieved on July 1, 2012, from http://www.eubusiness.com/topics/trade/customs-2010/.

Stern, P. (1985, September 1). Foreign product counterfeiting. *Vital Speeches of the Day*, Vol. LI, No. 22.

Stewart, C. (2005). *Brand piracy: A victimless crime? Americans want stricter counterfeiting and piracy laws.* Retrieved June 8, 2008, from http://www.nam.org/s_nam/bin.asp?CID=201820&DID=233395&DOC=FILE.PDF.

Stolte, K. M. (1998). How early did Anglo-American trademark law begin? An answer to Schechter's conundrum. *Fordham Intellectual Property, Media and Entertainment Law Journal, 8*(2), 505–547.

Stone, B. (2008, July 15). EBay cleared in site's sales of knockoffs. *New York Times*, p. C1.

Stopfakes.gov. (2012). *How do I register... abroad?* (2012). Retrieved June 4, 2012, from http://origin.www.stopfakes.gov/faqs/how-do-i-register-my-trademark-patent-or-copyright-abroad.

Strategy targeting organized piracy cracks down on pirates who steal from American workers. (2004). *Global News Wire*. Retrieved July 1, 2005, from http://www.ustr.gov/archive/assets/Document_Library/Fact_Sheets/2004/asset_upload_file507_6462.pdf.

Stumpf, S., & Chaudhry, P. (2010). Country matters: Executives weigh in on the causes and counter measures of counterfeit trade. *Business Horizons, 53*(3), 305–314.

Stumpf, S. A., Chaudhry, P. E., & Perretta, L. (2011). Fake: Can business stanch the flow of counterfeit products? *Journal of Business Strategy, 32*(2), 4–12.

Swinyard, W. R., Rinne, H., & Kau, A. K. (1990). The morality of software piracy: A cross-cultural analysis. *Journal of the Academy of Marketing Science, 29*(1), 16–35.

Šemeta, A. (2012). Taking stock of the EU-China cooperation in customs. Retrieved September 1, 2012, from http://ec.europa.eu/commission_2010-2014/semeta/headlines/news/2012/06/20120625_en.htm.

Tabata, Y. (2003). *Anti-counterfeits activities by Japanese companies in China.* Retrieved June 15, 2009, from www.aipla.org/Content/Microsites152/IP_Practice_in_Japan/Committee_Meetings/.../Tabata-Anti-counterfeitsActivities(Tab16).ppt.

Taylor, P. (2012, May 25). *G8 summit highlights counterfeit medicines.* Retrieved June 13, 2012, from http://www.securingpharma.com/g8-summit-highlights-counterfeit-medicines/s40/a1250/.

The impact of counterfeiting. (2012). Retrieved June 15, 2012, from http://www.ul.com/global/eng/pages/offerings/services/programs/anticounterfeitingoperations/counterfeiting/.

The intricacies of protecting your intellectual property rights in China. (1999, May 3). *Journal of Commerce*, p. 3A.

The long march to be a superpower. (2007, August 4). *The Economist*, pp. 21–23.

Thom, R. (2012, June 29). *European Council reaches agreement on the seat of the Unified Patent Court.* Retrieved June 30, 2012, from http://www.eupatent.com/news/.

Thomas, D. (2007, August 30). Terror's purse strings. *New York Times*, p. A23.

Tobacco plain packaging regulations. (2011). Select Legislative Instrument 2011 No. 263. Retrieved January 24, 2012, from http://AustraliaTobacco%20Plain%20Packaging%20Regulation.

Top 10 most pirated movies on BitTorrent. (2012). Retrieved on June 30, 2012, from http://torrentfreak.com/top-10-most-pirated-movies-on-bittorrent-121022/.

Top ten countries with highest video piracy. (2012). Retrieved on July 1, 2012 from http://www.mapsofworld.com/world-top-ten/world-top-ten-video-piracy-countries-map.html.

Tom, G., Garibaldi, B., Zeng, Y., & Pilcher, J. (1998). Consumer demand for counterfeit goods. *Psychology and Marketing, 15*(5), 405–421.

Toth, W. (2007). The quest for copycat purses leads underground. *New York Press.* Retrieved November 18, 2007, from http://www.nypress.com/20/13/news&columns/feature2.cfm.

Transcending the genre – Few Indian firms are creating drugs, rather than recreating them (2007, November 8). *The Economist.* Retrieved on May 1, 2008, from http://www.economist.com/node/10053133.

TRIPS, AIDS and generic drugs. (2007). Avert. Retrieved December 27, 2007, from http://www.avert.org/generic.htm.

UNCTAD's FDI database. (2012). Retrieved April 20, 2012, from http://unctadstat.unctad.org/ReportFolders/reportFolders.aspx?sRF_ActivePath=P,5,27&sRF_Expanded=,P,5,27.

United Nations Economic Commission for Europe. (2007). *Counterfeit goods endanger life and cost the economy billions of dollars.* Retrieved November 21, 2007, from http://www.unece.org/press/pr2007/07trade_p07e.htm.

United Nations Office on Drugs and Crime. (2010). *The globalization of crime: A transnational organized crime threat assessment.* Retrieved June 15, 2012, from http://www.unodc.org/documents/data-and-analysis/tocta/TOCTA_Report_2010_low_res.pdf.

US Chamber of Commerce. (2007). *Stopping fakes: Building awareness; a private sector perspective on I P public education campaigns.* Retrieved February 6, 2008, from http://www.thetruecosts.org/NR/rdonlyres/ehuu4mhgx44rhfhlkqzsymlppubamwdgnsrhkxtnbxvvre46oktgwhi3mf7u2g53my3zjvguv6zmfjtjsnt4oiyb5rf/13608APECBookrdc.pdf.

United States Customs and Border Protection. (2009). *Annual seizure reports for FY2003–2008.* Retrieved June 15, 2012, from http://www.cbp.gov/xp/cgov/trade/priority_trade/ipr/ipr_communications/seizure/trading/.

United States Customs and Border Protection. (2011). *FY 2011 seizure statistics.* Retrieved January 13, 2012, from http://www.cbp.gov/linkhandler/cgov/trade/priority_trade/ipr/pubs/seizure/ipr_seizures_fy2011.ctt/ipr_seizure_fy2011.pdf.

United States Customs and Border Protection. (2012). *Intellectual property rights—Fiscal year 2011 seizure statistics.* Retrieved May 3, 2012, from http://www.cbp.gov/xp/cgov/newsroom/news_releases/national/01092012.xml.

United States Department of Commerce. (2011). 22nd U.S.-China joint commission on commerce and trade signing ceremony fact sheet, November 21. Retrieved on June 1, 2012, from http://www.commerce.gov/news/fact-sheets/2011/11/21/22nd-us-china-joint-commission-commerce-and-trade-signing-ceremony-fact-.

United States Department of Homeland Security. (2008). *Tobacco and terror: How cigarette smuggling is funding our enemies abroad, republican staff report.* Retrieved January 21, 2012, from http://www.hsdl.org/?search=&page=1&advanced=&all=Tobacco+and+Terror%3A+How+Cigarette+Smuggling+is+Funding+our+Enemies+Abroad+%282008%29%2C+Republican+Staff+of+the+US+House+Committee+on+Homeland+Security&any=&exact=United+States.+Congress.+House.+Committee+on+Homeland+Security&without=&begindate=&enddate=&searchfield=publisher&collection=limited&submitted=Search.

United States Department of Justice. (2005). *Justice Department announces international internet piracy sweep.* Retrieved November 9, 2006, from http://www.usdoj.gov/opa/pr/2005/June/05_crm_353.htm.

United States Department of Justice. (2006a). *Operation buccaneer. Computer crime and intellectual property section, U.S. Department of Justice.* Retrieved February 1, 2008, from http://www.usdoj.gov/criminal/cybercrime/ob/OBMain.htm.

United States Department of Justice. (2006b). *Hi-tech pharmaceuticals and 11 individuals indicted for "generic" pill fraud scheme.* Retrieved December 24, 2006, from http://www.usdoj.gov/criminal/cybercrime/wheatIndict.htm.

United States Department of State. (2006). Focus on intellectual property rights: A message from Jackie Chan: Fakes cost more. Retrieved July 5, 2006, from http://usinfo.state.gov/products/pubs/intelprp/chan.htm.

United States Embassy, Beijing. (2012). *IPR toolkit.* Retrieved May 21, 2012, from http://beijing.usembassy-china.org.cn/protecting_ipr.html.

United States Government Accountability Office. (2005). *USTR would benefit from greater use of capital management principles* (Publication No. GAO-06-167). Washington, DC: United States Government Accountability Office.

United States Government Accountability Office. (2007). *Better data analysis and integration could help U.S. customs and border protection improve border enforcement efforts.* Retrieved November 21, 2007, from http://www.gao.gov/new.items/d07735.pdf.

United States Government Accountability Office. (2010). Report 10–423. *Observations on efforts to quantify the economic effects of counterfeit and pirated goods.* http://www.gao.gov/new.items/d10423.pdf. Cited 1 May 2010.

United States International Trade Commission. (2011). Investigation No. 332–519. *China: Effects of intellectual property infringement and indigenous innovation policies on the U.S. economy.* Washington: USITC, May 2011. Cited 10 July 2011.

United States Government Accountability Office. (2011). *Illicit tobacco: Various schemes are used to evade taxes*. Retrieved January 9, 2012, from http://www.gao.gov/new.items/d11313.pdf.
United States Immigration and Customs Enforcement. (2007). *ICE intellectual property rights investigations*. Retrieved August 31, 2007, from http://www.ice.gov/pi/news/factsheets/iproverview.htm.
United States State Department. (2006). *USINFO glossary of intellectual property terms*. Retrieved May 16, 2007, from http://www.america.gov/st/econenglish/2008/April/20080429233718eaifas0.3043067.html.
United States Trade Representative. (2002). *Special 301 report*. Retrieved July 15, 2008, from http://www.ustr.gov/reports/2002/special301-pwl.htm.
United States Trade Representative. (2004). *U.S. announces major new initiative to fight global trade in fakes*. Retrieved July 1, 2005, from http://www.ustr.gov.
United States Trade Representative. (2007a). *Foreign trade barriers—Mexico*. Retrieved December 14, 2007, from http://www.ustr.gov/assets/Document_Library/Reports_Publications/2007/2007_NTE_Report/asset_upload_file720_10964.pdf.
United States Trade Representative. (2007b). *Report to congress on China's WTO compliance*. Retrieved January 21, 2008, from http://www.ustr.gov/assets/Document_Library/Reports_Publications/2007/asset_upload_file625_13692.pdf.
United States Trade Representative. (2007c). *Special 301 report*. Retrieved December 21, 2007, from http://www.ustr.gov/assets/Document_Library/Reports_Publications/2007/2007_Special_301_Review/asset_upload_file230_11122.pdf.
United States Trade Representative. (2011a, December 20). *Out of cycle review of notorious markets*. Retrieved March 30, 2012, from http://www.ustr.gov/webfm_send/3215.
United States Trade Representative. (2011b). *Report to congress on China's WTO compliance*. Retrieved January 17, 2012, from http://www.ustr.gov/about-us/press-office/reports-and-publications/2011/2010-report-congress-china%E2%80%99s-wto-compliance.
United States Trade Representative. (2012). *2012 special 301 report*. Retrieved May 18, 2012, from http://www.ustr.gov/sites/default/files/2012%20Special%20301%20Report.pdf.
United States Trademark Act (Title 15 of the United States Code). (n.d.). *Construction and definitions; intent of chapter*. Retrieved November 15, 2007, from http://www.bitlaw.com/source/15usc/1127.html.
U.S. Customs and Border Protection. (2008). *U.S. customs and border protection and European Union announce joint operation in combating pirated goods*. Retrieved July 15, 2008, from http://useu.usmission.gov/Dossiers/IPR/Feb2008_Operation_Infrastructure.asp.
U.S., EU adopt action strategy for the enforcement of intellectual property rights. (2006). Retrieved July 1, 2006, from http://useu.usmission.gov/Dossiers/IPR/June2006_IPR_Strategy.asp.
U.S. Department of State. (2006). Focus on intellectual property rights: A message from Jackie Chan: Fakes cost more. Retrieved July 5, 2006, from http://usinfo.state.gov/products/pubs/intelprp/chan.htm.
UNODC. (2010). *The globalization of crime: A transnational organized crime threat assessment*. Chapter 8. Retrieved May 3, 2012, from http://www.unodc.org/documents/data-and-analysis/tocta/TOCTA_Report_2010_low_res.pdf.
Varney, S. (2012). *Law seeks to stop fake prescription drugs*. Retrieved June 1, 2012, from http://blogs.kqed.org/stateofhealth/2012/02/20/law-seeks-to-stop-fake-prescription-drugs/#more-3112.
Vitell, S. J., & Muncy, J. (1992). Consumer ethics: An empirical investigation of factors influencing ethical judgments of the final consumer. *Journal of Business Ethics, 11*(8), 585–597.
Vitell, S. J., & Muncy, J. (2005). The Muncy-Vitell consumer ethics scale: A modification and application. *Journal of Business Ethics, 62*(3), 267–275.
Von Lampe, K., Kurti, M. K., Shen, A., & Antonopoulos, G. A. (2012). The changing role of China in the global illicit cigarette trade. *International Criminal Justice Review, 22*, 43–67.
Wald, J., & Holleran, J. (2007). Counterfeit products and default the supply chain: Eight Johnson and Johnson brand integrity case studies. *Risk Management, 54*(4), 58–61.
Wan, W., Luk, C., Yau, O., Tse, A., Sin, L., Kwong, K., et al. (2009). Do traditional Chinese cultural values nourish a market for pirated CDs? *Journal of Business Ethics, 88*, 185–196.

Wang, F., Zhang, H., Zang, H., & Ouyang, M. (2005). Purchasing pirated software: An initial examination of Chinese consumers. *Journal of Consumer Marketing, 22*(6), 340–351.

Wang, S. (2010). Piracy and the DVD/VCD market: Contradictions and paradoxes. In Y. Zhu & S. Rosen (Ed.), *Art politics and commerce in Chinese cinema*. Hong Kong: Hong Kong University Press.

Weaver, C., Whalen, J., & Faucon, B. (2012, March 7). Drug distributor is tied to imports of fakes. *The Wall Street Journal*. Retrieved March 15, 2012, from http://online.wsj.com/article/SB100014240529702033706045772613439742141 10.html.

Wee, C., Tan, S., & Cheok, K. (1995). Non-price determinants of intention to purchase counterfeit goods. *International Marketing Review, 12*(6), 19–46.

What are the DMCA's anti-circumvention provisions? (2008). Retrieved May 1, 2008, from http://www.chillingeffects.org.

Why fakes are booming. (2008, January). *Consumer reports*. Retrieved December 28, 2007, from http://www.consumerreports.org/cro/money/shopping/shopping-tips/counterfeit-products-1–08/why-fakes-are-booming/counterfeit-why-fakes-are-booming.htm.

Why protect intellectual property? (2007). Retrieved March 30, 2008, from http://www.stopfakes.gov/sf_why.asp.

Wilcox, K., Kim, H., & Sen, S. (2009). Why do consumers buy counterfeit luxury brands? *Journal of Marketing Research, 46*(2), 247–259.

Williams, F. (2008). *Doha trade talks face 'moment of truth' in Geneva*. Retrieved July 26, 2008, from http://www.ft.com/cms/s/0/1ec9c98e-56bc-11dd-8686–000077b07658.html.

Willson, K. (29 June, 2009). Terrorism and tobacco—how cigarette smuggling finances Jihad and insurgency worldwide. *The Cutting Edge*. Retrieved January 24, 2012, from http://www.thecuttingedgenews.com/index.php?article=11427&pageid=&pagename=.

Winterfeldt, B. J., Dow, L., & Albertson, P. (2002). *Historical trademarks: In use since…; 4000 BC*. International Trademark Association. Retrieved November 13, 2007, from http://www.inta.org/index.php?option=com_content&task=view&id=213&Itemid=126&getcontent=1.

Wong, G. (2011, May 17). *Netflix is doing its job to reduce piracy in North America*. Retrieved June 16, 2012, from http://www.ubergizmo.com/2011/05/netflix-reduce-piracy-north-america/.

World Bank. (2011). *Tariffs*. Retrieved June 5, 2012, from http://data.worldbank.org/indicator/TM.TAX.MRCH.WM.AR.ZS.

World Health Organization. (2003). WHO launches campaign against counterfeit medicines. *WHO News*. Retrieved November 5, 2004, from http://www.who.int/bulletin/volumes/81/12/WHONews.pdf.

World Health Organization. (2007). *IMPACT! International medical products anti-counterfeiting taskforce*. Retrieved July 31, 2008, from http://www.who.int/impact/activities/counterfeit_drugs_small.jpg.

World Health Organization. (2010). *Fact sheet number 275*. Retrieved February 3, 2012, from http://www.who.int/mediacentre/factsheets/fs275/en/.

World Intellectual Property Organization. (2007). *About intellectual property*. Retrieved May 16, 2007, from http://www.wipo.int/about-ip/en/index.html.

World Intellectual Property Organization. (n.d.a.). *Contracting parties*. Retrieved July 31, 2007, from http://www.wipo.int/treaties/en/ShowResults.jsp?lang=en&treaty_id=2.

World Trade Organization. (2009, January 28). *Dispute settlement: Dispute DS362 China—Measures affecting the protection and enforcement of intellectual property rights*. Retrieved April 1, 2012, from http://www.wto.org/english/tratop_e/dispu_e/cases_e/ds362_e.htm.

World Trade Organization. (2010). China – Measures affecting the protection and enforcement of intellectual property rights. Retrieved on June 1, 2012, from http://www.wto.org/english/tratop_e/dispu_e/cases_e/ds362_e.htm.

World Trade Organization. (2011a). *Comments by Cuban and Nicaraguan governments to the Committee on Technical Barriers to Trade (G./TBT/M./54). [Minutes of regular meetings of the TBT Committee (Document code G/TBT/M/*)]*. Retrieved January 25, 2012, from http://www.wto.org/english/tratop_e/tbt_e/tbt_work_docs_e.htm21June.

World Trade Organization. (2011b). *Statement by the Dominican Republic to the committee on technical barriers to trade (G./TBT/W./339).* Retrieved January 25, 2012, from http://docsonline.wto.org/GEN_highLightParent.asp?qu=+%28%40meta%5FSymbol+G%FCTBT%FCW%FC%2A+%29+and+%28+%40Doc%5FDate+%3E%3D+2011%2F01%2F01+00%3A00%3A00+%29+and+%28+%40Doc%5FDate+%3C%3D+2011%2F12%2F31+23%3A59%3A59+%29&doc=D%3A%2FDDFDOCUMENTS%2FT%2FG%2FTBT%2FW339%2EDOC%2EHTM&curdoc=6&popTitle=G%2FTBT%2FW%2F339.

World Trade Organization. (2011c). *World trade in 2010—Overview.* Retrieved January 6, 2012, from http://www.wto.org/english/res_e/booksp_e/anrep_e/world_trade_report10_e.pdf.

World Trade Organization (WTO). (2012). *Dispute settlement: DS362 China—Measures affecting the protection and enforcement of intellectual property rights.* Retrieved May 21, 2012, from http://www.wto.org/english/tratop_e/dispu_e/cases_e/ds362_e.htm.

Wu, H. X. (2000). China's GDP level and growth performance: Alternative estimates and the implications. *Review of Income and Wealth, 46*(4), 475–499.

Yankelovich, D. (1992, October 5). How public opinion really works. *Fortune*, pp. 102–106.

Yung, K. (2006, July 17). In slow pursuit of counterfeiters: Heelys maker finds China is spinning its wheels. *Dallas Morning News*. Retrieved July 17, 2007, from http://dallasnews.com.

Zhao, C., & Graham, J. M. (2006). The PRC's evolving standards system: Institutions and strategy. *Asia Policy, 2*, 63–87.

Zhu, Z. (2005, November 3). Top foreign brands sue silk street market. *China Daily*, p. 2.

Zimmerman, A., & Chaudhry, P. (2009). Protecting intellectual property rights: The special case of China. *Journal of Asia-Pacific Business, 10*(4), 308–325.

MIX
Papier aus verantwortungsvollen Quellen
Paper from responsible sources
FSC® C105338

If you have any concerns about our products,
you can contact us on
ProductSafety@springernature.com

In case Publisher is established outside the EU,
the EU authorized representative is:
Springer Nature Customer Service Center GmbH
Europaplatz 3, 69115 Heidelberg, Germany

Printed by Libri Plureos GmbH
in Hamburg, Germany